The Constrained Court

The Constrained Court

LAW, POLITICS, AND THE
DECISIONS JUSTICES MAKE

Michael A. Bailey
Forrest Maltzman

PRINCETON UNIVERSITY PRESS
PRINCETON AND OXFORD

Published by Princeton University Press, 41 William Street, Princeton, New Jersey 08540
In the United Kingdom: Princeton University Press, 6 Oxford Street, Woodstock,
Oxfordshire OX20 1TW

press.princeton.edu

Library of Congress Cataloging-in-Publication Data

Bailey, Michael A., 1969–
The constrained court : law, politics, and the decisions justices make / Michael A. Bailey,
Forrest Maltzman.
p.   cm.
Includes bibliographical references and index.
ISBN 978-0-691-15104-5 (hardcover : alk. paper) — ISBN 978-0-691-15105-2
(pbk. : alk. paper)   1. United States. Supreme Court.   2. Political questions and judicial
power—United States.   I. Maltzman, Forrest, 1963–   II. Title.
KF8748.B237   2011
347.73′26—dc22   2011012707

British Library Cataloging-in-Publication Data is available

This book has been composed in Sabon
Printed on acid-free paper.∞
Printed in the United States of America

1 3 5 7 9 10 8 6 4 2

This book is dedicated to our parents

Who gave us worlds with few constraints

CONTENTS

Preface   ix

1. Introduction   1

2. The Measure of Law: Estimating Preferences across
   Institutions and Time   17

PART I. *Legal Value Constraints*

3. Disentangling Law and Policy Preferences   47

4. Law Matters   64

5. Causes and Consequences of Diverse Legal Values   80

PART II. *Political Constraints*

6. Separation of Powers and the Strategic Constraint   95

7. Signals from the Executive   121

8. Conclusion   140

Appendix. Statistical Details   156

Notes   175

References   185

Index   203

PREFACE

FEW DECISIONS IN AMERICAN POLITICS are more important than those reached by the justices of the United States Supreme Court. These nine judges routinely make decisions involving the most significant social and political issues in the country. They decide, among other things, whether government can mandate health insurance, detain suspected terrorists without a trial, ban abortion, or execute criminals who are mentally impaired.

How do justices make these momentous decisions? Many political scientists claim justices have essentially no constraints and, as political creatures, use their positions on the bench to pursue their ideological predilections. In this view, law does not matter. Likewise, according to this view the preferences of elected officials do not matter. Instead, justices themselves are like elected officials who use the power of their office to advance their policy goals.

This explanation has much to recommend for it. It moves past naive views of justices as apolitical legal sages. And it is consistent with empirical evidence that suggests that the votes cast by the justices frequently split along predictable ideological lines. For this reason, it has become a part of the political science canon.

But is it right? Do justices simply base their decisions on the policy preferences they bring to the bench? Many lawyers, students of American politics, judges, and political scientists believe that there is more to justices' decision-making. Elaborate opinions, cites to precedent, and even the robes suggest something beyond a purely political Court. Without denying the role of politics, many scholars and lawyers argue that law really does matter. According to this view, legal doctrine, not just policy preferences, constrains the decisions justices reach. Others argue that the legislative and executive branches also can constrain justices. In this view, the Supreme Court and its justices act interdependently with the other branches that make up the American political system. As such, the actions of justices depend in part upon the preferences of elected political actors.

While such explanations are intuitive, they are hard to prove empirically. Throughout this book, we provide evidence that justices are not simply pursuing their policy preferences. Instead, they are subject to constraints, whether they come from their internal value systems or from external political forces. We have wrestled with this task for eight years, and the result is a model that allows us statistically to identify legal and institutional influences on justices. To test this model, we have created a

large original data set of judicial and non-judicial position-taking on Supreme Court cases. We have read and coded scores of opinions. We have
tapped the latest improvements in measurement theory.

The results give us confidence that judicial policy preferences provide
only a starting point for explaining judicial decision-making. Justices' values also matter. Just as justices have attitudes about policy, they have attitudes about the law. Some value precedent; some believe in judicial deference; others interpret the First Amendment strictly. Expressions of these
values are not always smoke screens. They routinely affect how justices
decide cases. In addition, we show that justices are not independent of the
rest of the political system. They act differently when Congress and the
president are united against them. And, they are informationally inter-
dependent on external actors, especially the solicitor general. In short,
the view that justices are purely political animals who utilize their positions in pursuit of their policy preferences is too simplistic. And the view
that justices are robotic creatures neutrally enforcing the decisions of
others or interpreting the law misses the complexity of the decisions the
justices make.

We could not have pursued a project of this scope without the wisdom
and support of many colleagues and friends. We have been fortunate to
have benefited from a very able and generous scholarly community. Most
notably, we thank Brandon Bartels, Chris Bonneau, Saul Brenner, Cliff
Carrubba, Kelly Chang, Tom Clark, John Ferejohn, Josh Fischman, Barry
Friedman, Michael Giles, Tom Hammond, Robert Howard, Brian Ka-
moie, Bob Katzmann, Eric Lawrence, Jeff Lax, Jeff Lewis, Andrew Mar-
tin, Hans Noel, Kevin Quinn, Doug Reed, Jeff Segal, Lee Sigelman, Jim
Spriggs, Paul Wahlbeck, Barry Weingast, and participants at seminars at
Dartmouth, Emory University, the University of Georgia, Georgetown
University, George Washington University, the University of Minnesota,
New York University, the University of Pittsburgh, SUNY-Stony Brook,
Washington University in St. Louis, William and Mary, and the 2005
Summer Meeting of the Society for Political Methodology. Keith Poole
generously provided congressional vote data. Sarah Binder, Kevin Mc-
Guire, and Chuck Shipan read the entire manuscript and commented
extensively. We also appreciate the assistance of Maeve Carey, Chris Dre-
wry, Stephen de Man, Cynthia Fleming, Greg Fortelny, Elliott Fullmer,
Carroll Ganier, Mike Griffin, Matt Hard, Jake Haselswerdt, Alex Kar-
jeker, Laura Miller, Karen Miranda, Michael Schroeder, Alexis Teagar-
den, and Caroline Wells. Fully unpacking the contributions that have
gone into this book may be more difficult than unpacking influences on
judicial decision-making. Nevertheless, we appreciate the willingness of
so many to help us in so many ways, either knowingly or not.

We are also grateful to the National Science Foundation for financial support (SES-0351469 and SES-03151763) and to Georgetown University and George Washington University for supporting us as we worked on this project.

Finally, we wish to recognize our children, Jack, Emi, and Ken Bailey and Noa and Mica Maltzman. They may not always comply with the doctrines we prescribe, but our love for them has no bounds. Even more, this book would not exist without the patience and love shown by Mari Bailey and Sarah Binder. Above all, this book originates in the laws and values taught to us by our parents, Donald and Katherine Bailey and Charlene and Richard Maltzman, and we therefore dedicate this book to them.

The Constrained Court

Chapter 1

INTRODUCTION

IMMEDIATELY FOLLOWING the Supreme Court's ruling in *Bush v. Gore* (2000), George Washington University law professor Jeffrey Rosen expressed shock that the justices in the majority did "not even bother to cloak their willfulness in legal arguments intelligible to people of good faith." Rosen believed that the decision "made it impossible for citizens of the United States to sustain any kind of faith in the rule of law as something larger than the self-interested political preferences of William Rehnquist, Antonin Scalia, Clarence Thomas, Anthony Kennedy, and Sandra Day O'Connor" (2000).

Rosen was not alone within the legal academy. Over five hundred law professors wrote a public letter "as teachers whose lives have been dedicated to the rule of law" to condemn the Court's decision (Berkowitz and Wittes 2001). They argued that the majority of justices had acted as "political proponents for candidate Bush, not as judges." One signatory "deplored the fact that one of his primary teachings to his students over a 40-year career in constitutional law—that the U.S. Supreme Court acts as a nonpartisan institution despite differing judicial philosophies—had been rendered null and void by the actions of the five justices who stopped the count" (Dickenson 2001).

Not all Court critics think justices are right-wing partisans. Conservatives, too, routinely attack the Court for pursuing political, not legal, aims. Onetime Supreme Court nominee and conservative icon Robert Bork characterizes the Supreme Court as "an active partisan on one side of our culture wars" (quoted in Boot 1998, vi). Conservative columnist Thomas Sowell claims "Supreme Court decisions suggest that too many justices are not satisfied with their role, and seek more sweeping powers as supreme policy-makers, grand second-guessers or philosopher-kings" (2010).

Many political scientists see politics on the Court as business as usual. Much of the discipline has long embraced the notion that judicial outcomes primarily reflect judicial policy preferences (see discussions in Friedman 2006; Tamanaha 2010). Indeed, seven years before *Bush v. Gore* political scientists Jeffrey Segal and Harold Spaeth predicted that "if a case on the outcome of a presidential election should reach the Supreme Court, . . . the Court's decision might well turn on the personal preferences

of the justices" (1993, 70). *Bush v. Gore* made Segal and Spaeth look like
the oracles of Delphi.

If justices are indeed pursuing their personal policy preferences, those
who believe that an independent judiciary undermines our democratic
system have a strong argument. And the fears that were expressed at the
founding will have come to pass. *Federalist 78* noted that if the courts
"should be disposed to exercise will instead of judgment, the consequence would be the substitution of their pleasure for that of the legislative body." The only democratic recourse would be the appointments
process, which would, we could hope, elevate individuals to the bench
who share the views of the people (Dahl 1957). However, if justices are
unconstrained policymakers they need not remain in accord with popular
wishes. And with the recent trends of appointing younger justices and the
greater longevity of sitting justices, there is more reason to worry that the
policy preferences of the Court could become disconnected from the popular will.

Not everyone believes justices are unconstrained policymakers, however. Many believe justices feel constrained to follow established legal
principles. The operation of the Court and the norms of the legal community clearly support this. Justices parse legal doctrine in detailed opinions. Law students and journals analyze legal doctrine. Sitting judges express bafflement at the idea that law does not matter (Edwards 1998;
Wald 1999). And we suspect that the law professors who objected to
Bush v. Gore continue to teach that legal doctrines provide useful tools
for understanding Court decisions.

One reason the legal model may rise above the ashes of *Bush v. Gore*
is that justices routinely make decisions that appear to be inconsistent
with their policy preferences. For example, in *Dickerson v. United States*
(2000) the Court assessed the constitutionality of a law overturning *Miranda v. Arizona* (1966). Conservatives had long railed against *Miranda*
and many saw *Dickerson* as a chance for conservative, Republican-
appointed justices to reshape constitutional law. Surprisingly, though, the
Court stood behind *Miranda* by a 7–2 majority. No less a conservative
than Justice Rehnquist wrote an opinion that defended precedent and argued that since *Miranda* was a constitutionally based decision, Congress
could not alter the Court's ruling by statute.

In addition, the Court is often unanimous. From 1950 to 2004, about
38 percent of Court decisions had no votes against the majority (Epstein,
Segal, Spaeth, and Walker 2007, 227). This suggests that justices share
legal values that can supersede policy preferences. While it is possible that
policy-motivated justices can be unanimous if the alternative or legal status quo (e.g., upholding the lower court) has policy implications that are
so extreme that no justice views this as a viable alternative, it is unlikely

that they would do so as frequently as they do. The legal explanation of unanimous votes is that the "roughly similar forms of legal education and professional experience" of justices lead them to agree on cases for legal, not policy, reasons (Breyer 2005, 110).

Justices may also be subject to external constraints. In particular, the legislative and executive branches may be able to push the Court in favored directions with threats and persuasion, thereby attenuating the danger that the Court becomes a policymaker divorced from public will. Perhaps the most prominent example of such external influence is the "switch in time that saved nine" on *West Coast Hotel v. Parrish* (1937). After the Court struck down several New Deal laws, elected leaders became increasingly aggressive toward the Court, culminating in President Roosevelt's plan to "pack" the Court with more justices (Friedman 2009). One of the justices who frequently voted to strike government intervention in the economy, Justice Owen Roberts, suddenly voted to allow a Washington state minimum wage law. Roberts's change in tune relieved political pressure on the Court and sunk Roosevelt's Court-packing plan.

Hence we are faced with competing views about the role of the Supreme Court in the constitutional order. Many political scientists view the Court as a largely unconstrained policymaking body. Others believe there are constraints, either internal or external. Can empirical analysis resolve this debate? We believe it can. As social scientists, we agree with Segal and Spaeth (1994), who wrote that "it is a basic tenet of science, whether social, political or natural, that an untestable model has no explanatory power." We do not believe there is—nor does social science promise—an easy and definitive answer, but we are optimistic that advances in theory, data collection, and measurement can help us progress.

There are many benefits to understanding whether policy, law, or interinstitutional pressure shapes decisions made by justices. First, we can better explain the development of law. Many important cases have been decided by 5–4 votes, from *Lochner v. New York* (1905) to *Escobedo v. Illinois* (1964) to *Miranda v. Arizona* (1966) to *Furman v. Georgia* (1972) to *Regents of the University of California v. Bakke* (1978) to *Texas v. Johnson* (1989) (see, e.g., discussion in Tribe 1985, 32). If legal or political constraints switched votes in these cases, history and politics in the United States would be quite different.

Second, understanding the constraints faced by justices helps us assess and possibly even reform the Court. Whether justices simply follow their policy preferences affects the manner in which Congress and the president should interact with the judiciary. The optimal appointment process for justices who act as unelected policymakers looks different than one for justices who operate within legal and institutional constraints. If justices are purely political beings, judicial term limits may make sense in order to ensure that voters and their elected representatives have regular opportunities to influence who sits on the bench. Likewise, if justices are unconstrained policymakers the nomination and approval process for justices should perhaps be even more political. In addition, some argue that limits on the jurisdiction of the Court or challenges to its authority are reasonable if the Court is primarily policy oriented (Tushnet 1999).

Finally, how we view constraints on the Court affects our normative views of the Court. Is the Court legitimate? The executive and legislative branches derive their legitimacy from elections. Some argue that the Court can represent the public as well as the elected branches (Peretti 1999), but most believe that the Court derives its legitimacy from fealty to the Constitution and the law. A Court that is no different from a legislature may not have any moral standing (Ely 1991). As John Adams wrote in the Massachusetts Constitution of 1780, "the judicial shall never exercise the legislative and executive powers, or either of them: to the end it may be a government of laws and not of men" (Adams, Adams, and Bowdoin 1780). Even Rosen (2006, 3–7), who believes that the Court does and should follow public opinion, believes that the legitimacy of the Court depends on judicial decisions being "accepted by the country as being rooted in constitutional principles rather than political expediency."

The Attitudinal Model and the Absence of Constraints

We begin our consideration of constraints on the Court with a model that says there are none—the attitudinal model. This model assumes that justices are "decision makers who always vote their unconstrained attitudes" (Epstein and Knight 1995, 2). As Segal and Spaeth summarize it, "simply put, Rehnquist votes the way he does because he is extremely conservative; Marshall voted the way he did because he is extremely liberal" (1993, 65).

> **Attitudinal Model Claim:** Justices' decisions reflect their unconstrained policy preferences.

Empirically oriented scholars have produced decades of research indicating that policy motivations best explain Supreme Court behavior (Spaeth 1961, 1964, 1979; Rohde and Spaeth 1976; Hagle and Spaeth 1992, 1993; Segal and Spaeth 1993, 2002; Segal and Cover 1989). Segal and Spaeth's book *The Supreme Court and the Attitudinal Model* has become required reading for students of the Court. The model is so influential that empirically oriented political scientists have "an almost pathological skepticism that law matters" (Friedman 2006, 261; see also Tamanaha 2010, 232). The attitudinal model builds on two intellectual foundations.

First, legal realism in the early twentieth century highlighted the indeterminacy of law. This indeterminacy allows justices to inject their personal views (perhaps unconsciously) into the development of the law (Frank 2009 [1930]; Llewellyn 1962; Stephenson 2009; Tamanaha 2010). Second, the behavioral revolution in the middle of the twentieth century moved political science away from simple description and proscription toward theory building and testing (see Maltzman, Spriggs, and Wahlbeck 1999, 44; Tamanaha 2010, 111). Research in this vein emphasized observation and measurement, with Spaeth (1965) famously urging scholars to look at what justices do rather than what they say.

The attitudinal model is based on three premises. First, Supreme Court justices are subject to little or no oversight. Within the judicial branch justices face no oversight given the Supreme Court's position at the top of a judicial hierarchy (Segal and Spaeth 2002, 111; Posner 2005, 42). They arguably face little beyond the judicial branch due to the practical difficulty of overturning Supreme Court cases. Former solicitor general Ken Starr (2002) goes so far as to consider the Court "first among equals" in the constitutional order. While we will discuss the possibility of political oversight in both this chapter and chapter 6, it is plausible that, practically speaking, the Court has the final say on constitutional law in the United States given the relatively few instances in which Congress or a constitutional amendment has explicitly overruled the Supreme Court (J. Barnes 2004).

Second, the law is ambiguous enough to permit multiple interpretations (Segal and Spaeth 2002, 72). This is due not only to constitutional and statutory vagueness but also to the winnowing process that sends only a small fraction of all legal disputes to the Supreme Court. These are the truly tough cases and they are only before the justices because the proper legal conclusion is not straightforward (Cross 1997, 285). Posner (2005, 40) sums up this view when he writes, "Almost a quarter century as federal appellate judge has convinced me that it is rarely possible to say with a straight face of a Supreme Court constitutional decision that it was decided correctly or incorrectly." If both sides of a case have plausible legal grounds (and justices are subject to no oversight), justices can easily choose the side they prefer on policy grounds while maintaining an appearance of upholding the law.

The third premise of the attitudinal model is that justices care only about policy (Segal and Spaeth 2002, 111). Court cases often have profound policy implications—touching issues ranging from terrorism to segregation to abortion to elections to the death penalty and beyond—and attitudinalists argue that justices focus only on policy when deciding cases. In the attitudinal model, the legal views justices express in their opinions are simply smoke screens to cover their pursuit of policy.

In this book, we focus on two predictions of the attitudinal model. The first is that law does not matter. In *The Supreme Court and the Attitudinal Model*, Segal and Spaeth scoured Supreme Court history looking for influences of law. They concluded "we have not discovered any narrowly defined issues in which variables of a non-attitudinal sort operate" (1993, 359). They went on to write a book-length refutation of the claim that precedent influences Supreme Court behavior (Spaeth and Segal 1999; see also Brenner and Spaeth 1995). Bolstered by the partisan outcomes in *Bush v. Gore*, they describe a Supreme Court that is "activist and conservative . . . [and] blatantly partisan" (2002, 430). Law in this view is "a low form of rational behavior," no more science than "creative writing, necromancy or finger painting" (Spaeth 1979, 64; cited in Gillman 2001, 470).

A second prediction of the attitudinal model holds that external actors do not influence justices. This prediction implies that a host of potential influences does not matter, including the legislative and executive branches. It is consistent with the Founders' intent of creating an independent judicial branch by providing justices with lifetime appointments and protection from a salary reduction (Hamilton, Madison, and Jay 2011, #78, #79). This corollary suggests that Congress will not be able to otherwise threaten the Court and the president will not be able to use the power, prestige, and legal infrastructure of the executive branch to influence the Court.[1]

Neither of the attitudinal model predictions is foreordained. Segal and Spaeth developed the attitudinal model based on empirical evidence. It is possible that justices follow legal values or defer to Congress and the president; attitudinalists claim that as a matter of fact justices do not exhibit these behaviors.

CONSTRAINED BY LEGAL VALUES

Not everyone agrees that justices are unconstrained. Many in law argue that the main constraint on justices "is an internal one: the judge's integrity and degree of commitment to engage in an unbiased search for the correct legal answer" (Tamanaha 2010, 189). Even legal realists thought that such constraints could and should matter (Stephenson 2009, 206). In its starkest form, this view suggests that justices vote in accordance with legal principles, irrespective of the policy implications. Justice Elena Kagan expressed such a view during her confirmation hearings. After admitting that "I've been a Democrat my whole life, my political views are generally progressive," she said her policy preferences would not influence her decisions as a judge: "You are looking at law all the way

down, not your political preferences, not your personal preferences"
(Kagan 2010).

Legal Model Claim: Legal doctrines guide the decisions justices
   make.

Proponents of this view accept that justices gain considerable latitude
from being at the top of the judicial hierarchy and that cases can be legally indeterminate. They differ at the third step of the attitudinal model
logic: the idea that policy is the only thing that matters to justices. In
other words, legalist scholars grant attitudinal model claims that justices
have the ability to do what they want but contest whether justices only
want policy outcomes.

Legalist scholars instead contend that justices value the law in and of
itself (see, e.g., Cross 1997, 297). Kahn argues that judicial values arise
from "a distinctive set of institutional norms and customs, including legal
principles and theories" (1999, 175; see also R. Smith 1988). Baum
(1997) and Gibson (1978, 1983) attribute these values to justices' social-
ization in law schools and the legal community. Gillman and Clayton
(1999, 4) attribute these values to the nature of the institutional position
justices occupy. In particular, the roles of the justices lead them to feel
obligated to follow legal principles. This "role orientation" of judges
(Gibson 1977, 1978; Ulmer 1973; Glick and Vines 1969) pushes judges
to believe that "to regard oneself and be regarded by others, especially
one's peers, as a good judge requires conformity to the accepted norms of
judging" (Posner 2008, 61). Even Walter Murphy, a scholar most prominent for arguing that justices strategically pursue policy goals, admits
that "much of the force of self-restraint can be traced to individual justices' concepts of their proper role in American government" (1964, 29).

The law can matter in rational choice perspectives as well. After all,
rational choice models posit utility maximization, not the object of utility.
Ferejohn and Weingast (1992, 277) present a rational choice theory of
statutory interpretation and argue that "in the past, positive political theory has relied too exclusively on the assumption that judges are political
actors with ideological motives identical to elected officials. While this assumption undoubtedly captures an important aspect of judicial decision-
making, it hardly exhausts the range of judicial behavior and the manifold
normative bases of judicial decisions" (see also Baum 1997, 61). Segal and
Spaeth (2002, 111) explicitly reject such an approach.

Judges may also follow legal principals in order to minimize effort (Tiller and Cross 2006, 530; Posner 2008). Judges may value avoiding work
on what can sometimes be tedious cases, cases that D.C. Circuit of the
U.S. Court of Appeals judge Patricia Wald notes often revolve around

such scintillating topics as "appropriate regulatory standards for 'retro-fitted cell-burners' as opposed to 'wall-fired electric utility boilers'" (1999, 237, 241). Faced with such a case, judges may be able to use legal rules and norms to resolve the dispute; without such principles ad hoc rulings could be harder to devise and defend.

Which legal principles might constrain justices? A full accounting would fill a law library (and already has). Here we focus on three prominent possibilities: stare decisis, judicial restraint, and strict construction of the Constitution.

Stare Decisis

Stare decisis is the doctrine that decisions should be consistent with past decisions. The doctrine is central to all legal perspectives (Levi 1949; Dworkin 1978; Kahn 1999; Gillman and Clayton 1999). According to George and Epstein, "at its core, legalism centers around a rather simple assumption about judicial decision making, namely, that legal doctrine, generated by past cases, is the primary determinant of extant case outcomes" (1992, 324). Spaeth and Segal characterize stare decisis as "the lifeblood of the legal model" (2001, 314). Judges themselves emphasize precedent more frequently than any other legal factor (Knight and Epstein 1996).

The Court benefits in a number of ways when it follows precedent. First, precedent is a useful heuristic. How did other judges interpret the Constitution when faced with similar problems? How did they balance competing values? How did they resolve ambiguity? Precedent encapsulates the answers of previous judges to these questions.

Second, the Court can smooth the operation of the judicial branch by respecting precedent. Lower court judges will struggle to apply case law as a guide if there is too much ambiguity and incoherence. If the Supreme Court sticks to precedent, though, lower court judges will have clearer standards to guide them. As Justice Louis Brandeis once argued, "stare decisis is usually the wise policy, because in most matters it is more important that the applicable rule of law be settled than that it be settled right" (1932, 406).

Third, justices can use precedent to indirectly pursue policy goals; in other words, "judges [may] care about precedent because they care about policy" (Bueno de Mesquita and Stephenson 2002, 755). Justices following precedent may "lose" in policy terms on a case, but the outcome may strengthen the Court's ability to control lower courts by maintaining the norm of stare decisis (Bueno de Mesquita and Stephenson 2002; Hansford and Spriggs 2006, 19–20; Landes and Posner 1975). In addition, the justices may be better able to achieve policy goals the more the Court is viewed as legitimate (Peretti 1999, 81). If the Court disregards precedent too often, individuals and organizations affected by the law could come to see the Court as a political institution not deserving of legitimacy and compliance (Hansford and Spriggs 2006, 20; Kahn 1999, 189).

Judicial Restraint

Another doctrine that may constrain justices is judicial restraint. Judicial restraint implies that justices should defer to elected officials as much as possible within the bounds established by the Constitution (and, depending on one's view of stare decisis).[2] In this view, an ideal judge's temperament "is marked by modesty, by caution, by deference to others in different roles with different responsibilities" (Kronman 2006).[3]

There are two ways of justifying this doctrine. The first is a normative claim that if justices exercise restraint, they will be less likely to usurp legitimate democratic will. Law is, as we have seen, complicated and many cases are amenable to multiple legitimate decisions. If justices are the final source for choosing among such alternatives, there is little recourse, as justices are not elected and overturning their decisions is very difficult with democratic means. On the other hand, if justices defer to the judgment of elected officials, voters have a chance to discipline these officials at the ballot box if they make poor decisions. Therefore, Thayer (1893), Wechsler (1959), and many others have argued that justices should not overturn laws unless the laws clearly conflict with constitutional provisions.

A second justification for judicial restraint is more practical: the less the Court challenges legislative actors, the less likely those actors will threaten its legitimacy. The Court requires the consent of the executive branch and states to enforce its decisions. If it challenges elected actors too often, those actors may become less inclined to value the Court and find more reason to disobey. The tenuousness of Court power led Ferejohn and Kramer to observe that "the judiciary is a self-regulator: it has created a system of self-imposed institutional and doctrinal constraints that keep judges within the bounds required by institutional vulnerability" (2006, 163). Rosen summarizes this view: "history suggests that courts can best maintain their democratic legitimacy . . . by practicing judicial restraint" (2006, 13).

Justices frequently espouse judicial restraint. Justice Oliver Wendell Holmes quipped, "if my fellow citizens want to go to hell I will help them. It's my job" (1920, cited in Howe 1953). Justice Harlan Fiske Stone lamented, "the truth is that I feel obliged to uphold some laws which turn my stomach" (quoted in Dunne 1977, 199). Felix Frankfurter said that the philosophy of judicial restraint was "the alpha and omega of our job" (quoted in Urofsky 1991, 31), and Justice John Marshall Harlan II made the case that

> the Constitution is not a panacea for every blot upon the public welfare, nor should this Court, ordained as a judicial body, be thought of as a general haven for reform movements. This Court, limited in function in accordance with that premise, does not serve its high purpose when it exceeds its authority, even to satisfy justified impatience with the slow workings of the political process. (1964, 624–25)

Contemporary justices espouse judicial deference as well. Justice Kagan testified that "every judge has to be committed to the policies of restraint" (2010). Future Chief Justice John Roberts testified during his D.C. Circuit confirmation hearing that "the Supreme Court has, throughout its history, on many occasions described the deference that is due to legislative judgments. . . . It's a principle that is easily stated and needs to be observed in practice, as well as in theory" (2003, 49). Justices Sonia Sotomayor and Samuel Alito, too, made strong statements in support of judicial deference in their confirmation hearings (Sotomayor 2009; Alito 2006).

Members of Congress agree. In announcing his vote to confirm Roberts as Chief Justice, Senator Patrick Leahy (D, Vermont) urged "appropriate deference to congressional action taken by the people's elected representatives" (2005). Senator Jeff Bingaman (D, New Mexico) said he voted for Roberts because Roberts's testimony convinced him that Roberts would show "adequate deference to Congress" (2005). Likewise, Senator Al Franken (D, Minnesota) stated at the Sotomayor confirmation hearings that "I am wary of judicial activism and I believe in judicial restraint. Except under the most exceptional circumstances, the judicial branch is designed to show deep deference to Congress and not make policy by itself" (2009).

Judicial restraint is complicated by the fact that complete deference to elected officials nullifies a major purpose of the judiciary. Courts are necessary because legislatures and executives might violate or misconstrue the Constitution and somebody needs to resist such encroachments. Hence visions of judicial restraint often come with conditions—and these conditions can vary dramatically from justice to justice. Justice Stephen Breyer's constitutional vision centers on "judicial modesty" (2005, 5), as he wants the Court to let legislators use their values and expertise to develop laws acceptable to the public. He sees limits to judicial modesty when the political process malfunctions (see also Ely 1980).

The famous footnote 4 of *United States v. Carolene Products* (1938) provides a slightly different view of judicial restraint. In it, Justice Stone argued that while the Court should presume the constitutionality of legislation whenever possible, it should subject to a higher level of scrutiny any legislation that affects personal rights or that may be a result of "prejudice against discrete and insular minorities." This view of judicial restraint led the Court to accept economic legislation unless it was very clearly in violation of the Constitution and to be skeptical toward legislation that harmed minorities or non-economic rights.

Yet other views of judicial restraint provide different guidance. In a textualist reading of the Constitution, the Court should defer to the judgment of legislatures and executives unless there is specific language in the Constitution banning the action in question (Scalia 1997). And if there is doubt as to what is and is not allowed under the Constitution, originalists (often, but not always, allied with textualists) look to the beliefs and practices accepted at the time of the Constitution's drafting or ratification of an amendment (Bork 1990). In practice, textualists have been less willing to strike laws and actions that may harm minorities or individual rights and have been more willing to strike laws and actions that threaten economic rights.

This discussion makes it clear that legal values are nuanced, and it is possible that justices will embrace legal values that are at odds with the legal values endorsed by their colleagues on the bench. Legal values may also conflict. For example, Breyer's commitment to deference to legislative will comes into tension with his commitment to precedent cases about state regulations on abortion.

Strict Construction

Another prominent legal principle is strict construction of constitutional and statutory texts. Cases invariably arise where the disputed legal language conflicts with common sense, with another law, or with a judge's sense of justice. Judges come down in varying places on what to do in these situations. Some are easily swayed from legal texts by contextual factors; they are loose constructionists. Others stick to the text, easily when they agree with the outcome but also when they do not; they are strict constructionists. They do not let purpose trump the plain meaning of laws and will rule consistently with the law as written even if the outcome in a particular case appears unjust.

The early debate over the Bank of the United States provides a classic example of the distinction (Zavodnyik 2007). Alexander Hamilton proposed the First National Bank in order to improve the scope and efficiency of the nation's financial system. There was no explicit constitutional provision for the bank, but Hamilton was a loose constructionist and saw the power to incorporate and to regulate as clearly inherent in the constitutional governance structure. Thomas Jefferson took a strict constructionist view and argued that the bank was unconstitutional since the Constitution did not explicitly authorize such a bank.

Strict constructionists view the Constitution as a contract that describes how to determine government policies and how to change the terms of the contract. The job of the courts is to enforce the contract. If justices impose their values or interpretations or allow other considerations to intervene, they are usurping the law. The result would not be law but policymaking via a mechanism that was not agreed to by the parties to the contract. We are using strict constructionism in a general sense to indicate avowed adherence to the text of the Constitution and the intent of its framers. There are many permutations. For example, Scalia advocates textualism over strict construction, saying, "A text should not be construed strictly and it should not be construed leniently. It should be construed reasonably, to contain all that it fairly means" (quoted in Taylor 2005, 2354).

All perspectives under this rubric, however, share a starting point that the Constitution must be enforced as written. If a law is allowable under the original intent of the Constitution, a justice should not strike it, no matter how personally objectionable the justice finds it. In Bork's view, "we administer justice according to law. Justice in a larger sense, justice according to morality, is for Congress and the President to administer, if they see fit, through the creation of new law" (1990, 6). Bork therefore controversially rejected popular Supreme Court decisions including one that banned racial covenants (*Shelley v. Kramer* [1948]) and one that banned poll taxes (*Harper v. Virginia Board of Elections* [1966]) (Bork 1990).

The right to privacy is anathema to strict constructionists. This right was articulated by Justice William O. Douglas in his majority opinion in *Griswold v. Connecticut* (1965). Douglas argued that "specific guarantees in the Bill of Rights have penumbras, formed by emanations from those guarantees that help give them life and substance," and that a right to privacy included a right for married persons to make personal decisions about birth control. Strict constructionists look, in vain, for explicit text to justify this specific right and, absent it, would not hold legislatures to protecting it.

Strict constructionism is undeniably a major element of the legal landscape. Bush hailed his nominee for Chief Justice, John Roberts, as "a strict constructionist, somebody who looks at the words of the Constitution for what they are, somebody who will not legislate from the bench" (Stout 2005). President Nixon used the same term to describe his nominee for Chief Justice, Warren Burger (Nixon 1969). Senators commonly use the term to characterize their views on the Court. Senator Tom Coburn

(R, Oklahoma), for example, stated during the Kagan nomination hearings that

> There is a group in America, though, that believes in strict constructionism. We actually believe the founders had preeminent wisdom, that they were very rarely wrong, and—and that the modern idea that we can mold the Constitution to what we want it to be, rather than what that vision was, is something that's antithetical to a ton of people throughout this country. (2010)

For reasons we discuss in chapter 4, we are not able to measure the influence of strict constructionism broadly construed. We are able to investigate one aspect of it, which is strict construction of the First Amendment's free speech clause that "Congress shall make no law" prohibition on restricting speech. This is an area in which the modern Court in general has shown a strong commitment (Friedman 2009, 378). For example, Justice Hugo Black, widely reputed to be a strict constructionist (see, e.g., Ely 1980, 3; U.S. Congress 1971), famously repeated that "no law means no law" in justifying his votes to strike laws that he may well have agreed with but for his interpretation of the Constitution (Black 1969).

CONSTRAINED BY OTHER ACTORS

Another source of possible constraint on the Court is external. In contrast to both the attitudinal and legal models in which justices are isolated decision-makers, "separation of powers" models (perhaps more aptly called "checks and balances" models) assert that Congress and the president constrain justices.[4] In this view, justices may still primarily be interested in policy but may find that they cannot ignore the desires of the other branches of government if they want to achieve their policy goals. As Epstein and Knight put it, "justices are strategic actors who realize that their ability to achieve their goals depends upon a consideration of the preferences of other actors, the choices they expect others to make, and the institutional context in which they act" (1998, 10).

Separation-of-Powers Model Claim: The preferences of the legislative and executive branches shape the decisions justices make.

A large academic literature elaborates on the mechanism of such constraint (W. Murphy 1964; Eskridge 1991; Ferejohn and Shipan 1990; Ferejohn 1999; Gely and Spiller 1990; Spiller and Gely 1992; Eskridge, Ferejohn, and Gandhi 2002). In the standard version of the model, justices and elected officials have one-dimensional policy preferences (Marks 1989; Ferejohn and Weingast 1992), meaning we can line up justices, the president, and the medians of the House and Senate from most liberal to most conservative. If, when interpreting a law passed by Congress, the Court makes a decision that places the policy outcome outside the "po-litical pareto set" defined by the line segment that connects the president, House median, and Senate median, all three political actors will agree to new legislation overturning the Court. In contrast, a decision by the Court that is within the political pareto set will be protected as an effort to move policy to the right will be resisted by whatever political actor is to the left of the Court's decision and an effort to move policy to the left will be resisted by whatever political actor is to the right of the Court's decision. Cognizant of this, strategic justices should produce an opinion that reflects the policy outcome that is nearest to the Court median's ideal point and within the pareto set defined by elected officials (Bawn and Shipan 1997, 1). Doing so yields the best outcome for the Court median that will not be overturned.

On constitutional interpretation the model is more complicated as Congress and the president cannot, in principle, overturn the Court legis-latively. A constitutional amendment is possible but faces a high hurdle that requires the consent of Congress and most state legislatures. How-ever, the political branches can sanction the Court by not implementing its rulings, curtailing its jurisdiction, limiting its budget, manipulating the size of the bench, or even impeaching justices (W. Murphy 1964; Cross and Nelson 2001; Rosenberg 1991; McNollgast 1995; Friedman 1990, 1998; Ferejohn 1999; Peretti 1999; Epstein, Knight, and Martin 2004; J. Barnes 2004).

There could also be an informal basis for the Court to try to please Congress and the president: justices might desire to avoid conflict with the other branches (Baum 2006, 77). This might reflect a desire to protect the legitimacy of the Court or to be socially embraced by the Washington community and to maintain personal friendships with members of the executive and legislative branches.

Outline of the Book

We are left with an open question: are justices constrained? Segal and Spaeth argue justices are not and defend their view with voluminous and well-received empirical analysis. As for doubters, Segal and Spaeth's response is direct: show us the evidence (2002, chapter 2). They want specific measurable predictions from non-attitudinal models that can be tested empirically.

We take up Segal and Spaeth's challenge. We offer new approaches to assessing constraints on Supreme Court behavior. We rely heavily on two types of methodological advances. The first relates to measurement. In chapter 2, we describe recent statistical developments that allow us to measure the ideologies of justices, members of Congress, and the executive on the same ideological scale over time. These developments allow us to leverage cross-institutional and cross-time data to pin down legal and political constraints on justices. The second type of methodological advance relates to "identification." We expend considerable effort fleshing out exactly what kind of evidence is necessary to disentangle various influences on the Court. "Identifying" the effect of law, for example, requires careful theoretical development and new uses of data.

In chapters 3, 4, and 5, we explore if and how legal values influence justices. In chapter 3, we make the theoretical case that the influence of legal doctrines can get hidden in seemingly ideological behavior by justices. We also develop a technique for disentangling the effect of policy preferences and legal values. In chapter 4, we implement the technique, using the positions taken by non-Court actors, to identify the influence of stare decisis, judicial restraint, and strict construction of the First Amendment. We find that these legal doctrines influence justices although there is considerable diversity in how much each justice is affected by each factor. In chapter 5, we explore the sources and implications of this diversity.

In chapter 6, we assess whether the elected branches of government constrain the justices. We build on the extensive "separation of powers" literature to isolate the instances in which the threat of legislative response to Court actions is most likely to induce justices to defer to Congress and the president. We find substantial evidence that justices respond to the other branches on both statutory and constitutional interpretation, although there is again considerable diversity across justices.

In chapter 7, we evaluate whether the president can constrain the Court via his top lawyer, the solicitor general. The attitudinal model rejects the notion that justices are influenced by external actors. But we find evidence that the solicitor general influences justices. We use a signaling model and find that the persuasive ability of the executive branch varies across political contexts.

How justices decide cases is more than just an interesting puzzle. It is a question that has important normative implications. Indeed, how justices reach decisions may influence political support for the judiciary. Therefore, in the final chapter we conclude by presenting a series of survey experiments that demonstrate the importance of legal constraint for the public's acceptance of the judiciary.

Our evidence suggests a nuanced portrait of the Supreme Court and the choices justices make, a portrait of policy-motivated but legally and institutionally constrained justices. Law matters, although how it matters to individual justices is highly variable. Inter-institutional politics matters too. Sometimes justices value judicial restraint enough to defer to elected officials' judgment; other times justices defer to elected officials out of fear (as in separation-of-powers models) or persuasion (as in signaling models). No unicausal explanation can account for all the choices justices make, but we can nonetheless understand the Court in analytically meaningful ways.

Chapter 2

THE MEASURE OF LAW

Estimating Preferences across Institutions and Time

RICHARD NIXON CAMPAIGNED for president in 1968 on the platform of defending the "silent majority" against the perditions of an overly liberal Supreme Court. He promised to appoint justices who would "strengthen the peace forces as against the criminal forces in the land" and appreciate the tenets of "laws and order" (quoted in Abraham 1999, 9).

In short order, fate gave Nixon a chance to fundamentally remake the Court. Chief Justice Earl Warren stepped aside in June 1968 in an effort to ensure that President Johnson could name his successor (Ward 2003, 171). But Warren's plan came undone when Justice Abe Fortas, Johnson's nominee for Chief Justice, resigned from the bench after financial irregularities came to light. This gave Nixon two seats to fill. Two more retirements came in September 1971, giving Nixon a total of four appointments in his first term.

Did the Nixon appointees fundamentally remake the Court? Martin and Quinn's widely cited measures of judicial ideology (Martin and Quinn 2002; Liptak 2010) provide one answer. Figure 2.1 presents the Martin and Quinn ideology scores of the Court median over time; higher values indicate a more conservative Court median. The scores indicate that the Court median was conservative during the 1950s, became quite liberal in the 1960s, and then became very conservative in the early 1970s after Nixon came to office. Indeed, by 1973 the Court median reached a conservative peak that it has seldom reached before or since. By this measure, Nixon and conservatives should have been ecstatic with the new Court.

Of course, the story is more complicated. Most summaries of the Burger Court view it as a brake on what the liberal Warren Court had done rather than a fundamental change (Lindquist and Cross 2009, 6; Posner 2008, 55). And, in some ways, the Burger Court and its four Nixon nominees not only protected the Warren Court legacy but extended it. In fact, in the early 1970s when the Martin and Quinn scores indicate that the Court was at the height of its postwar conservatism, the Court issued two of the most liberal decisions in its history: in *Roe v. Wade* (1973) the Court said that there is a constitutional right to abortion, and in *Furman v. Georgia* (1972) the Court imposed a nationwide moratorium on the death penalty.

Figure 2.1. Martin and Quinn estimates of Supreme Court median over time

The Court's history during the first half of the 1970s undermines the face validity of the Martin and Quinn measure. But if this widely employed measure is flawed, how can one measure judicial preferences? Because our task in the remainder of the book is to ascertain how justices reach the decisions they do and because the conventional wisdom suggests that policy preferences guide justices, it is imperative that we design and employ a valid measure of judicial ideology. Because our examination of the decisions justices make will span almost half a century, it is important that we employ a preference measurement strategy that works over time.

In this chapter, we articulate the challenges that any empirically oriented scholar would have in devising a measure of judicial preferences. We show that it is impossible to make robust across-time comparisons using only Court voting. However, if we incorporate additional data we can create a measure of ideology that meets our needs and has face validity. The estimates we produce accord much better with the general understanding of Court movements over time as they indicate that Nixon's appointees moved the Court modestly to the right but that the Court remained quite moderate in historical terms in the early 1970s (see also Bailey 2007).

The fundamental challenge is that it is hard to separate preference change from agenda change. That is, we might see more conservative votes (as occurred in the early Burger Court), but how much of this is because the justices moved decisively to the right (Martin and Quinn's explanation) and how much of this is due to the agenda of the Court being quite liberal?

This book tackles both this question and an even more difficult challenge. Since we seek to assess whether justices are constrained by the separation-of-powers system, we need to compare preferences across institutions, as well as over time. The good news on this front is that statisticians and political scientists have developed a number of sophisticated methods for measuring preferences within institutions. The bad news is that these approaches do not travel well across institutional boundaries.

Since the most prominent legislative, executive, and judicial measures of ideology are based on different scales and on different agendas, comparing them directly would be as problematic as comparing students' test scores on different tests in different courses. Does a student who scores 75 on one test have the same mathematical ability as a student who scored 75 on a different test? Of course, the answer depends on the tests. Surely a student who gets a 75 on a test of simple addition is less mathematically capable than a student who got a 75 solving differential equations. Similarly, if Justice William Brennan voted conservatively 19 percent of the time on the Court and Representative Connie Morella (R, Maryland) voted conservatively 20 percent of the time in the House of Representatives (as they did in the samples of votes in our data set), would we have any confidence in saying that they have the same preferences? It depends on the sets of votes each actor faced (or, analogously, the "tests"). Directly comparing Congresswoman Morella's and Justice Brennan's voting records requires that we identify a comparable set of votes.

This chapter provides a framework for addressing these issues. First, we establish that measurement matters. While no one doubts the technical basis for concerns about cross-institutional and cross-time comparability, some may believe that simple measures provide valid results without the headache inherent in more technically sophisticated approaches. In this context, however, simple does not suffice. In fact, even some of the most prominent approaches are flawed. We show that not only Martin and Quinn's Supreme Court measures but also Poole and Rosenthal's (1997) congressional preference measures fail to capture certain commonsense notions about how politics have evolved in the postwar era.

Second, we build an inter-institutional and inter-temporal measurement model that we use to generate preference estimates for justices, members of Congress, and presidents from 1950 to 2008; these estimates are available at our website.[1] Key to the approach is the use of "bridging" techniques that link actors across time and institutions. To bridge across institutions, we incorporate data on presidents and members of Congress taking positions on Supreme Court cases. To bridge across time, we incorporate observations of individuals taking positions on cases and votes in the past and use information about the substantive implications of cases and legislation. The statistical analysis uses flexible and powerful Bayesian Markov Chain Monte Carlo methods (see, e.g., Jackman 2000). In subsequent chapters we build on the approach to assess legal and political influences on the Court.

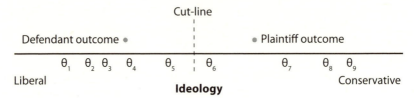

Figure 2.2. Basic spatial model

A Spatial Model of Supreme Court Decision-Making

Spatial models provide the foundation for measuring Supreme Court preferences. These models have a long pedigree and are standard in the literature (Downs 1957; Martin, Quinn, and Epstein 2005). In them, individuals have "ideal points" in policy space that maximize their utility. Policy alternatives are points in that preference space, and individuals prefer spatially closer alternatives.

Figure 2.2 illustrates the classic spatial model. Each justice has an ideal point at θ_i. Following standard spatial theory, a justice will vote for the defendant if his or her ideal point is on the same side of the midway point between the outcomes associated with voting for the defendant and plaintiff (which we refer to as the vote "cutpoint"). In the figure, justices one through five support the defendant and justices six through nine support the plaintiff. More concretely, suppose a liberal justice such as Justice Stevens has an ideal point of −1 while a conservative justice such as Justice Scalia has an ideal point of +1. If a case presented justices with the alternatives of voting to free a defendant (with a hypothetical policy outcome of −0.8) or to convict a defendant (with a hypothetical policy outcome of +0.6), Stevens would prefer to free the defendant and Scalia would prefer to convict.

Comparing Preferences across Institutions

Our first task is to estimate preferences in a manner that allows us to directly compare preferences of actors who operate in different institutions. This would be a simple task if justices voted on congressional roll calls and members of Congress voted on Supreme Court cases. In that case, we could directly apply any of the advanced measurement approaches in the literature (Bailey 2001; Clinton, Jackman, and Rivers 2004; Poole and Rosenthal 1997). Unfortunately reality is not so accommodating.

One solution commonly employed assumes that preference estimates for members of one institution are directly comparable to preference

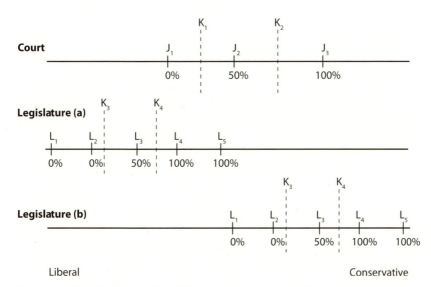

Figure 2.3. The challenge of making inter-institutional preference comparisons

estimates produced for another institution. For example, Segal (1997) assumed that a preference measure for justices based upon an analysis of newspaper editorials written while a nomination was pending (Segal and Cover 1989) were directly comparable to scores for members of Congress produced by Americans for Democratic Action based upon key roll-call votes (commonly known as ADA scores). Moraski and Shipan (1999) assumed that percent-liberal scores for justices were directly comparable to adjusted ADA scores from Groseclose, Levitt, and Snyder (1999).[2]

Scholars have long recognized the problem with this approach. Indeed, Segal (1997, 36) employed a direct comparison and noted that such comparison was "obviously not an example of textbook scaling."[3] The problem with the direct comparison approach is that it only works if the distributions of vote cutpoints facing judicial and legislative actors are the same. Figure 2.3 demonstrates what can go wrong if this assumption does not hold. At the top is a hypothetical court with judges with ideal points at J_1, J_2, and J_3. This court ruled on two cases. In the first, the cutpoint between the two alternatives was K_1; in the second, the cutpoint was K_2. The ideal point of the judge J_3 is greater than both cutpoints. If there is no randomness, this judge will vote conservatively 100 percent of the time. The ideal point of the median judge (J_2) is greater than K_1 but less than K_2, leading this judge to vote liberally once and conservatively once. The ideal point of the most liberal judge is less than both cutpoints, yielding no conservative votes.

In the next two panels are hypothetical legislatures whose legislators have ideal points at L_1 through L_5. The legislature voted on legislation that had cutpoints at K_3 and K_4. Two conservative legislators had ideal points above both cutpoints, implying a 100 percent conservative rating. The median legislator's ideal point was higher than the first cutpoint (implying one conservative vote) and lower than the second cutpoint (implying one liberal vote). Two liberal legislators' ideal points were below both cutpoints, implying a 0 percent conservative rating.

If we measure preferences based on voting within each of the two institutions, we cannot know whether the depiction in the middle panel (where the legislative median is far to the left of the Court median) or the bottom panel (where the legislative median is far to the right of the Court median) is correct. Either depiction is logically possible, even as they differ dramatically from each other. More sophisticated within-institution preference estimation will not solve this fundamental inter-institutional problem.

This is not merely a technical problem. Figure 2.4 compares two plausible ways to implement direct comparability. The first treats percent-liberal judicial scores as comparable to ADA scores. The second treats Poole and Rosenthal Common Space scores for senators and presidents as comparable to Martin and Quinn scores for justices.[4] The figure presents the estimated preferences of the Court median, the Senate median, and the president for these two approaches over time.[5]

Even casual observation suggests stark differences between the two approaches. For example, in the 1950s, the ADA measure indicates the Court was the most liberal and the Senate was the most conservative. The measures based on Poole and Rosenthal and Martin and Quinn scores, on the other hand, has the opposite, with the Senate the most liberal and the Court the most conservative. The fact that these approaches differ this decisively illustrates the need to employ measurement theory while developing measurement strategies.

COMPARING PREFERENCES OVER TIME

A related challenge is ensuring that preference measures are comparable over time. To see the issue, suppose we wish to compare the conservatism of two Courts: one that voted 7–2 in favor of a liberal outcome on *Roe v. Wade* (1973) and another that voted 5–4 in favor of a conservative outcome on *Webster v. Reproductive Health* (1989), a case in which the Court upheld a Missouri law that banned abortions in public facilities and placed other limits on abortions.

Figure 2.5 presents a hypothetical depiction of preferences of the justices on each case. In the top panel, the seven justices who voted liberally

(a)

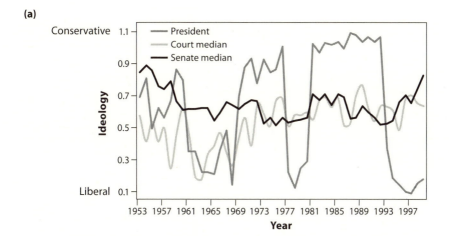

(b)

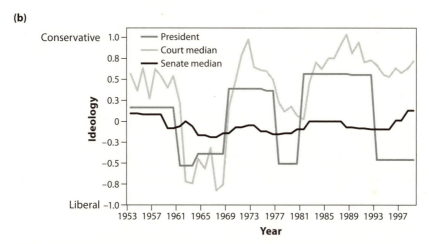

Figure 2.4. Inter-institutional comparisons assuming direct comparability. ADA Measure (*top*): inter-institutional comparison assuming adjusted ADA scores are comparable to judicial percent-liberal scores; PRMQ Measure (*bottom*): inter-institutional comparison assuming Poole and Rosenthal scores are comparable to Martin and Quinn scores.

on *Roe* are to the left of the cutpoint and the two who voted conservatively are on the right. The next panels depict hypothetical preferences of the justices who voted on *Webster*. Again, those who voted liberally are to the left of the cutpoint and those who voted conservatively are to the right. Here, though, we see the problem: Do we believe scenario 1 in which the vote cutpoint is similar to that of *Roe*? Or do we believe scenario 2 in which the vote cutpoint has shifted to the left? Or is the correct

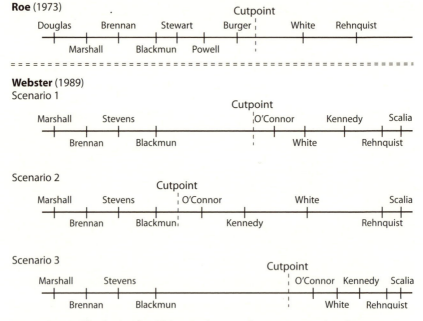

Figure 2.5. Difficulty in identifying preference change or cutpoint change

view scenario 3 in which the cutpoint has shifted to the right? Based on only the vote information, we cannot say.

The stakes are high for estimating preference change over time: If we believe scenario 1, for example, there is little to indicate a significant change in Court preferences. If we believe scenario 3, however, the bench has shifted significantly to the right. And given Baum's (1988) results that the agenda has in fact changed over time, this problem could well be quite real.

In fact, widely used preference measures struggle with across-time preference estimation. Consider first Martin and Quinn's estimates of the median of the Supreme Court as presented in Figure 2.1 (see, e.g., Epstein, Friedman, and Staudt 2008). Because the Supreme Court operates under more or less open rules and appears to mostly divide along one-dimensional lines, scholars frequently use the Court median to summarize the Court's preferences for any given point in time. As discussed earlier in this chapter, the Martin and Quinn scores imply the Court reached its postwar conservative peak in 1973.

The challenge of inter-temporal preference estimation extends to Congress. Poole and Rosenthal (1997) argue that congressional voting can be explained across long time periods with a one-dimensional spatial model of preferences; only in limited periods does a second dimension signifi-

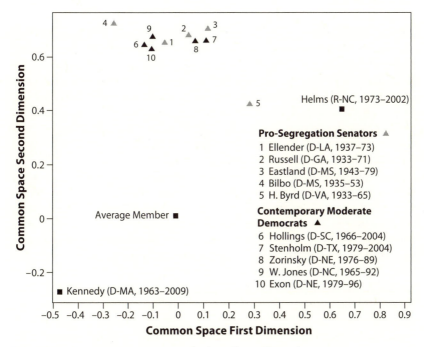

Figure 2.6. Common Space scores of selected members of Congress

cantly help explain voting. One of the products of this research agenda
has been Common Space scores that "place the members of the House
and Senate in the same space . . . [allowing] members to be compared
across Chambers and across Congresses" (Poole 2004; see also Poole
1998). These scores are routinely employed by legislative scholars.

Figure 2.6 plots Common Space scores of selected members of Congress. The first dimension captures "party loyalty" and explains most votes
in Congress. The second dimension—the so-called race dimension (Poole
and Rosenthal 1997, 46–48)—was important in the 1950s and 1960s but
faded considerably with the Republican realignment in the South in the
1980s. Average preferences are roughly (0, 0). Senators Helms and Kennedy are included as reference points, as these two often are treated as
anchors on the conservative and liberal extremes on both dimensions.

Most striking about the figure is that southern segregationist senators
are indistinguishable from modern moderate Democrats on both dimensions. Senator Fritz Hollings (D, South Carolina)—who, among other
things, voted to override President Bush's 1988 veto of the Civil Rights
Restoration Act and voted for the 1991 Civil Rights Act—is measured to
be at least as conservative as Senator Harry Byrd (D, Virginia), who advocated "massive resistance" to civil rights rulings by the Court at a time

when African Americans were routinely denied voting rights and segregated in public. Byrd (not to be confused with Senator Robert Byrd of West Virginia) stated, "we should exclude the Negro population" from voting and that "non-segregation would be most unwise and I will certainly oppose it in every way I can" (quoted in Heineman 1996, 318). Hollings also has a similar score to that of Senator James Eastland (D, Mississippi), who had stated, "I assert that the Negro race is an inferior race. . . . I know that the white race is a superior race. . . . It is responsible for all the progress on earth" (quoted in DeParle 2004, 32, citing *Congressional Record*, 79th Cong., June 29, 1945, p. S7000).[6]

Why do these immensely influential preference estimates contradict our understandings of the ideology of Supreme Court justices and members of Congress? Why do these measures lack face validity? The problem is that it is very hard to estimate preferences when the underlying policy agenda is changing. Poole and Rosenthal's Common Space scores, like the Martin and Quinn judicial ideology measures, use only vote data, implicitly assuming that the distributions of vote cutpoints over time do not vary.[7] However, without information on the relative location of vote cutpoints, the estimation has no reason to favor any one of the bottom three scenarios in Figure 2.5 and will, on average, assume that the cutpoint has not changed. This can cause a problem if there is a rapid increase in the number of conservative votes (as occurred in the early 1970s). The cutpoint distribution is by default assumed to be the same or to the right, meaning that the estimation procedure will lean toward the alignment in scenario 3 even if, in fact, scenario 1 or 2 reflects reality.

These problems do not go away if we focus on just one of Poole and Rosenthal's two dimensions. If we were to use only first dimension scores, we would have a poor measure for issues, such as school prayer and busing, that loaded heavily on the second dimension and were central to the Court's agenda. For example, the Common Space scores of Senators Max Baucus (D, Montana), Evan Bayh (D, Indiana), Harry Reid (D, Nevada), and Edward Brooke (R, Massachusetts) are more conservative on the first dimension than the indisputably racist Senator Theodore Bilbo (D, Mississippi), who served from 1935 to 1947 and infamously wrote an anti–civil rights tract entitled *Take Your Choice: Separation or Mongrelization*. In fact, the Common Space scores of most moderate Republicans are more conservative on the first dimension than those of most signers of the segregationist Southern Manifesto of 1956. One may consider using second dimension scores, but this dimension faded to near irrelevance by the late 1980s, making these scores useless for analysis of what is happening at the start of the twenty-first century.[8]

The point of these examples is that measurement matters. As scholars we need to reflect carefully on if and how the preference measures we use are consistent with the political concepts we are trying to measure. In many cases, the easiest to acquire measures will not be appropriate for the question at hand. For example, in our efforts to isolate political preferences on cases before the Court, we cannot use preference measures that imply that the modern southern Democrats are the same as their segregationist predecessors. Or, in the same spirit, as we try to assess political constraints on the Court, we may be reluctant to use preference measures that place the Supreme Court near its conservative peak in a time when it was handing down decidedly liberal opinions.

GENERATING COMPARABLE PREFERENCES

Our goal is to build a measurement model that can span institutions and time. Key to our approach will be "bridge" observations of judges and elected officials taking positions on cases and votes in other institutions and other periods of time. These observations help us pin down preferences of a diverse set of actors in a common space.

Educational testers face an analogous and mathematically isomorphic problem when trying to create scores that are comparable across students who take exams with different test questions (see, e.g., Baker 1992). Educational testers model each student as having some "ability" and each question as having some "difficulty." If every student took the same test, then it would be straightforward to compare students' abilities as they were faced with questions of the same difficulty. However, if standardized tests are made up of the same questions year in and year out, students could prepare for the exam using the actual questions. Thus, standardized tests usually ask different questions to different cohorts. The challenge is to make these scores comparable. The solution is to have a modest number of questions that are asked across the cohorts. For these overlapping questions, the difficulty is the same, facilitating estimation of ability across test-taking cohorts; this in turn facilitates comparable estimation of the difficulty of different questions.

We pursue an analogous strategy. We model each justice as having some "ideology" and each case as having (as above) some cutpoint. Our "overlapping questions" are of two kinds. The first is Supreme Court cases where members of Congress take public positions such as the 2008 *District of Columbia v. Heller* gun control case on which 322 members of Congress joined amicus briefs. We also obtain bridging observations from Supreme Court cases where non-contemporaneous justices take positions. For example, on the *Atkins v. Virginia* (2002) death penalty case, justices took positions on the previous *Penry v. Lynaugh* (1989) case, with some affirming the earlier decisions and others rejecting it. For members

(a)

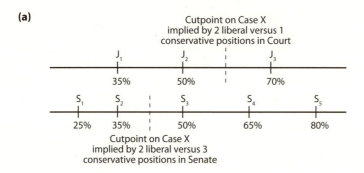

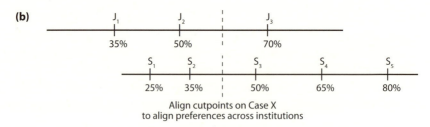

Figure 2.7. Identifying preferences in an inter-institutional context

of Congress, we have similar bridging over time on Supreme Court cases and, occasionally, on votes in earlier sessions of Congress.

Our approach therefore uses the following pieces of information: justices' votes on questions presented to the Court, the votes of members of Congress on the questions (roll calls) presented to Congress and presidents, and the positions of some members of Congress on *some* questions presented to the Supreme Court. The conservatism of political actors is analogous to test-taking ability, and the cases on which non-judicial actors have taken positions are analogous to the overlapping questions (Bailey and Chang 2001).

These bridge observations provide fixed references against which the preferences of actors across institutional boundaries can be judged. Suppose we are interested in comparing preferences of a three-person Court (with justices J_1, J_2, and J_3) to a five-person Senate (with senators S_1, S_2, S_3, S_4, and S_5). These hypothetical individuals are aligned from liberal to conservative in each institutional context in Figure 2.7(a). We also include the percentage of the time each of our hypothetical senators and justices votes in a conservative manner as a tool for illustrating again the weakness of assuming direct comparability of ideology scores. As discussed earlier, we cannot calibrate preferences across the two contexts based only on votes within the respective contexts. However, if we observe the position of the justices and senators on "Case X" we have information that is very helpful. In the example, two justices were liberal and one was conservative on Case X while two senators were liberal and three were conservative on the same case. Using the cutpoint of Case X as a fixed reference, we can align the preferences across the two institutions as in Figure 2.7(b). Using this basic insight, the statistical model described below incorporates such information in a large-scale, fully specified dichotomous choice statistical model.

Our approach is to find fixed reference points that allow preferences to be estimated even when preferences change over time. It follows a similar reasoning as for the inter-institutional bridges. To see the logic, first suppose that instead of having two separate institutions, we have the same institution at two separate points in time. There may be some overlap of membership, but if we allow preferences to change over time, we will not be able to align preferences across time without additional information or assumptions. One very useful source of information is the existence of cases (such as Case X) on which individuals at both points in time took positions. This produces comparability just as in Figure 2.7. For example, when Justice Thomas wrote in *Planned Parenthood v. Casey* (1992) that *Roe* was "wrongly decided," he provided an indication of his preferences in 1992 relative to *Roe*, a case decided well before he came to the Court by justices with whom he did not generally overlap.

Incorporating these bridge observations has the additional salutary effect of increasing information about case parameters. As Londregan (1999) has emphasized, cutpoint estimates for institutions with a small number of actors—such as the Supreme Court—will be poorly estimated. The best way to mitigate the problem is to add "votes" whenever possible and to incorporate other sources of information about vote parameters (see also Clinton and Meirowitz 2001).

We also employ information based on the relative position of vote cutpoints. Doing this allows us to incorporate substantive information about agenda changes when it is available. We know, for example, that the 1964 Civil Rights Act was more liberal than the 1960 Civil Rights Act that in turn was more liberal than the 1957 Civil Rights Act. Using this information allows us to more precisely measure preferences across time in a way that is comparable across time. Figure 2.8 illustrates how this works with a specific example involving two death penalty cases. In *Thompson v. Oklahoma* (1988) the Court assessed whether execution of people under sixteen was permissible; in *Stanford v. Kentucky* (1989) the Court assessed whether execution of people between sixteen and eighteen years old was permissible. The key point for our purposes is that allowing execution of minors under sixteen logically implies execution of individuals over sixteen is acceptable. If we do not incorporate this relative cutpoint information

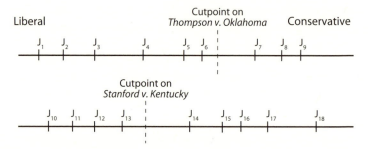

Figure 2.8. Identifying relative cutpoint locations

the estimation could, for the reasons laid out in the discussion of Figure 2.5 estimate the cutpoint for *Thompson* to be to the left of the cutpoint for *Stanford*. When we do incorporate the constraint on cutpoints, however, we ensure that on this vote the implied ideal point for justices 7 through 9 are to the right of the cutpoint on *Stanford* and the implied ideal points for justices 10 through 13 are to the left of the cutpoint in *Thompson*.[9]

To identify the relative position of cutpoints does not mean that we can characterize all justices' implicit positions on the other case. In our example, the cutpoint information does not determine positions for justices 1 through 6 and justices 14 through 18 on the other case in the example. For example, our knowing the cutpoint on *Stanford* does not rule out the possibility that all liberals on *Thompson* would have been conservative on *Stanford* (unlike what is in the figure).

We have many inter-institutional examples. The abortion issue provides several cases where the relative location of the cutpoints can clearly be identified. In many of the abortion cases that followed *Roe* (including, for example, *Webster*) the Court was asked to rule on legislation that regulated but did not outlaw abortion. If one thought that states could outlaw abortion as did conservatives on *Roe*, then, logically, states must be able to regulate it in a manner that stops short of outlawing it, as was true in all these cases. Hence, someone to the right of *Roe* must be to the right on these cases that do less than outlaw abortion, implying the cutpoints of these cases must be to the left of *Roe*. Sometimes the cutpoint information spans institutions. For example, senators voted on April 28, 1976, on a "right to life" amendment that deemed fetuses people with legal rights. Voting in favor of this amendment implied that a senator thought not only that states could regulate abortion (which was at issue in *Roe v. Wade*) but that states should ban it. Hence, the cutpoint on the right to life vote is to the right of the cutpoint in *Roe*.

A few other issues account for a large proportion of the substantive cutpoint linkages. As referenced earlier, civil rights legislation over the years became progressively more liberal; if you were liberal on the 1991

Civil Rights Act, which expanded the ability of minorities to succeed with discrimination claims, you would certainly approve of the 1964 Civil Rights Act, which established certain basic principles of non-discrimination. There were also many Court cases and congressional votes on busing; if one was liberal on busing, that meant one had to be liberal on *Brown v. Board of Education* (1954); in our terms, this means the cutpoint on busing cases and votes was to the left of the cutpoint in *Brown*. There are also many death penalty votes and cases with cutpoint constraints. The cutpoint on a vote in Congress expanding the death penalty to "drug kingpins" will be to the right of the cutpoint in *Gregg v. Georgia* (1976). Liberals on *Gregg* were willing to strike all death penalties even after post-*Furman* reforms; they would certainly be liberal on efforts to expand the death penalty.

Information on the relative position of case cutpoints was drawn from a variety of sources. Legal reference books such as that by O'Brien (2003) were used to follow the case evolution of specific issue areas. Congressional votes that had potential relations either to Court cases or to congressional votes in previous Congresses were investigated, typically using the relevant edition of Congressional Quarterly's *Congressional Almanac*.

Statistical Model

In this section we formalize our model; readers not interested in statistical details may wish to skip to the data description section. Readers interested in more details can refer to the book's appendix.

The model builds on the canonical formulation of latent preferences in the ideal point estimation literature (see, e.g., Bailey 2001; Clinton, Jackman, and Rivers 2004). Let $i = 1, \ldots, N$ index individuals and $v = 1, \ldots, V$ index votes. The utility of actor i of voting for the conservative alternative is

$$u_i(\lambda_v^C) = -(\theta_{it} - \lambda_v^C)^2 + \varepsilon_{iv}^C$$

where λ_v^C is the spatial location of the conservative alternative, θ_{it} is the ideal point of the actor at the time of proposal t, and ε_{iv}^C is a random shock. The utility of voting for the liberal alternative with spatial location of λ_v^L is analogous.

Let y_{itv}^* be the utility difference between the conservative and liberal alternatives. It is

$$\begin{aligned} y_{itv}^* &= -(\theta_{it} - \lambda_v^C)^2 + \varepsilon_{iv}^C + (\theta_{it} - \lambda_v^L)^2 - \varepsilon_{iv}^L \\ &= 2\theta_{it}(\lambda_v^C - \lambda_v^L) + \lambda_v^{L2} - \lambda_v^{C2} + \varepsilon_{iv}^C - \varepsilon_{iv}^L \\ &= (\lambda_v^C - \lambda_v^L)(2\theta_{it} - (\lambda_v^L + \lambda_v^C)) + \varepsilon_{iv}^C - \varepsilon_{iv}^L. \end{aligned}$$

At this point we treat ideology as a single-dimensional characteristic of individual justices that best predicts voting. That is, we are measuring revealed preferences, preferences that may be affected by more than the justices' personal ideological preferences. For example, a justice may be affected by stare decisis, by public opinion, by strategic considerations with regard to Congress, and so forth. The goal of subsequent chapters is to add such considerations to the framework developed here.

Let $\kappa_v = \frac{\lambda_v^L + \lambda_v^C}{2}$ be the vote "cutpoint" (the midway point between the spatial location of the yea and nay alternatives), $\alpha_v = 2(\lambda_v^C - \lambda_v^L)$ be the vote "discrimination parameter,"[10] and $\varepsilon_{iv} = \varepsilon_{iv}^C - \varepsilon_{iv}^L$ be a $N(0, 1)$ random variable that is uncorrelated with other errors; then

$$y_{itv}^* = \alpha_v(\theta_{it} - \kappa_v) + \varepsilon_{iv},$$

which implies that

$$\text{Prob}(y_{itv} = 1) = \Phi(\alpha_v(\theta_{it} - \kappa_v)). \tag{2.1}$$

Assuming independence across individuals and votes, the joint posterior probability of the observed data is

$$g(\theta, \alpha, \kappa | Y) \propto L(\theta, \alpha, \kappa | Y)\, g(\theta, \alpha, \kappa)$$

where

$$L(\theta, \alpha, \kappa | Y) = \prod_{i=1}^{N} \prod_{v=1}^{V} \Phi(\alpha_v(\theta_{it} - \kappa_v))^{y_{iv}} \times (1 - \Phi(\alpha_v(\theta_{it} - \kappa_v)))^{1 - y_{iv}}$$

and $g(\theta, \alpha, \kappa)$ is the prior distribution over the parameters to be estimated.

For cases and votes that are identical across voting bodies (mostly votes on conference legislation taken in the House and Senate) we constrain the cutpoints to be the same by relabeling the votes with a common label. For cases and votes for which we have information on the relative locations of the cutpoints, we constrain the cutpoints to satisfy the inequality constraint implied by the information. This is implemented in the Bayesian sampling process via rejection sampling.

The ideal points of individuals vary over time in order to account for the ideological evolution of justices and long-serving senators and representatives. For justices, there is a broad consensus that at least some individuals exhibited substantial preference evolution over the course of their service (see, e.g., Bailey and Chang 2001; Martin and Quinn 2002; Epstein et al. 1998); for members of Congress, this is more debatable, as

Poole and Rosenthal (1997) find little preference change. As we shall see, the results here provide evidence of substantial preference evolution of members of Congress (which is consistent with the anecdotal evidence on Senator Hollings discussed earlier).

There is a broad consensus that the preferences of at least some justices change over time (Epstein et al. 1988). Therefore, for long-serving individuals (those who served more than twenty-four years), we assume that the ideology of individual i at time t is

$$\theta_{it} = \gamma_{0i} + \gamma_{1i}X_{it} + \gamma_{2i}X_{it}^2 + \gamma_{3i}X_{it}^3$$

where the γ parameters are preference parameters to be estimated, and X_{it} is the years the individual has been in office.[11] For justices and members of Congress who serve between sixteen and twenty-four years, we estimate their preferences with a quadratic equation (meaning we estimate γ_{0i}, γ_{1i}, and γ_{2i}). For justices and members of Congress who serve between nine and sixteen years, we estimate their preferences with a linear equation (meaning we estimate γ_{0i} and γ_{1i}). We assume individuals who served eight or fewer years have fixed preferences (meaning we estimate only γ_{0i}).

This functional form represents a tradeoff between flexibility and computation. The third order polynomial estimates four parameters to represent non-linear patterns of ideal point evolution. In contrast, Martin and Quinn estimate preferences for each term, with a Bayesian prior that preferences are similar to those in the previous term. This provides more flexibility but increases complexity and computational time. In addition, the patterns of preference evolution that they do find with their method seem generally explicable in terms of a quadratic equation or, what we have here, a third order polynomial.

The model is estimated with Markov Chain Monte Carlo methods. These methods repeatedly sample from the posterior density of the parameter distribution. The mode, mean, and standard error of the distribution of the parameters can then easily be derived from the mode, mean, and standard error of the sampled observations. The appendix and references provide additional information.[12]

Data

The data consist of canonical data sets on Court cases and congressional roll calls merged with an originally collected data set of bridge observations. The core data set consists of four variables: an identifier for each member of Congress, justice, or president; an identifier for each case or roll call; a variable indicating the year of the observation; and the dependent variable, which is a dichotomous variable coded 1 if the individual was conservative on the vote in question and 0 if not. There are 495,624 total observations: 464,812 are by members of Congress, 29,524 are by justices, and 1,288 are by presidents. These include 17,882 bridge observations of actors taking positions on cases or roll calls in another institution. These bridge observations are the crucial link to identifying preferences across institutions and time. Although all of the presidential observations are bridged, the legislative and Court observations that are not are still useful for precisely aligning individuals within the same institution.

The data reflect the preference of the actor at the time the statement is made. That is, if we have an observation from 2001 of President George W. Bush applauding *Brown v. Board of Education*, this only reflects Bush's position in 2001. This is not to be taken that we are saying that Bush would have approved of *Brown* in 1954; instead these observations are about the positions of the actors at the time the comments are made.

For both the Congress and the Supreme Court, we look only at votes and cases related to the major topics addressed by the Court in the postwar era, including crime, civil rights, free speech, religion, abortion, and privacy. Concentrating on these issues allows us to focus on the most relevant areas of political-judicial exchange and to minimize chances that our results are affected by behavior on secondary issues that did not necessarily have the same structure of preferences (W. Murphy 1962, 75; Dean 2001, 41). Nonetheless, it seems that in recent years positions on the issues we focus on appear to correlate highly with positions on economic and other matters (see, e.g., Martin and Quinn 2002).

We begin in 1950. Even as more data from earlier eras become available, we believe this remains an appropriate starting point as the ideological splits of the New Deal era revolved around economic legislation associated with the New Deal, topics that were quite different than those of the Vinson Court (1949–53) and beyond when "social issues" such as race, civil rights, and privacy dominated the Court's agenda. Given our assumption of a single policy dimension, we do not want to push too far into the past when this assumption becomes increasingly difficult to defend.

Presidents

Presidential positions on Supreme Court cases are drawn from two sources. One is a set of all statements by presidents on Supreme Court cases. We searched presidential public papers, presidential library websites, and other sources for references to the Supreme Court and then coded all comments where a president or high-ranking officials in his administration took a position on a specific case. For example, George H. W.

Bush on June 24, 1992, stated he was "very disappointed" by the Supreme Court's ruling in *Lee v. Weisman* (1992) that a religious figure could not deliver an invocation at a public school graduation ceremony (see Table A.1).

We also obtained presidential positions on Supreme Court cases from solicitor general amicus filings.[13] Given the influence of the president in the selection of the solicitor general and the power of the president to overrule or remove him or her, these can be treated as administration positions. Others make a similar assumption (Segal 1989; Stimson, Mackuen, and Erikson 1995).

Several institutional and historical factors support the use of these filings for this purpose. The overt sources of presidential influence on the solicitor general are clear: "the clearest and most important institutional linkage is with the President. It is the President who, by statute, nominates the Solicitor General and at whose pleasure he serves. Should he care to, the President has the coercive language to direct the activities of even a reticent Solicitor General" (Cooper 1990, 681). These institutional powers may lead to influence even if we seldom see the president coercing the solicitor general. First, solicitor general appointees often share the preferences of the appointing president. As one of Reagan's former solicitors general, Charles Fried, said, "I have no trouble saying what the Attorney General and his crew want me to, because I'm more conservative than they are" (quoted in Cooper 1990, 681). Reagan surely anticipated Fried's preferences before appointing him. Second, even when the preferences of the solicitor general and the president diverge, the solicitor general may choose to do the president's bidding, out of deference or out of a desire to avert explicit intervention by the president.

In general, the evidence suggests that solicitors general follow the desires of presidents. Meinhold and Shull (1998) found that presidential policy statements predicted solicitor general amicus curiae briefs. In addition, examples in which presidents guide solicitor general activities sometimes make it to the public sphere. Presidents Clinton and Bush both ordered their solicitors general to change positions on cases (Fraley 1996, 1236). President Kennedy had frequent contact with Solicitor General Archibald Cox (Segal 1989, 142), and President Eisenhower personally added several sentences to the government's brief in *Brown v. Board of Education* (Days 1994, 492). President Bush (at the urging of White House Counsel Alberto Gonzales) had the administration brief on *Grutter v. Bollinger* rewritten to be more accepting of affirmative action (Novak 2003). In addition, when solicitors general take positions that run contrary to what the president wants, presidents have the ability to replace them. Reagan essentially fired Solicitor General Rex Lee when Lee expressed reluctance in pursuing Reagan's agenda (Norman-Major 1994).

Nixon forced out Solicitor General Erwin Griswold in 1972 due to a perception that Griswold was too liberal (Salokar 1992, 41).

Presidential positions on Senate and House votes are based on Congressional Quarterly data provided by Keith Poole. Work by McCarty and Poole (1995) and Poole (1998) led the way in estimating presidential preferences simultaneously with members of Congress by including presidents' positions on roll-call votes.

Senators and Representatives

Congressional positions on Supreme Court cases are based on amicus filings by members of Congress, statements in support of or in opposition to specific decisions by the Supreme Court, sponsorship data for legislation that explicitly or implicitly took a position on Supreme Court cases, and roll-call votes that explicitly took a position on specific Supreme Court cases.[14] For example, Senator Paul Douglas (D, Illinois) characterized *Brown* as a "correct and noble decision" (*Congressional Record* 110: 20910) while almost one hundred southern Democrats signed the Southern Manifesto, stating the decision was "a clear abuse of judicial power" (*Congressional Record* 102: 4459). A good example of a congressional vote that provided many bridge observations is an October 1999 vote in the Senate on an amendment stating that *Roe* was "an appropriate decision and secures an important constitutional right." (See Tables A.2 and A.3 for more congressional comments on Supreme Court cases.)

Justices

Data on Supreme Court voting from 1951 to 2008 are available in Spaeth 2009. We include all cases with bridge or linkage information or that were "important."[15] The observations of justices taking positions on cases that arose prior to the justices' arrival on the bench were taken from written opinions. Opinions were identified by (1) searching for the phrases such as "wrongly decided" or "correctly decided," (2) examining every case that overturned precedent, and (3) working through issue-specific discussions in legal reference books. An example is Justice Thomas's position on *Roe* discussed above. (See Table A.4 for more examples.)

When a case clearly and directly overturned a precedent, a vote in favor of overturning the precedent was also coded as a vote against the original decision. For example, in *Roper v. Simmons* (2005), the Court explicitly overruled *Stanford v. Kentucky* (1989). A vote in favor of *Roper* was coded as a vote against *Stanford*. In some instances, such as this one, a justice changed his or her position on a case. In this case, Justice Kennedy was conservative on the original case and liberal on the later case.

Such observations are useful in gauging the ideological evolution of individual justices.

Data Validity

Even though using position-taking that crosses institutional boundaries helps us solve some problems, doing so raises new questions. First, is non-voting position-taking less consequential than Court and congressional voting and thus less valid? This is a good question that cuts to the heart of the approach here. Three factors lead us to believe that this is not a fundamental problem. First, these observations tend to reflect commitment to the positions stated. They are, in one way or another, based on official acts (ranging from amicus filings to bill co-sponsorship to statements on the floor of Congress). In addition, the member publicly stated his or her position more than one time for more than 20 percent of the observations (although we do not use or count repeat observations in the analysis unless they are separated by more than five years). Second, public position-taking on Supreme Court cases has clear electoral and political consequences. No contemporary politician would treat his or her position on *Roe* as a trivial act, nor would politicians in the 1950s and 1960s treat their public pronouncements on *Brown* or busing cases as inconsequential. Even comments on less prominent cases can be politically relevant, as happened when Senator Rick Santorum (R, Pennsylvania) created a controversy with comments on *Texas v. Lawrence* (2003) (Loughlin 2003).[16] Indeed, it is the importance of such statements that has made the use of non-voting data for the purpose of preference measurement more common. For example, presidential NOMINATE and ADA scores are partially based on presidential position-taking. Likewise, Ansolabehere, Snyder, and Stewart (2001) use comment data from candidate surveys to identify legislators' preferences. Third, we must not overstate the consequences of most roll-call votes. Because most roll-call votes are decided by more than one vote, legislators have considerable leeway to vote based on position-taking rather than substance. In addition, Poole and Rosenthal (1997, 69) provide evidence that "roll call voting is concerned with position-taking rather than policy-making."

A second question is whether non-vote data are fundamentally different because of their more optional nature. Members may virtually be forced to take positions via roll-call votes but may easily avoid making public statements about Supreme Court cases. One consequence is that a non-random selection of legislators may take public positions on Supreme Court cases, something that in fact comes to pass in our data (see Figure A.4). A non-representative sample of legislators taking positions is not enough to bias the estimation; instead what causes bias is a correlation of the error in the selection equation (the equation that governs whether a legislator takes a position) with the error in the preference equation (the equation that governs the position actually taken) (Greene 2000, 976). In other words, there is no bias if, once we control for ideology, whether a legislator takes a position is uncorrelated with the position he or she takes.

Hence the more statistically important concern is that unmeasured factors that affect whether to take a position also affect the position taken. That is, bias can occur if, for example, members of Congress are more likely to take positions when they are more conservative than usual. In statistical terms, the concern is that errors in the selection equation are associated with errors in the position-taking equation. This would imply that the preferences of legislators are different when they choose to take positions than when they vote on cases or roll calls.[17] In this case, the error in the selection equation would be correlated with error in the outcome and selection bias would be possible. This could occur if, for example, a member of Congress only takes positions on Court cases in order to look conservative (and does not do that on roll calls, the above notwithstanding). While it would appear reasonable to assume that the public persona politicians would like to exhibit would be similar whether acting on roll calls or other public acts, we cannot know for certain that this is the case. To test for the possibility of selection bias, we compare preferences expressed via roll-call votes and preferences expressed via non-vote public positions. To do so, we generated two sets of preference estimates: one based only on Senate roll-call votes and the other based on Court data and voluntary Senate data such as public statements and amicus filings. Clear differences in preference ordering across these two estimation procedures would indicate that the ordinal ranking of senators based on voluntary observations was markedly different from senatorial behavior on roll-call observations. This does not appear to be the case, however, as the correlation between the two preference estimates is 0.89.[18]

PREFERENCE ESTIMATES

The method produces estimates of the preferences for justices, members of Congress, and presidents from 1950 to 2008.[19] We plot the ideal points for Supreme Court justices in Figures 2.9 and 2.10. The scale in each plot is the same, allowing us to see that the results accord with intuition. Rehnquist and Thomas are at the conservative end of the spectrum, O'Connor is toward the middle, and Stevens and Souter are at the liberal end. Souter began his career on the Supreme Court close to O'Connor but moved left over time. Harlan's estimated ideal points were generally

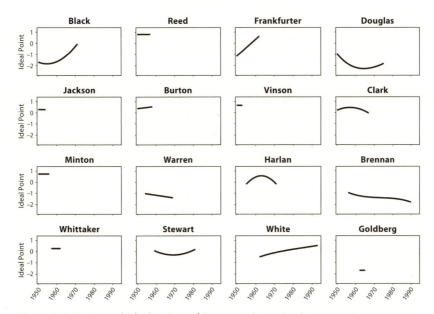

Figure 2.9. Estimated ideal points of Supreme Court justices, page 1

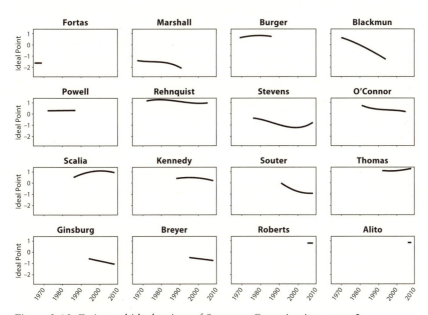

Figure 2.10. Estimated ideal points of Supreme Court justices, page 2

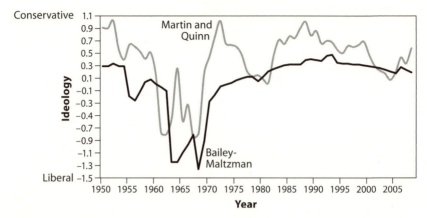

Figure 2.11. Martin and Quinn estimates of Supreme Court median over time

between those estimated for O'Connor and Souter, while Brennan's were consistently to the left of Stevens and the rest.

The estimates also accord well with conventional views about how the Court has evolved. Figure 2.11 plots the Court median over time as estimated by our method and by Martin and Quinn (2009). As discussed earlier, the Martin and Quinn scores present some startling patterns, including an implication that the Court was more conservative in the 1970s than at any other time, including the current Court. Our approach, on the other hand, uses additional information to better pin down the relative changes on the Court and produces something more in line with conventional views: the Court did indeed become more conservative in the early 1970s, but it was still relatively moderate and instead of becoming markedly more liberal over the 1970s (as in Martin and Quinn's estimates) it became gradually more conservative over time.

Our approach generates ideal points for all members of Congress who served between 1950 and 2008. In this section, we focus on how they relate to Common Space scores, which, as we have seen in Figure 2.6, exhibit serious anomalies with regard to cross-temporal comparisons. Our estimates do not exhibit such anomalies. Consider the preferences of southern Democrats over time. Figure 2.12 depicts the preferences over time of a southern segregationist senator (Eastland) and a moderate modern Democrat (Hollings). (Bayesian 90 percent confidence intervals are indicated with light lines around the estimates.) In contrast to Common Space preference estimates, our results show clear differences between these two; our results also are consistent with evidence that at least some members of Congress changed preferences over time. Bailey (2007) shows that ideal points based on the bridging approach are better able to explain

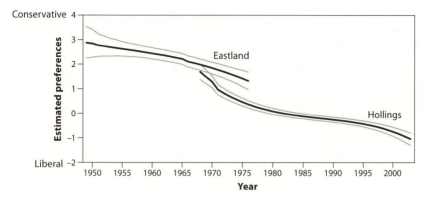

Figure 2.12. Estimated preferences for selected senators

Senate voting on Supreme Court nominations than Epstein et al.'s (2006) estimation approach that builds on Common Space scores.

There are two factors behind the differences in our results from the Common Space scores. First, our data are limited to "social issues" broadly construed (e.g., civil rights, civil liberties, speech, crime, abortion). Poole and Rosenthal scores are based on all votes across years in which dimensionality changes. To see to what extent this explains the seemingly better fit with reality for our measures, we used Poole and Rosenthal's NOMINATE procedures to estimate preferences based only on the roll calls in the sample.[20] In these estimates, the modern and segregationist southern Democrats are distinguishable; for example, Senators Eastland and Allen Ellender (D, Louisiana) each have estimated ideal points of 0.23 while Senators J. J. Exon (D, Nebraska) and Hollings have estimated ideal points of 0.04 and 0.06, respectively (with the NOMINATE-produced conditional standard errors in the range of 0.01 to 0.03). This implies that the similarity of southern segregationist and modern moderate Democrats in both dimensions of Common Space scores was due to shifting mapping of issues onto the underlying latent space, a complication we avoid in this book by limiting the analysis to a more focused set of issues.

But sample selection is far from the whole story. The NOMINATE scores from the restricted sample produce results that imply, for example, that the cutpoint for the 1991 Civil Rights Act was to the right of the 1964 Civil Rights Act (meaning someone who opposed the 1991 Civil Rights Act would have opposed the 1964 act when in fact many who opposed the 1991 act were strong supporters of the 1964 act). The restricted sample NOMINATE measures also imply, for example, that the Senate median was more or less constant from 1961 to 1980 and that the Senate median was not affected by the 1958 elections. The methods and data

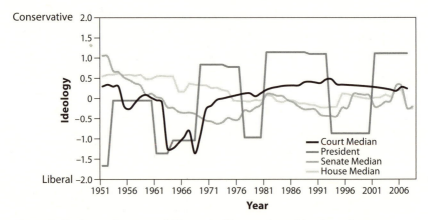

Figure 2.13. Court, Senate, and House medians and president's preferences

described in this chapter are specifically designed to facilitate careful analysis of whether we believe such results and, as it happens, produce quite different results (note the evolution of Senate preferences in Figure 2.13).

The results also allow us to examine Court preferences in relation to other branches. Is the Court out of line with Congress and the president? When does the Court move relative to the elected branches? Is it true that the appointment process disciplines the Court to keep it within the mainstream of political views?

Figure 2.13 plots the estimated preferences of the Court median, the president, Senate median, and the House median.[21] In the 1950s, the Court median started between the president and the Senate and then moved to the left of even the president. After efforts in the 1950s to curb the Court, the Court median moved back to the middle. In the 1960s, the Court moved firmly in the liberal direction, especially after Goldberg replaced Frankfurter in 1962. After a big rightward shift during the early Burger Court, the Court median trended conservative in the 1970s and 1980s. In the 1990s, the Court median was more conservative than President Clinton and congressional medians. The Court remained to the right of the congressional medians in George W. Bush's first term; the congressional medians then briefly converged to where the Court was in 2005 and 2006 but then moved clearly to the left after the Democratic victories in the 2006 elections.

CONCLUSION

Accurate measurement is essential for quantitative theory testing. If we cannot characterize preferences with confidence, we cannot determine the forces that shape them or how they in turn affect outcomes. In the case of research crossing institutional boundaries and spanning time, it has been particularly challenging to generate comparable preference estimates, a fact that has left several research agendas waiting on the development of valid preference measures that are comparable over time and across institutions.

In this chapter, we offer two contributions. First, we show that measurement matters. We highlight theoretical challenges and show the relevance of these issues for active research. Ad hoc and equally plausible approaches to inter-institutional comparisons yield starkly different conclusions about the relative policy preferences of the president and congressional medians. Martin and Quinn's and Poole and Rosenthal's widely used preference estimates imply temporal preference relations that are, in some respects, hard to believe. The examples and analysis here not only set the stage for the rest of the book but also point scholars toward being more critically reflective about the preference measures they use.

Second, we provide a method and data for producing preference estimates that are comparable across time and institutions. We use three types of information: "bridge" observations of actors taking positions on cases or votes in another institution; "bridge" observations of actors taking positions on cases or votes in a previous time period; and substantive information about the relationship of vote cutpoints over time. These data are incorporated into a spatial ideal point model estimated via Bayesian Markov chain simulation methods. The payoff is that the method produces preference estimates that avoid the anomalies found with other widely used measures, estimates that can be used to address a broad array of questions in the literature.

PART 1

Legal Value Constraints

Chapter 3

DISENTANGLING LAW AND POLICY PREFERENCES

IN RESPONSE TO A NEIGHBOR'S false report about a man "going crazy" with a gun, an armed Harris County sheriff's deputy entered John Lawrence's unlocked apartment on September 17, 1998. Instead of finding a dangerous situation, the deputy found an awkward one: Lawrence and another man were engaged in intimate sexual acts. The deputy arrested both men based on a Texas anti-sodomy law that prohibited anal and oral sex between members of the same sex. They spent the night in jail and were eventually fined $200.

Lawrence challenged his conviction on the grounds that the law itself violated both his constitutional right to privacy and the equal protection clause of the Fourteenth Amendment. The case made its way to the United States Supreme Court where six justices voted to overturn the Texas law in *Lawrence v. Texas* (2003). In so doing, the justices overturned the precedent in *Bowers v. Hardwick* (1986) in which the Court had upheld a similar law.

Both sides were quick to see politics at work. Conservatives said that the justices who voted to strike the Texas law (Stephen Breyer, Ruth Bader Ginsburg, Anthony Kennedy, Sandra Day O'Connor, David Souter, and John Paul Stevens) had trampled precedent to get to their desired policy outcome. Liberals said the three justices who voted to uphold the Texas law (William Rehnquist, Antonin Scalia, and Clarence Thomas) were simply promoting homophobic policy preferences (Pinello 2003, 100).

Even in this politically charged environment, however, each side justified itself in legal terms. Justice Kennedy's majority opinion argued that the due process clause of the Fourteenth Amendment protected consensual intimate physical relationships and that *Romer v. Evans* (1996) meant that class-based legislation directed at homosexuals violated the equal protection clause. On the other side, Justice Thomas argued that even though on policy grounds he found Texas's law against homosexual sex "uncommonly silly," the Constitution provided no grounds for overturning it. He said that were he a member of the Texas state legislature—and presumably acting on policy instead of legal grounds—he would vote to repeal the law.

In this case, like so many, political and legal explanations weave together in a complex knot. As a result, separating these influences is very difficult. The goal of this chapter is to provide a theoretical framework for disentangling the political and legal perspectives on Court behavior. We show that, indeed, the problem is knotty and how it is impossible to fully separate legal from policy-motivated behavior using only Supreme Court voting data.

The knottiness of the problem is exacerbated by the fact that legal factors can exert a decisive effect on a Supreme Court case even when the voting breaks down along ideological lines. This is an incredibly important point. The relentless flow of cases in which justices break down in ideologically sensible ways should not be taken as evidence that justices' decisions are dominated by ideological policy orientations. Instead, the model makes it clear that law can be decisive even when we observe ideological patterns in Court voting. This is especially true when the justices share a consensus about the legal values in question. The model also guides us out of the thicket. In particular, if we want to estimate the effect of both law and policy on Supreme Court voting, we need to find some additional information that will help us identify the policy implications.

A Model of Law and Policy

We use spatial theory to guide our thinking about the problem of disentangling legal and policy motivations. As in chapter 2, policies are viewed as points in space. Political actors have preferences over these policies and each actor has a most preferred policy that we refer to as his or her "ideal point." If there is only a single policy dimension (as is the case in Figure 3.1), ideal points can be placed on a line. This corresponds to everyday notions of politics. For example, we say without hesitation that President George W. Bush was to the right of President Obama.

In Figure 3.1, each justice has an ideal point at θ_i, represented by his or her location on the x-axis. The utility of justice i of voting for the petitioner is a function of the distance between the justice's ideal point and the spatial location of an outcome favoring the petitioner. Specifically, a justice's utility of voting for the petitioner's claim is a quadratic loss function: $U_i^P = -(\theta_i - \gamma^P)^2$ where γ^P is the spatial location of the outcome associated with voting for the petitioner. The utility of voting for the respondent is analogous: $U_i^R = -(\theta_i - \gamma^R)^2$ where γ^R is the spatial location of the outcome associated with voting for the respondent. In the figure, the outcome preferred by the plaintiff has policy implications located between the preferred points of θ_2 and θ_3; the outcome preferred by the respondent has policy implications located between the preferred points of θ_7 and θ_8. Following standard spatial theory, a justice will vote for the petitioner if his or her ideal point is on the same side of the midway point

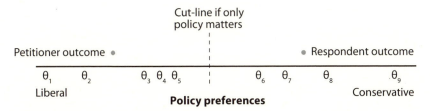

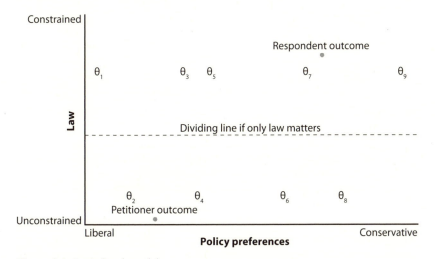

Figure 3.1. Basic spatial model

Figure 3.2. Basic legal model

between the outcomes associated with voting for the petitioner and respondent (which we will refer to as a cut-line).

In Figure 3.1, justices with ideal points θ_1, θ_2, θ_3, θ_4, and θ_5 support the
petitioner, and justices with ideal points θ_6 through θ_9 support the respondent. This pattern suggests a 5–4 liberal vote, with a cut-line between
θ_5 and θ_6. Behavior here is completely consistent with the attitudinalist
position that justices vote exclusively on policy preferences.

In Figure 3.2, we add a legal dimension (e.g., adherence to precedent or
originalism) to the model. For simplicity, we refer to this second dimension simply as the "Law."[1] The ideal points now refer to preferred outcomes for justices in both policy and legal space. Justice 1 prefers liberal
outcomes and values the law highly; justice 2 is nearly as liberal but does
not value this aspect of law. If we assume justices base their decision only
on their legal preferences (and completely ignore policy), the situation
looks like Figure 3.2. A horizontal legal cut-line divides the odd-numbered
justices (who vote for the respondent outcome) from the even-numbered

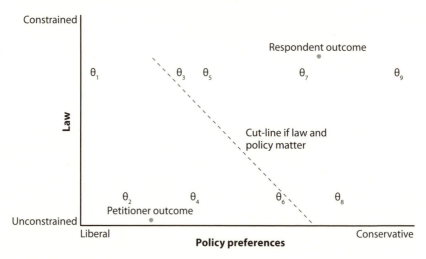

Figure 3.3. Law and policy model

justices (who vote for the petitioner outcome). The odd-numbered justices vote for the politically conservative outcome preferred by the respondent because such an outcome is more consistent with their legal
views even though some of them have liberal policy views.

Few scholars would claim that such a stark legal model captures the
way Supreme Court justices decide what opinion to embrace. Therefore,
Figure 3.3 presents a situation where *both* law and policy matter. Law here
"generates some gravitational force" on the justices (Gillman 2001, 481).
The justices base their decisions on both the policy implications of a case
and the legal merits of the parties' positions. The dividing line between
those who support the petitioner's conservative and legally advantaged
position and those who support the respondent's liberal and legally dis-
advantaged position is represented by the diagonal cut-line in the figure.[2]
It suggests that justices 1, 2, 4, and 6 will support the petitioner and the
other five justices will support the politically conservative respondent position. The petitioner and respondent outcomes have the same policy implications, but the outcome is markedly different than in Figure 3.1. Relative to the policy-only world, the votes of justices 3 and 5 have switched
from liberal to conservative and the vote of justice 6 has switched from
conservative to liberal. In other words, law has led the Court to go against
its ideological inclinations (seen in Figure 3.1) to support the respondent's conservative position.

We can use *Gonzales v. Raich* (2005) to illustrate how the model works.
When California voters approved a ballot proposition legalizing the medical use of marijuana in 1996, they put California law in conflict with

federal law that banned the possession of marijuana. The Court had to decide whether the State of California or the federal government had a better claim.

Our expectations about the case vary depending on whether we think policy or legal views dominate decision-making. If we approach the case in policy-only terms, as in Figure 3.1, it is pretty easy to align justices according to their sympathy with legalizing marijuana. The medical marijuana movement in California was a liberal political movement with previous efforts passed in San Francisco and supported by liberals in the state legislature. Liberal benefactors, such as George Soros, also invested in the marijuana legalization effort (Goldberg 1996). The movement was opposed by conservatives, including the Traditional Values Coalition and Republican governor Pete Wilson, who vetoed a related bill in 1993. Viewed in this light, the liberals on the Court—Breyer, Ginsburg, Souter, Stevens—would be expected to sympathize with the California law and the conservatives on the Court—Rehnquist, Scalia, and Thomas—would be expected to side with the anti-marijuana position of the federal government. How the moderates—Kennedy and O'Connor—would vote was unclear.

On the other hand, if we approach the case in only legal-only terms, as in Figure 3.2, we would expect the voting to accord with views about the appropriate role of federal power in regulating the economy. We would expect justices less sympathetic to federal power (Kennedy, O'Connor, Rehnquist, Scalia, Thomas; see Dorf 2009) to favor the politically liberal pro–medical marijuana side and the justices more sympathetic to federal power (Breyer, Ginsburg, Souter, Stevens) to favor the politically conservative anti–medical marijuana side.

In the end, the Court ruled 6–3 in favor of the federal government. Four pro–federal government anti-marijuana votes came from liberals (Breyer, Ginsburg, Souter, Stevens) and two came from more conservative justices (Kennedy and Scalia). The three pro-marijuana votes came from the conservative end of the Court spectrum (O'Connor, Rehnquist, Thomas). Cornell law professor Michael Dorf noted that "only Justices Scalia and Kennedy voted in line with what we might presume to be their policy preferences—rather than with their broader views about federalism" (2009).

Figure 3.4 provides a rough guide as to how this came about. Policy preferences are on the horizontal axis; legal views about the appropriate scope of the federal government are on the vertical axis. We illustrate the cleavage on the case by placing justices based on their reputations. There are four justices in the lower left corner, which indicates they have generally liberal policy preferences and tend to side with the federal government on federalism issues. Justices Scalia, Rehnquist, and Thomas are in

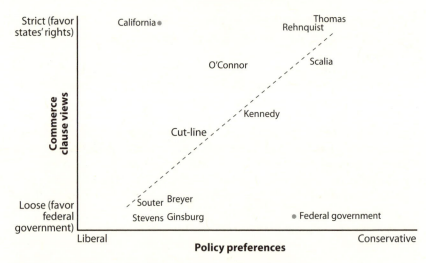

Figure 3.4. Preferences and voting on *Gonzales v. Raich*

the upper right corner, indicating they have generally conservative policy preferences and tend to side with states on federalism issues. Justices O'Connor and Kennedy are in the middle on both dimensions. We have drawn in hypothetical positions associated with the California and federal government positions and an associated cut-line that divides those voting for the pro–federal government, anti-marijuana outcome (mostly, the liberals in the lower left, ironically) from those voting for the pro-states, pro-marijuana outcome (mostly those in the upper right, ironically).

In the *Raich* case, the voting coalition did not break cleanly along ideological lines. Liberals and a strong conservative aligned against two conservatives and a moderate. In such a case, it is intuitive that non-ideological factors played a role. But what about cases that break along ideological lines? Aren't these cases most easily understood in terms of ideology? And given that the vast majority of non-unanimous cases on the Court do break down along ideological lines, isn't this evidence that the Court is dominated by ideology? The answer is no.

To see this, Figure 3.5 shows a case similar to the previous one except that now justices have the same legal views. Suppose, for example, that all justices value adhering to precedent. We can follow the standard spatial theory prescription for identifying who is closer to the petitioner and outcome, draw in the appropriate diagonal cut-line, and find a 7–2 vote in favor of the respondent. That this is a straightforward result of the assumptions should not mask how important this is for thinking about the Supreme Court. We saw in Figure 3.1 that with the same policy implications and a policy-only Court, the petitioner won this case. When we add

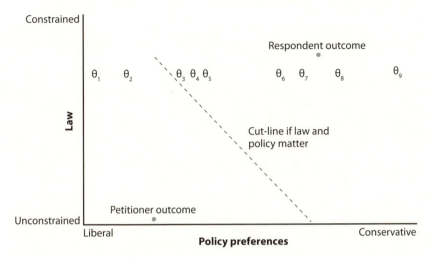

Figure 3.5. Law and policy model with contiguous ideological coalitions

law, the respondent won. Law clearly determined the outcome. *And yet, even though law decisively influences this case, the voting appears ideological.* That is, we observe seven "conservatives" versus two "liberals" (when in fact Figure 3.1 makes it clear that there are five liberals and four conservatives in terms of policy only).

This example highlights a key point: the presence of ideological voting patterns does not preclude the law shaping outcomes. On cases in which justices vary on the relevant legal value (such as in Figure 3.3), then law mattering can produce ideologically jumbled coalitions. But on cases in which justices share views on a relevant legal value (such as in Figure 3.5), law can matter yet be hidden in a thicket of seemingly ideological behavior. While the ideological patterns disappear in a world where only law matters, they persist in a world in where both law and policy matter. Hence, our observations of term after term of cases with ideologically coherent voting coalitions is not necessarily evidence that ideology dominates; such outcomes are equally consistent with a model in which law matters and justices have a general consensus about the legal value in question.

IDENTIFICATION

Our goal is to use this model to help us test if and how law and policy preferences affect Supreme Court decision-making. This model helps us see how difficult this is, as it shows that law and policy effects are not "identified." An identification problem occurs when there are two or

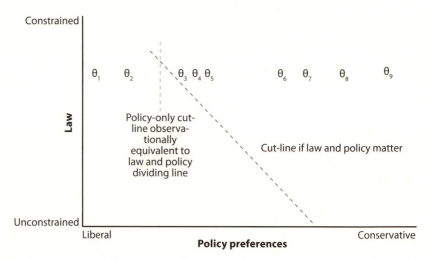

Figure 3.6. The challenge of identification

more two equally valid solutions to a problem. A classic identification problem is from early algebra. The parameter X is identified in the equation X + 4 = 10 but is not identified in the equation X + Y = 10. X is six in the first equation, but in the second any value of X can be offset by a particular value of Y. This second equation essentially characterizes our challenge. We can make X big (i.e., attribute a lot of influence to legal factors) and adjust Y (the influence of policy) downward, or we can make X small (i.e., attribute minimal influence to legal factors) and adjust Y (the influence of policy) upward.

Figure 3.6 plots two different explanations of observed patterns of behavior on the Court to illustrate the identification problem. One has the policy implications of the petitioner and respondent outcomes exactly as plotted in Figure 3.5. As a result, a diagonal cut-line explains the decisions justices make on the merits. There is another, equally valid way to explain this vote, however. We could simply shift the petitioner and respondent outcomes to the left (these are, after all, unobservable quantities) such that there is a vertical cut-line between justices 2 and 3. This cut-line would produce the same 7–2 outcome. In other words, we have two equally compelling interpretations. In the first one, justices 3, 4, and 5 were compelled to vote against their policy preferences by the superior legal merit of the respondent's case (as we showed with Figure 3.4); in the second interpretation, it was all policy, as the case's ideological cut-line between justices 2 and 3 was sufficient to completely explain voting. Hence, simply observing this—or any other—ideologically contiguous coalition cannot tell us whether the attitudinalists or legalists are correct.

Another way to see the identification problem is to examine the voting equation implied by the model. Building on standard measurement theory, we can write the probability of a conservative vote as a function of ideology and law:[3]

$$Pr(y_{iv} = 1) = \Phi(\theta_i - \kappa_v + \delta_i Law_v) \qquad (3.1)$$

where θ_i is the ideal point of justice i, κ_v is the cutpoint on vote v, δ_i is the weight justice i places on law, and *Law* is the legal merit of the conservative position (for now we treat this very abstractly; later we will discuss in detail how we code this variable in the statistical analysis).

Add and subtract the average of δ_is $(\bar{\delta}) \times Law_v$ and regroup:

$$Pr(y_{iv} = 1) = \Phi(\theta_i - \kappa_v + \delta_i Law_v + \bar{\delta} Law_v - \bar{\delta} Law_v)$$
$$= \Phi(\theta_i - \kappa_v + (\delta_i - \bar{\delta}) Law_v + \bar{\delta} Law_v).$$

If we relabel variables by letting $\bar{\kappa}_v = \kappa_v + \bar{\delta} Law_v$ and $\bar{\delta}_i = (\delta_i - \bar{\delta})$, then

$$Pr(y_{iv} = 1) = \Phi(\theta_i - \bar{\kappa}_v + \bar{\delta}_i Law_v). \qquad (3.2)$$

Because we can get the same predicted probabilities with two different parameter formulations, the model is unidentified. In the first formulation (Equation 3.1), the cutpoint (κ) contains no legal elements and the estimated δ is the weight on the law variable. In the second formulation (Equation 3.2) the cutpoint $(\bar{\kappa})$ contains the average weight on the law and the estimated $(\bar{\delta})$ is deviated from the mean weight on law.

SEGAL AND SPAETH'S TEST FOR THE EFFECT OF PRECEDENT

How can we untangle ideological and legal influences given the identification problem? Before proposing our own approach, let us first consider Segal and Spaeth's (1996; Spaeth and Segal 1999) influential test for an independent effect of law. They focused on whether individual justices who dissented on landmark cases subsequently supported the precedent in future progeny cases. For example, if an original case had a liberal majority, they interpret the legal model to mean that the conservatives on the original case should vote liberally on progeny cases. Because they found that justices' votes rarely change on progeny cases, they infer that precedent exerts little effect.

The Segal and Spaeth standard for testing the legal model means that following precedent requires voting in the same direction as the precedent on any new case on the same issue. We believe this is questionable.

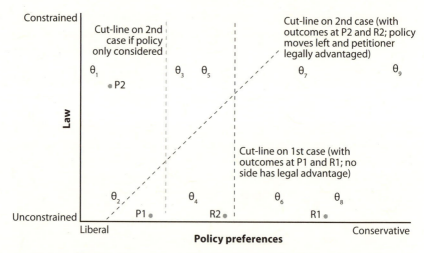

Figure 3.7. Considering Segal and Spaeth's approach in terms of law and policy model

The legal precedent of a constitutional right to an abortion in the first two trimesters (*Roe*) does necessarily imply a constitutional right to an abortion in a non-hospital facility (the question in *Planned Parenthood v. Ashcroft* [1983]). Yet, in Segal and Spaeth's coding, all precedent-upholding justices should be voting liberally on all subsequent abortion cases (see Spaeth and Segal 1999, 213). Of course, a precedent-upholding justice might reasonably maintain that one could act consistently with precedent and not vote liberally; that is, one could uphold the right to abortion but still believe that states could regulate it as a medical procedure.

We can use our model to reassess expectations about voting on progeny cases in a world in which both law and policy matter to justices. Figure 3.7 provides an example to illustrate the predictions for progeny cases. In the original precedent case, P1 is the spatial location of the petitioner and R1 is the spatial location of the respondent. By assumption, neither case is legally advantaged. The justices split according to the vertical line on the right, leading to a 5–4 liberal victory.

The figure illustrates a subsequent progeny case where the petitioner's and respondent's outcomes have moved to the left. This move means that all else equal, justices are more likely to vote conservatively as the choices are between more liberal options than on the original case. In the figure, the respondent's outcome is at R2, which is left of R1 along the bottom of the figure. The petitioner's outcome has shifted left and, because it is now legally advantaged as per Segal and Spaeth's logic, it has also shifted up such that it is in the upper left-hand corner. The choice between R2 and P2 induces a diagonal cut-line as indicated in the figure.[4]

Even though precedent actually matters on the progeny case, Segal and Spaeth's method would find no effect of precedent. To see that precedent matters, note that the policy-only vote on the progeny case would separate justices according to the light gray vertical line on the left, which is a vertical line halfway between the policy value of R2 and P2; this would be a 7–2 conservative vote. In fact, two justices who would on policy-only grounds vote for the conservative position (justices 3 and 5) vote for the liberal position due to its legally advantageous position. Segal and Spaeth's logic would require a justice who voted conservatively on the first case to vote for the liberal position on subsequent cases.

Another possibility is that the spatial locations of the progeny case move to the right. That is, the policy cutpoint of the progeny case could shift to the right. As a result, justices are, on policy grounds, more likely to vote liberally on the progeny case than on the original case. For example, suppose the Court struck a law banning late-term abortion in the original case and the progeny case was a law banning abortion from day one of a pregnancy; on policy grounds alone, some moderates might be willing to allow late-term abortion bans but not support a complete ban on abortion. In this instance, the locations of the petitioner and respondent outcomes (P2 and R2, respectively) would be to the right of P1 and R1 in the figure and the cut-line would shift right as well. More justices would be voting liberally on the progeny case, but it would not be due to deference to precedent but simply to the policy implications of the progeny case. Segal and Spaeth's approach, however, would take the new liberal votes as evidence for stare decisis. In both examples, precedent matters, but Segal and Spaeth's approach would give different answers depending on the shift in the policy implications.

We should note that there are institutional reasons to expect shifts in petitioner and respondent positions in the direction that causes Segal and Spaeth's method to understate deference to precedent rather than in the direction that overstates deference to precedent. If the original precedent case is decided liberally, litigants and overturn-averse lower courts would not want to send a case to the Supreme Court that is even less likely to pass on policy grounds (Kastellec and Lax 2008). That is, if the Supreme Court rules there is a right to abortion in the first two trimesters, lower court judges in general would not want to be associated with allowing a ban on morning-after pills (arguably a ban on abortion in the first day); a higher court would in all likelihood say that if there is a right to an abortion in the sixth month of a pregnancy, there is a right to an abortion on the first day. On the other hand, it makes more sense for litigants and lower court judges to be willing to test the Court on cases where the policy implications would move policy further in the direction of the initial case. For example, in order to find the boundary on the rights defined by the Supreme Court, a lower court judge could accept a right to abortion in the first two trimesters but also hold that a waiting period or medical licensing requirement is unacceptable—cases in which the outcomes would move to the left.[5] This implies that Segal and Spaeth's results may reflect predictable agenda dynamics in the Court rather than levels of support for stare decisis.

USING NON-COURT ACTORS TO IDENTIFY THE EFFECT OF LAW

We pursue a different approach to identifying the independent effect of law on justices. Since the identification problem means that the behavior of justices can be seen through two equally valid lenses, we need additional evidence that will pin down which lens is empirically more accurate. If we knew, for example, where the ideological cut-line κ was for a given case, it is as if one of the two variables in our $X + Y = 10$ example were pinned down. Then solving for the effect of law becomes as tractable as solving for X when we have another equation for Y.

The key to our identification strategy is using data from actors who are not affected by the legal parameters in question. As we will discuss in the next chapter, the bridge observations we have from members of Congress are the primary source of such observations. If we assume they do not share the justices' legal values, then their behavior depends only on the policy implications of a case. With enough of these observations we can pin down the ideological cut-line κ, allowing us to use the justices' behavior to assess whether law mattered. In terms of Figure 3.6, the control actors allow us to pin down the location of the policy cutpoint, which in turn lets us isolate the effect of law. If justices exhibit the same behavior conditional on policy preferences as do elected officials on cases in which legal concepts are clearly implicated, we can infer that these legal concepts do not influence behavior. On the other hand, if, conditional on policy preferences, justices differ from elected officials in a manner consistent with legal doctrine, we can infer that law matters.

Figures 3.8(a) and 3.8(b) illustrate our identification strategy via an example in which the conservative respondent's side is legally advantaged. Actors are located at their ideal points. A triangle indicates that an actor with an ideal point at that location voted liberally; a square indicates that an actor with an ideal point at that location voted conservatively. The justices are on top as they are allowed to value both law and policy. The non-Court actors are arrayed at the bottom because they are assumed to have no interest in law.

In our hypothetical vote the Court was 7–2 for the conservative respondent's position. As discussed above, based on the vote alone, we cannot

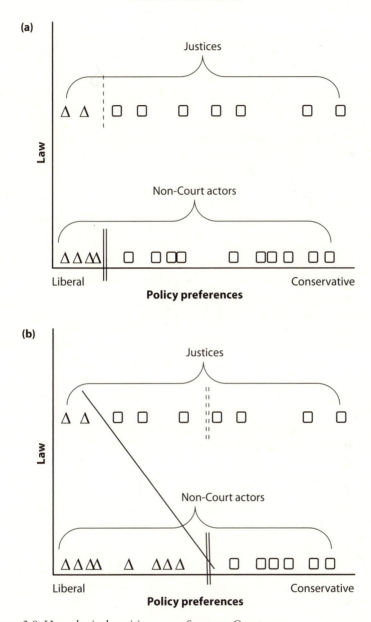

Figure 3.8. Hypothetical positions on a Supreme Court case

tell if ideology alone determined the vote or if legal considerations moved some votes. If we have non-legal actors, however, we can make these distinctions. Suppose that we observe fourteen members of Congress take positions on the case; their positions are based only on ideology. If we observe something like panel (a) in which the non-legal actors break at the same point as the Supreme Court justices, the dividing line (κ) is at the same ideological location for both institutions, which implies that there is nothing distinctive about the Court. The ideological implications of the cases explain Court voting perfectly well.

On the other hand, our conclusion is different if we observe something like panel (b) in which the members of Congress divide at a different point than do the justices. In this case, the non-Court actors divide roughly in the middle of the ideological space, quite differently than the justices' 7–2 division. The three justices to the left of the dashed double line in panel (b) would have been expected to vote liberally if they voted in accord with their co-ideologues in the policy-only world. However, they voted in favor of the legally favored conservative respondent's position, implying a diagonal cut-line such as we have seen in the law and ideology models developed above. Without the non-Court actors we would not be able to pin down the ideological implications of a case (the double line in the figures and κ in the equations), meaning that we would not be able to distinguish between these very different interpretations of the 7–2 observed vote.

Our identification strategy can also work if we allow justices to take positions on non-contemporaneous Supreme Court cases. This approach specifically allows us to identify the effect of stare decisis on decision-making. (We will discuss our approach to stare decisis and other legal concepts in greater detail below.) The key to this approach is noting that justices who vote on a case with a clear precedent are potentially bound by precedent whereas justices voting on a case without a clear precedent are not so bound. Hence the justices who voted on the original case are not subject to precedent and we can use their behavior to help pin down the policy implications of a case.

Figure 3.9 shows how these observations provide additional leverage for identifying the effect, if any, of precedent. We place justices on similar ideological and legal scales as before but we are more specific about law (labeling it stare decisis). As a heuristic device we treat the justices deciding the original case as not valuing precedent (for even if they do value precedent, it does not matter in this as the precedent in question does not affect the original case). They are therefore at the bottom of the figure (analogous to the non-Court actors in the previous figures). Their behavior allows us to identify the ideological cut-line that, in turn, allows us to assess whether precedent influences position-taking. Justices on the original

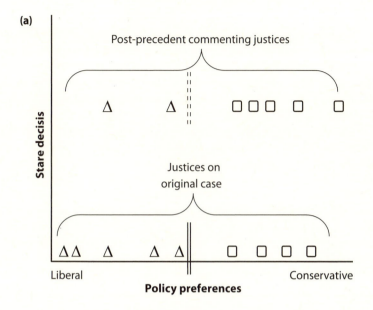

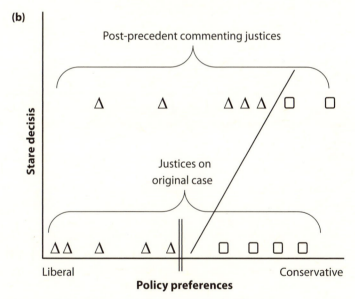

Figure 3.9. Using comments to identify the effect of precedent

Court and the post-precedent justices are different. To make it clear that the non-contemporaneous positions are not necessarily votes on cases, we depict seven rather than nine justices as the non-contemporaneous positions-taking justices.

We can look at possible outcomes to see how our identification approach works. In panel (a) of Figure 3.9 there is no evidence that precedent mattered. The ideological cut-line is the same on both cases. The distribution of votes is different only because the personnel of the Court changed, but there is no indication that the justices who took positions after the case are doing anything but following their policy preferences. In panel (b), on the other hand, there is evidence that precedent mattered as three justices to the right of the cut-line in the original case are now taking liberal positions even though their co-ideologues on the original case voted conservatively. The general idea in both of our identification strategies is to use situations in which we observe position-taking among some set of actors for which law does not matter and then see if, controlling for ideology, behavior changes when law does matter.

CONCLUSION

The question of how much justices are moved by policy and how much they are moved by law is fundamental to our evaluation of the judiciary. Observers of the courts have long recognized gaps in law that must be filled by the judgment of judges (Tamanaha 2010, 184) and have, at least since the legal realists, been concerned about the extent to which personal policy goals either consciously or unconsciously affect decisions (Stephenson 2009). Assessing the extent to which policy preferences creep in and possibly dominate legal considerations is difficult, however. Few doubt that a clever lawyer can make many positions, including a desired policy outcome, appear mandated by some aspect of the law.

In this chapter we have formalized this challenge as manifested in the quantitative study of the Court. No matter how much Supreme Court voting data we have, it will not suffice to distinguish legal and policy motivations. Policy and legal motivations are statistically unidentified with only votes on Supreme Court cases. We can, for example, observe a 6–3 vote in favor of a conservative outcome and explain it equally well with a voting equation in which law matters and one in which policy matters.

The first implication of our results is that we should be cautious about over-imputing policy motivations from Supreme Court cases that divide along ideological lines. An ideologically divided vote on the Court does not rule out the logical possibility that justices were substantially influenced by legal factors. In fact, we showed a particular example in which legal factors were decisive in turning a decision away from a policy-only outcome and yet the voting aligned along an ideological cleavage. The second implication of this is that the only way around the identification problem is to get outside data. The model implies that if we were to obtain positions on Supreme Court cases taken by actors who are not motivated by law, this will pin down the ideological component of a case, solving the identification problem. We turn in the next chapter to implementing such a model, using elected politicians as our primary non-Court actors who provide statistical identification to the problem.

Chapter 4

LAW MATTERS

ON MARCH 24, 1998, a divided Supreme Court upheld Hugo Almendarez-Torres' eighty-five-month sentence for reentering the United States after a previous deportation. The reason Almendarez-Torres was sentenced to more than seven years in jail for this crime was that he had had a burglary conviction prior to his first deportation. Without this prior conviction, the maximum statutory penalty for reentering was less than a third of the sentence he received. The Supreme Court held that this much stiffer sentence could be imposed on Almendarez-Torres even though the indictment did not mention and the jury did not establish that a prior conviction had taken place.

The central question in the case was whether the prior conviction was part of the second criminal act (reentering the United States) or whether it was part of the sentencing phase and thus not subject to the protections afforded by the Sixth Amendment's right to a jury. Justice Stephen Breyer's majority opinion for the Court concluded that the prior conviction "is a penalty provision, which simply authorizes a court to increase the sentence. . . . It does not define a separate crime." In the dissent, Justice Antonin Scalia argued that the prior conviction was an element of the crime and thus should be determined by a jury.

The case was the opening gambit in what has become one of the most confusing areas of the law: criminal sentencing requirements. It is also one of many cases where the opinions and the positions of the justices seem to contradict the attitudinal model. A liberal justice (Breyer) wrote the pro-punishment majority opinion and two moderates (Kennedy and O'Connor) and two conservatives (Thomas and Rehnquist) joined him. Against them, a conservative (Scalia) wrote a pro-defendant dissent, joined by three liberals (Stevens, Souter, and Ginsburg).

Two years later, the Supreme Court went in a different direction in *Apprendi v. New Jersey* (2000). In this case, the Court used the Sixth Amendment to overturn a sentence that went beyond a statutory maximum based upon facts that were not established by a jury. One of the justices who changed course was Clarence Thomas, who argued that he "succumbed" to error in *Almendarez-Torres* and that the Court should simply reverse itself. In contrast, Justice Stevens, who had been on the losing side in *Almendarez-Torres*, made it clear that "even though it is arguable that

Almendarez-Torres was incorrectly decided . . . we need not revisit it for purposes of our decision today" (2000).

Stevens's respect for precedent in this case was not merely window dressing. *Rangel-Reyes v. United States* (2006) presented a case quite similar to *Almendarez-Torres*, thereby offering Stevens a chance to overturn the conservative precedent. However, Stevens wrote, "While I continue to believe that *Almendarez-Torres v. United States* was wrongly decided, that is not a sufficient reason for revisiting the issue. . . . The doctrine of stare decisis provides a sufficient basis for the denial of cert" (2006b). Characteristically, Thomas continued to want to overturn precedent— one that he originally supported—writing that the "Court should address the ongoing validity of the *Almendarez-Torres* exception" (2006).

The sentencing guideline cases do not fit the attitudinal model's claim that *justices' decisions reflect their unconstrained policy preferences*. It appears that Justices Stevens and Scalia, in particular, were influenced by legal values and that these beliefs led them to support outcomes that did not necessarily correspond to their policy preferences. Without legal influences, one would expect Stevens to have embraced a pro-defendant stance; for Scalia, a policy-only perspective would lead one to expect him to consistently support a tough-on-criminals approach.

As suggestive as these stories are, they are, of course, insufficient to lead us to reject the attitudinal model. After all, we can just as easily produce stories of justices voting against legal doctrines in favor of their presumed policy preferences. Indeed, Stevens is hardly immune from overturning precedent, and although Scalia steadfastly claims that the textual interpretation drives his statutory interpretation (see Scalia 1998), evidence suggests that he is not beyond abandoning a textual interpretation of statutes (see McGowan 2008). Hence, while these anecdotes can raise doubts about both attitudinal and legal perspectives, we need more general social scientific tests to support one or another view.

Effective empirical tests, however, have proven elusive. This stems in large part from the difficulty of disentangling the justices' legal and policy motivations discussed in the previous chapter. To get around this problem, we use the approach developed there to test the extent to which prominent legal doctrines constrain the justices' decisions. Key to the approach is the use of the bridge observations: because elected officials are less likely to be influenced by legal doctrines than are justices, their revealed behavior helps us pin down the policy implications of each case. This, in turn, enables us to isolate and statistically identify the effects on justices of legal doctrines such as precedent, judicial restraint, and a strict interpretation of the First Amendment.

We find that law matters. But it matters to different justices in different ways. The legal values do not completely supplant policy preferences, but clearly the relationship between the Court and policy is much more complicated than it would be if the Court were simply a small legislature of nine unelected politicians.

LEGAL INFLUENCES ON THE COURT

Building on the theoretical model of the previous chapter, we seek to actually assess whether "law" affects judicial decisions independently of policy preferences. Numerous legal doctrines may shape judicial decision-making, including stare decisis, originalism, plain meaning, the promotion of democratic participation, and doctrines with regard to specific elements of the Constitution such as the Bill of Rights or the commerce clause (Tiller and Cross 2006). We concentrate on three legal doctrines (stare decisis, strict interpretation of the Constitution, and judicial restraint) that are both prominent and clearly more likely to play a role in structuring decision-making on some cases than on others.[1] Our doctrines are not necessarily canons of jurisprudence that are universally shared; they are principles that are widely acknowledged in the legal world as appropriately influencing constitutional interpretation.

Stare Decisis

The most widely celebrated legal influence is stare decisis, the notion that judges' decisions should follow prior decisions. Public law scholars and Supreme Court justices routinely argue that precedent shapes the decisions of the Court (Levi 1949; Dworkin 1978; Kahn 1999; Gillman and Clayton 1999; Hansford and Spriggs 2006). There are many examples in which justices seem to truly be influenced by precedent. For example, in *Baze v. Rees* (2008) Justice Stevens announced that he opposed the death penalty in all cases but that he would respect the precedents of the Court and join the majority in upholding lethal injections (Toobin 2007, 400). While precedent is at the heart of all legal methods, it may nonetheless have some instrumental value to justices (Bueno de Mesquita and Stephenson 2002; Hansford and Spriggs 2006).

Quantitative evidence in support of stare decisis has been mixed. As discussed earlier, Segal and Spaeth's (1996; Spaeth and Segal 1999) and Brenner and Spaeth's (1995) work rejecting the influence of precedent has been quite influential. Others, however, conclude precedent does matter. Richards and Kritzer (2002) find evidence that doctrinal changes in First Amendment case law led to measurable changes in the determinants of case outcomes. George and Epstein (1992) conclude that both law and ideology affect death penalty cases. Likewise, Hansford and Spriggs (2006) found precedents to be a constraint on justices if the precedents achieved a favored status by being employed repeatedly over a lengthy period of time.

Judicial Deference

Another legal doctrine that may shape judicial decision-making is judicial deference to legislatures. This factor comes into play when justices argue, as in Thomas's "uncommonly silly" comment on *Lawrence*, that although they do not agree with a given case outcome, it is the task of duly elected legislators, not unelected judges, to change policy. Justices can be among the most forceful advocates for judicial restraint. Justice John Marshall Harlan II wrote: "This Court, limited in function, does not serve its high purpose when it exceeds its authority, even to satisfy justified impatience with the slow workings of the political process" (1964, 624–25). More recently, Chief Justice Roberts elaborated on his belief in judicial restraint: "Members of Congress have been chosen by hundreds of thousands of people, millions of people. Not a single person has voted for me. And that is, to me, an important constraint. It means that I'm not there to make a judgment based on my personal policy preferences or my political preferences" (quoted in R. Barnes 2006). Other behavioral patterns of the Court suggest that it is inclined to defer to Congress. The Court invalidates a tiny proportion of legislative statutes—0.0075 percent according to Zeppos (1993)—and it is hard to believe that the Court is in such high agreement on policy grounds with the other branches. In addition, justices often use Court opinions to invite Congress to fix things as opposed to doing it themselves, as one might expect unconstrained policymakers to do (Hausegger and Baum 1999).

Strict Interpretation of the First Amendment

We also want to assess strict versus loose adherence to the Constitution. Knowing what constitutes strict versus loose construction is difficult. In many instances, objectively coding one side or another of a case as implying strict or loose construction is not feasible. But there is a sub-area of constitutional interpretation that we believe is relatively amenable to such coding: the interpretation of the First Amendment. We will discuss coding later, but here we wish to consider the legal importance of this issue area.

The concept of strictly interpreting the Constitution when interpreting the First Amendment emerged in the early twentieth century. Justices Holmes and Brandeis played a major role. In 1919, Justice Holmes used a "clear and present" danger standard to justify jailing socialists under the Espionage Act for urging opposition to the draft and wrote a majority opinion upholding the jailing of socialist leader Eugene Debs even as he was writing personal letters saying he thought Debs should be freed from jail (A. Lewis 2009). After a barrage of criticism, Holmes dissented in a subsequent case in which the Court upheld another Espionage Act conviction. This was the "first Supreme Court opinion, ever, that treated freedom of speech as a fundamental value under the Constitution. The Court had never found that any suppression of speech violated the First Amendment's guarantee of free expression" (A. Lewis 2009, 46). Holmes and Brandeis continued to resist the Court majority on speech, and finally in 1931 a majority of the Court for the first time struck a law based on the First Amendment.

Since then the Court has frequently taken a firm stand on the First Amendment (Friedman 2009, 378). Several justices, particularly those with strict interpretation orientations, have vigorously defended the First Amendment's "Congress shall make no law" prohibition on restricting speech. For example, Justice Hugo Black—stating that "no law means no law"—would vote to strike laws that he may well have agreed with but for his interpretation of the Constitution (Black 1969). Justice Scalia is one of the contemporary justices associated with a strong stand on the First Amendment (Tushnet 2005). He has cast a number of votes that have resulted in alliances that span the ideological spectrum. Perhaps the most prominent examples are Scalia's votes to join Justice Brennan in striking down state (*Texas v. Johnson* [1989]) and federal (*United States v. Eichman* [1990]) laws prohibiting flag burning. While delivering a speech at the University of Mississippi School of Law, Scalia explained that he cast the deciding vote for Gregory Lee Johnson in the *Texas v. Johnson* case even though "I would have been delighted to throw Mr. Johnson in jail. Unfortunately, as I understand the First Amendment, I couldn't do it" (UM Lawyer 2003, 1).

Modeling and Estimating the Role of Law

To ascertain whether legal doctrines do indeed constrain justices, we model the positions taken by justices, presidents, and members of Congress on both Supreme Court cases and congressional roll calls as a function of ideology (for all actors) and legal factors (justices only). The model is derived in the appendix from Equation 3.1 using the standard techniques of random utility models and ideal point preference estimation. The dependent variable indicates whether or not an individual voted conservatively. The model estimated is

$$Pr(y_{itv} = 1) = \Phi(\alpha_v(\theta_{it} - \kappa_v) + \pi_i Precedent_v + \delta_i Deference_v + \sigma_i Speech_v)$$

$$(4.1)$$

where y_{itv} is 1 if individual i takes a conservative position at time t on vote v, α_v is the vote discrimination parameter,[2] θ_{it} is the policy preference of individual i at time t (the higher the value, the more conservative), κ_v is the vote cutpoint, π_i, δ_i, and σ_i are the weights justice i places on precedent, legislative deference, and protection of speech, respectively, and *Precedent$_v$*, *Deference$_v$*, and *Speech$_v$* are the precedent, deference, and speech variables, coded as described below. Policy preferences are permitted to vary over the course of an individual's career (see appendix).

The identification assumption is $\pi_i = \delta_i = \sigma_i = 0$ for all non-justices, which means that we are identifying the effect of these factors on justices relative to any effect they may have on non-justices. Finding $\pi_i > 0$ or $\delta_i > 0$ or $\sigma_i > 0$ for at least some justices would be consistent with the idea that legal factors exert a real effect independent of judicial policy preferences.

As we explained in the previous chapter, key to our use of members of Congress and presidents to identify the policy cutpoints is an assumption that these elected actors are not affected by law. This is a reasonable approximation of congressional behavior. Pickerill (2004, 8) carefully studies the role of law in congressional deliberation and concludes that "members of Congress and other lawmakers frequently consider constitutional arguments in an instrumental and strategic manner, the main objective being to pass or sustain popular public policies." Presidents appear similar; Justice Frankfurter anticipated our approach when he criticized Chief Justice Charles Evans Hughes, saying, "My kick against the Chief Justice in a single word is that he has been just as political as the President" (quoted in Dunne 1997, 187). And Justice Kagan made our distinction clear when she asserted that how she would vote as a legislator is different than how she would vote as a judge (2010).

The reason that members of Congress care less about law per se is, in the words of legal historian Leonard Levy, because "the public cares about results and has little patience for reasons" (cited in Friedman 2009, 281). Senator William Borah (R, Idaho) put it more colorfully when explaining why opponents of the New Deal made little headway with their legal arguments: they "offered the Constitution—but the people can't eat the Constitution" (quoted in Friedman 2009, 209). The literature on Congress instead points to ideology (Poole and Rosenthal 1997), party needs (Cox and McCubbins 1993), and constituencies (Arnold 1990) as the main motivations of members of Congress.

Of course, some members of Congress and politicians may at some times care about law independent of its policy effects (see, e.g., Peabody 2005). To the extent this is true, our estimated policy cut-line will not be completely purged of legal effects and we will be identifying the differential effect that the legal doctrines have on justices relative to members of Congress and the president. Nonetheless, it seems a reasonable

characterization of the legal model that justices on the Supreme Court
should care more about the law than do elected officials.

The model is estimated via a Bayesian Markov Chain Monte Carlo
(MCMC) algorithm that simultaneously estimates the parameters in
Equation 3.1. This approach is flexible enough to incorporate constraints
on cutpoints, and it readily produces standard errors of all estimated
quantities (see, e.g., Clinton, Jackman, and Rivers 2004; Clinton and
Meirowitz 2001).

DATA

The dependent variable is the position—conservative or not—taken by
justices, members of Congress, and presidents on 3,239 Supreme Court
cases and 1,538 congressional votes that occurred between 1950 and
2008.[3] No observation exists for those who did not take a position on a
given case or roll-call vote.

Identifying Policy Implications of Supreme Court Cases

The approach relies on the inter-institutional bridge observations, discussed in chapter 2 and in the appendix, to identify legal versus attitudinal behavior. These observations consist of members of Congress and
presidents taking positions on Supreme Court cases. While our interest
centers on the behavior of Supreme Court justices, we include congressional votes in order to estimate preferences of members of Congress
relative to one another. This, in turn, helps us pin down the policy implications of votes and enables us to use elected officials' positions to isolate
the effect of the law on Supreme Court justices.[4]

Coding Cases

Our key independent variables are the three legal concepts discussed
so far: precedent, deference to Congress, and the sanctity of the First
Amendment's free speech clause. At first blush, this may seem a daunting
task. Friedman (2006, 267), for example, notes that "law may seem frus-
trating to political scientists in that, because of the way it works, the
actions of legal actors are not so easily coded as they may like." And
clearly justices can use numerous legal principles to guide their decision
on any given case.

Nevertheless, we believe it is possible to objectively identify cases in
which the three legal doctrines imply a specific outcome. For example,

although every case could theoretically be used to overturn a precedent, stare decisis is a prominent issue in only some cases. An important question in *Webster*, for instance, was whether the *Roe* precedent should be upheld. The petitioner's brief, in fact, asked the Court to use the case as a vehicle for overturning *Roe* (Segal and Howard 2005, 435). In contrast, in *Texas v. Johnson* (1989) there was no serious question of overturning the precedent that established that the Constitution protected symbolic speech; in this case, none of the parties or justices involved in the case argued that a precedent needed to be reversed.

To denote cases in which precedent was particularly salient, we relied upon the actions of the justices and the litigants. Precedent was coded as at issue if (a) any of the parties or justices expressly supported overturning a specific precedent and (b) the votes divided justices into pro-precedent and anti-precedent camps; that is, we would not code precedent as being in play if some in the majority signed onto a concurring opinion that did not advocate overturning precedent. For 1984 to 1995, the coding of petitioner and respondent briefs is from Segal and Howard 2005. For the 1978–83 and 1995–2008 periods, we coded the petitioner and respondent briefs using a list of key words based on briefs coded by Segal and Howard and the data on briefs from Gale Cengage Learning 2005. Justices' positions on precedent are primarily from the *alter_du* variable in Benesh and Spaeth 2003. For the years not included in Benesh and Spaeth 2003, we relied upon both Spaeth's (2009) *alt_prec* variable and our own reading of the opinions.

The value of the precedent variable depends upon whether supporting the precedent in question implied a liberal or conservative vote. If a liberal decision overturned precedent, that would mean that conservatives were voting deferentially (to uphold the precedent), and the precedent variable would be coded as 1. If a conservative decision struck down precedent, the liberals were voting in favor of precedent and the precedent variable would be coded as −1. A good way to understand the logic is to refer to Equation 4.1: a positive value of π_i (the justice-specific coefficient on precedent) coupled with a positive value of the precedent variable would increase the probability of a conservative vote; a positive π_i coupled with a negative value of the precedent variable would decrease the probability of a conservative vote.

The coding of this variable has a built-in bias *against* finding an effect for precedent. All cases in which precedent was actually overturned were coded as having implicated precedent and had a majority voting against precedent. However, cases in which precedent did in fact influence justices but no one made an explicit argument for overturning precedent were not coded as having implicated precedent. It is easy to imagine the parties to a case would not advocate overturning a precedent if they did not believe they had a good chance of actually overturning precedent; one could also imagine that justices would be somewhat thrifty in their advocacy of overturning precedent given the social norms on the Court valuing precedent. For these reasons, one could interpret these results as a lower bound on the true effect of precedent.

Our deference variable indicates cases that involved the Court upholding or overturning the constitutionality of a law passed by Congress.[5] For example, a case involving a federal statute banning flag burning implicates legislative deference, while a case involving the constitutionality of a shopping center that bans leafleting does not. Likewise, a case involving a National Park Service ban against oversized placards on a national monument would implicate deference to a legislative body only if the question before the Court clearly involved a law adopted by Congress rather than an administrative decision of the Park Service.

The value of the deference variable depends on whether deference implied a liberal or conservative vote. For example, if an act of Congress authorized the attorney general to expel foreigners without a hearing and was challenged, a vote for deference (accepting the act's constitutionality) would imply a conservative outcome; the deference variable in this case would be coded as 1. Likewise, if an act of Congress mandated minority set asides in contracting, a vote for deference (accepting the act's constitutionality) would imply a liberal outcome; the deference variable in this case would be coded as –1.

Our coding with regard to the freedom of speech variable proceeded in a similar fashion. To ascertain whether each justice allowed a strict interpretation of the First Amendment's free speech protections to drive their decision-making, we relied upon Spaeth 2006 to identify constitutional cases in which freedom of speech questions were particularly prominent.[6] The value of the speech variable depends on whether protection of free speech implied a liberal or conservative vote. For example, in the Texas flag-burning case, a vote to protect speech would imply a liberal outcome; the speech variable in this case would be coded as –1. In *McConnell v. FEC* (2003), a case that considered the constitutionality of restrictions on campaign ads, the conservatives were voting for free speech while liberals who were voting to regulate ads in the interest of equalizing access to the political system were voting against it. In this case, the speech variable is coded as 1.

Putting the above sources of data together, we have a data structure in which there is a dependent variable (whether or not a given actor took a conservative or liberal position on a given case or roll call) and a series of parameters that allow us to estimate ideal points (θ), vote parameters (α and κ), and the law variables (π, δ, and σ) identified in Equation 4.1.

RESULTS

Table 4.1 reports the estimated precedent (π), congressional deference (δ), and speech (σ) parameters for the justices in the sample, as well as the Bayesian analog to a significance level for each parameter. The column headed $\pi = \delta = \sigma = 0$ has the Bayesian analog to a p-value for the null hypothesis that the coefficients on all legal parameters are equal to zero for that individual versus the alternative hypothesis that one of the coefficients is greater than zero. For twenty-four of the thirty-two justices we examine, we can reject the null that all legal parameters are zero or less at the 1 percent level; the number goes up to twenty-eight and thirty for the 5 and 10 percent significance levels, respectively.[7] These results strongly imply that legal factors affect most justices. In addition, three of the four justices for whom there is least evidence of legal effects have relatively few observations (Robert Jackson, Fred Vinson, and Abe Fortas), raising the possibility that low statistical power may be behind some of the null results.[8]

Breaking the results down by legal dimension, the precedent parameter for seven justices was significantly greater than zero at the 1 percent level and was significantly greater than zero at the 5 and 10 percent levels for eleven and fourteen justices, respectively. The deference parameter for five justices was significantly greater than zero at the 1 percent level and was significantly greater than zero at the 5 and 10 percent levels for eight and twelve justices, respectively. The free speech parameter for fifteen justices was significantly greater than zero at the 1 percent level and was significantly greater than zero at the 5 and 10 percent levels for sixteen and seventeen justices, respectively.[9]

Of course, we wish to get a sense of how much these factors mattered. The non-linear probit-like structure of the model renders direct interpretation of the parameters impossible. Therefore, we used the estimated parameters to simulate justices' probabilities of voting conservatively. Figure 4.1 shows one typical set of simulation results for the precedent parameter (in order to keep the figure simple, it only displays justices appointed after 1960). We assume that the cutpoint, κ, is zero. For each justice we calculated his or her average policy preference over the time period in the sample and then calculated the probability of voting conservatively given that precedent was implicated and implied a conservative vote (the dark bar in the figure) or a liberal vote (the lightly shaded bar). If after controlling for policy preferences a justice's votes were swayed by precedent, his or her dark bar will be higher than his or her light bar. For example, when precedent suggests a liberal outcome, O'Connor is simulated to vote in a conservative direction with 45 percent probability;

TABLE 4.1
Legal Parameter Estimates

	Legal measure			
Justice	Precedent (π)	Congress (δ)	Speech (σ)	π = δ = σ = 0
Black	−0.32 (p = 0.94)	−0.87 (p = 1.00)	1.02 (p = 0.001)	(p = 0.001)
Reed	−0.24 (p = 0.60)	2.49 (p = 0.003)	0.38 (p = 0.22)	(p = 0.001)
Frankfurter	−0.02 (p = 0.51)	0.49 (p = 0.09)	−0.33 (p = 0.87)	(p = 0.025)
Douglas	−0.20 (p = 0.74)	−0.86 (p = 0.99)	0.95 (p = 0.001)	(p = 0.001)
Jackson	0.79 (p = 0.19)	−0.93 (p = 0.87)	0.19 (p = 0.34)	(p = 0.066)
Burton	−0.25 (p = 0.68)	1.11 (p = 0.01)	0.00 (p = 0.49)	(p = 0.005)
Vinson	−1.47 (p = 0.83)	1.33 (p = 0.20)	−0.31 (p = 0.70)	(p = 0.110)
Clark	0.44 (p = 0.03)	0.32 (p = 0.14)	−0.28 (p = 0.91)	(p = 0.003)
Minton	−0.59 (p = 0.72)	1.25 (p = 0.03)	0.23 (p = 0.32)	(p = 0.008)
Warren	−0.36 (p = 0.91)	0.24 (p = 0.21)	0.31 (p = 0.09)	(p = 0.025)
Harlan	−0.02 (p = 0.54)	0.00 (p = 0.49)	−0.08 (p = 0.67)	(p = 0.181)
Brennan	−0.19 (p = 0.87)	0.23 (p = 0.08)	0.69 (p = 0.001)	(p = 0.001)
Whittaker	−0.13 (p = 0.63)	0.71 (p = 0.07)	−0.13 (p = 0.63)	(p = 0.031)
Stewart	0.20 (p = 0.11)	0.21 (p = 0.09)	0.80 (p = 0.001)	(p = 0.001)
White	0.24 (p = 0.05)	0.40 (p = 0.00)	0.06 (p = 0.29)	(p = 0.001)
Goldberg	−0.67 (p = 0.82)	−0.10 (p = 0.54)	1.46 (p = 0.04)	(p = 0.021)

Note: The "p" values are the Bayesian analogs to conventional p-values.

but when precedent suggests a conservative outcome, O'Connor is simulated to have an 85 percent probability of voting conservatively. On cases where respect for stare decisis was implicated, O'Connor tended to vote with precedent. In contrast, Scalia's dark and lightly shaded bars are relatively similar (and, if anything, suggest Scalia tends to vote against precedent), suggesting that stare decisis plays a relatively small role in his jurisprudence; in other words, our results indicate that regardless of the direction of the precedent Scalia embraces conservative positions.

Figures 4.2, 4.3, and 4.4 present averages of such simulations across multiple values of κ. For each justice, the bar indicates the average of the simulated change in probability of a justice casting a conservative vote when the precedent is implicated (Figure 4.2), when deference to Congress is implicated (Figure 4.3), or when a strict interpretation of the First Amendment suggests a particular outcome (Figure 4.4).[10] We also use a thin line to connect the 10th and 90th percentiles of the posterior distribution in order to indicate the precision of the parameter estimates. Some estimates are imprecise because some justices voted on only a few cases with legal concepts implicated.

Every justice who joined the bench after Warren Burger became Chief Justice has a significant stare decisis parameter except Clarence Thomas, Antonin Scalia, and Harry Blackmun. Thomas has a reputation for not

TABLE 4.1
(continued)

Justice	Precedent (π)	Congress (δ)	Speech (σ)	$\pi = \delta = \sigma = 0$
		Legal measure		
Fortas	−0.67 (p = 0.94)	−0.13 (p = 0.57)	−0.16 (p = 0.66)	(p = 0.367)
Marshall	−0.04 (p = 0.56)	0.14 (p = 0.23)	0.48 (p = 0.003)	(p = 0.002)
Burger	0.31 (p = 0.09)	0.41 (p = 0.02)	0.32 (p = 0.01)	(p = 0.001)
Blackmun	0.09 (p = 0.31)	0.41 (p = 0.01)	0.37 (p = 0.004)	(p = 0.001)
Powell	0.36 (p = 0.05)	0.56 (p = 0.004)	0.55 (p = 0.001)	(p = 0.001)
Rehnquist	0.23 (p = 0.07)	0.11 (p = 0.27)	0.15 (p = 0.15)	(p = 0.005)
Stevens	0.37 (p = 0.01)	0.29 (p = 0.03)	0.31 (p = 0.002)	(p = 0.001)
O'Connor	0.58 (p = 0.001)	−0.24 (p = 0.89)	0.34 (p = 0.01)	(p = 0.001)
Scalia	−0.18 (p = 0.89)	−0.59 (p = 0.99)	0.68 (p = 0.001)	(p = 0.001)
Kennedy	0.27 (p = 0.03)	−0.53 (p = 0.99)	1.05 (p = 0.001)	(p = 0.001)
Souter	0.77 (p = 0.001)	0.06 (p = 0.40)	0.71 (p = 0.001)	(p = 0.001)
Thomas	−0.50 (p = 0.99)	−0.91 (p = 1.00)	0.72 (p = 0.001)	(p = 0.001)
Ginsburg	0.67 (p = 0.001)	−0.35 (p = 0.91)	0.61 (p = 0.003)	(p = 0.001)
Breyer	0.64 (p = 0.001)	−0.11 (p = 0.67)	−0.05 (p = 0.58)	(p = 0.001)
Roberts	1.24 (p = 0.02)	0.00 (p = 0.50)	0.40 (p = 0.27)	(p = 0.006)
Alito	1.39 (p = 0.02)	0.17 (p = 0.44)	0.46 (p = 0.27)	(p = 0.002)

valuing precedent; Goldstein (2007) has written that Thomas "believes that precedent qua precedent concerning constitutional law has no value at all; he does not give stare decisis any weight. Justice Thomas's view is, at bottom, a doctrine of stare indecisis" (see also Toobin 2007, 119; Sunstein 2005, 34). That Justice Scalia is unconstrained by stare decisis is also not particularly surprising; as he himself has noted, "I do not myself believe in rigid adherence to stare decisis in constitutional cases" (2003). The pro-precedent justices are not surprising either. For example, Toobin (2007, 63) attributes to Anthony Kennedy the thought that "saving *Roe* would show the world that judges were something more than mere pols" at the time Kennedy joined David Souter and Sandra Day O'Connor to reaffirm the basic core of *Roe* in the *Casey* decision. Of justices appointed before Burger, only Byron White and Tom Clark exhibited pro-precedential behavior.

For the deference to Congress parameter, the results in Figure 4.3 indicate that Justices John Paul Stevens, Lewis Powell, Harry Blackmun, Warren Burger, Byron White, Potter Stewart, Charles Whittaker, William Brennan, Sherman Minton, Harold Burton, Felix Frankfurter, and Stanley Reed were significantly more likely to practice judicial restraint and defer to Congress. In contrast, Justices Clarence Thomas, Anthony Kennedy, Antonin Scalia, Sandra Day O'Connor, William Douglas, and Hugo

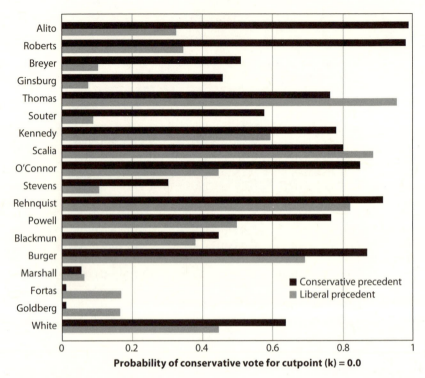

Figure 4.1. Simulated effect of precedent

Black have coefficients that are both negative and significant—suggesting the complete absence of any constraint based upon a notion of congressional deference.

The face validity of these results is strong. Two justices whom we estimate as among the most deferential—Frankfurter and Burton—were labeled "champions of restraint" by historian Arthur Schlesinger in 1947 (Lindquist and Cross 2009, 1) and those classified by Lindquist and Cross (2009) as most deferential include justices we estimate as being most deferential to Congress, including Frankfurter, Clark, Burger, White, Powell, and Blackmun.[11] Our findings are also compatible with Howard and Segal's (2004) finding that White and Powell are the two justices who most clearly showed a preference for deference when both liberals and conservatives sought to overturn a congressional act.[12]

Figure 4.4 indicates all justices appointed since Justice Whittaker in 1957, except Justices Breyer, Rehnquist, Fortas, and White, were significantly influenced by pro-speech sentiments. That is, after controlling for the ideological predispositions of these justices—many of whom would be ideologically predisposed to favor speech claims—most justices were

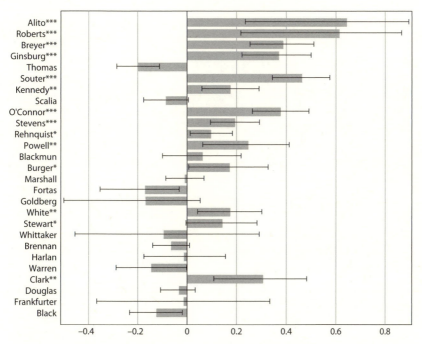

Figure 4.2. Effect of precedent. The shaded bar indicates the change in probability of a conservative vote when moving from *Precedent* = −1 to *Precedent* = 1. The line indicates a simulated 90 percent Bayesian confidence interval; ***change significantly > 0 at $p = .01$; **change significantly > 0 at $p = .05$; *change significantly > 0 at $p = .1$.

more favorable toward speech claims. The inclusion of members of Congress in the model allows us to identify these effects by pinning down the ideological cutpoint of cases in which speech was a central issue. Among the justices with the largest estimated parameters are Black and Stewart, consistent with Black's famous devotion to the First Amendment (see, e.g., Dunne 1977, 289; Cross 1997, 291) and Stewart's belief that "censorship reflects a society's lack of confidence in itself. It is a hallmark of an authoritarian regime" (1966, 498).

CONCLUSION

For years, many empirically oriented judicial scholars have maintained that there is no systematic evidence that legal doctrines constrain justices. In this chapter, we revisit this question by using the positions taken by members of Congress, presidents, and previous Supreme Court justices to

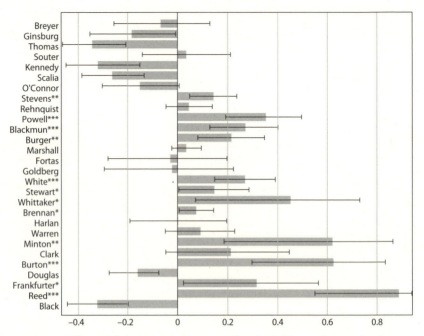

Figure 4.3. Effect of deference to Congress. The shaded bar indicates the change in probability of a conservative vote when moving from *Deference* = −1 to *Deference* = 1. The line indicates a simulated 90 percent Bayesian confidence interval; ***change significantly > 0 at p = .01; **change significantly > 0 at p = .05; *change significantly > 0 at p = .1.

identify distinctive effects of law and policy on Supreme Court decision-making. In contrast to the attitudinal model, we find strong evidence that legal principles are influential for the decisions made by most justices. We also find considerable heterogeneity as different justices value different legal doctrines.

Even though we find evidence that the decisions justices make are routinely constrained by notions of the law, we suspect that we have understated the effect of the law for three reasons. First, measurement of our three doctrines is imperfect, and measurement error typically attenuates results. Second, there are many doctrines that we have not examined and that may well influence justices. Third, justices who act inconsistently with a legal doctrine are also not necessarily letting their policy preferences override the law (Lindquist and Solberg 2007). In some cases, it may be that adherence to one legal concept may override adherence to another. For example, a justice who values a narrow reading of the commerce clause may be less likely to defer to Congress when Congress inserts itself into the gray area of federalism.

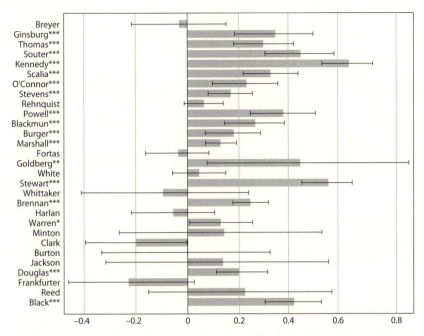

Figure 4.4. Effect of judicial free speech values. The shaded bar indicates the change in probability of a conservative vote when moving from *Speech* = −1 to *Speech* = 1. The line indicates a simulated 90 percent Bayesian confidence interval; ***change significantly > 0 at $p = .01$; **change significantly > 0 at $p = .05$; *change significantly > 0 at $p = .1$.

With solid evidence that law matters and that the way it matters varies across individual justices, the natural next question is: Where do these values come from? How does the variation in legal influences affect the operation of the Court and its relation to the rest of the political system? We turn to these questions in the next chapter.

Chapter 5

CAUSES AND CONSEQUENCES OF DIVERSE LEGAL VALUES

No one doubts Felix Frankfurter's liberal pedigree. Before serving on the Court, Frankfurter helped found the American Civil Liberties Union (ACLU), wrote a book criticizing death sentences for Nicola Sacco and Bartolomeo Vanzetti, and advised Franklin Roosevelt. However, on the Court, Frankfurter was widely viewed as a conservative jurist. He took conservative positions on anti-communist cases (Friedman 2009, 255) and labor cases (Spaeth and Altfeld 1986) and frequently butted heads with liberal justices (Urofsky 1991, 63; Ely 1980, 3). Statistical studies place him on the conservative end of the bench (Bailey 2007; Martin and Quinn 2002).

One source of Frankfurter's judicial conservatism was that he believed "unless a statute violates a clear constitutional prohibition, courts should not void a law because judges disagree with its premises" (Urofsky 1991, x). This led him to repeatedly vote to uphold legislation and government actions that he opposed on policy grounds. Frankfurter testified against the death penalty before the Royal Commission on Capital Punishment in London in 1950, but he did not systematically rule against it as a justice (Urofsky 1991, 215). He opposed anti-subversion acts such as the Smith Act of 1940, writing to Justice Brennan that "there isn't a man on the Court who personally disapproves more than I do of the un-American Committees, of all the Smith prosecutions, of the Attorney General's list etc etc," but he generally did not vote against such government activities (Friedman 2009, 255; Urofsky 1991, 115).[1]

Frankfurter's reluctance to strike laws or government actions makes sense in light of his personal history. In the early twentieth century when Frankfurter entered public life, the Supreme Court struck progressive legislation with relentless regularity. In *Pollack v. Farmers Loan and Trust* (1895) it struck the income tax. In *Lochner v. New York* (1905) it struck limits on the work week. In *Bailey v. Drexel Furniture* (1922) it struck child labor laws. In *Adkins v. Children's Hospital* (1923) and *Morehead v. New York* (1936) it struck minimum wage laws. And in *Schechter Poultry v. United States* (1935) it struck the New Deal's center-piece National Industrial Recovery Act. Not surprisingly, liberals were fed up with Court intervention.

Hence it is not surprising that a progressive leader like Frankfurter believed that "the role of the Court was to accept the verdict of democratically elected legislative majorities" (Levinson 1977, 83). Frankfurter particularly respected Justice Holmes, who took a famously restrained view of what the Court should do. Just before joining the Court, Frankfurter (1938, 22) wrote approvingly of Holmes that "it was not for him to prescribe for society or to deny it the right of experimentation with very wide limits. That was to be left for contest by the political forces in the state. The duty of the Court was to keep the ring free."[2]

Not all liberals in Frankfurter's era came to share his legal philosophy, however. Justices Black, Jackson, Reed, Douglas, and Frankfurter had all "originally been regarded as New Dealers, expected to take almost similar political philosophies to the Court" (Katcher 1967, 312), but Black and Douglas in particular showed little interest in judicial deference (Friedman 2009, 239). These presumably liberal justices clashed repeatedly, often with a great deal of animosity, making it clear that judicial values were not fully determined by ideology and historical context (Yalof 1999, 27).

What, then, can we say about the determinants of legal values on the Court? How much do legal values reflect the political context? What other factors matter? And what, in turn, is the effect of these heterogeneous values on the operation of the Court? As we will see, historical context and personal experiences affect the legal values of justices, but the connections are imperfect and unpredictable.

HISTORICAL "REGIMES" AND LEGAL VALUES

Figure 5.1 ranks the impact of our three legal variables across justices. The justices at the top are, relative to their brethren, more constrained by the legal doctrines reflected in each column. The results show clear changes over time in which legal factors matter the most. The top justices on the precedent variable tend to be of recent vintage; of the fourteen with statistically significant precedent coefficients, ten of them served on the Court after 2000. The top justices on the deference variable, in contrast, served much earlier. Most of the justices with statistically significant deference coefficients served in the 1950s and 1960s; only Justice Stevens served after 2000. The top justices on the speech parameter are more distributed over time. Some, such as Stewart, Goldberg, Black, and Brennan, served early in our time frame; others, such as Souter, Ginsburg, Scalia, and Thomas, are more recent occupants of the bench.

Figure 5.2 provides a schematic view of the evolving mix of legal values. The figure plots the median effect of each variable over time for the

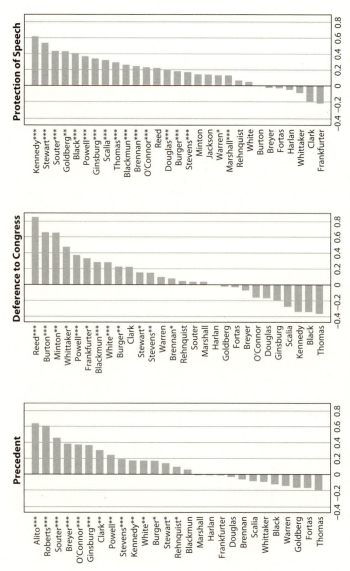

Figure 5.1. Effect of law: average percentage-point change in probability of conservative vote (for justices with more than ten non-zero observations for each independent variable); ∗∗∗significant at $p = .01$; ∗∗significant at $p = .05$; ∗significant at $p = .1$.

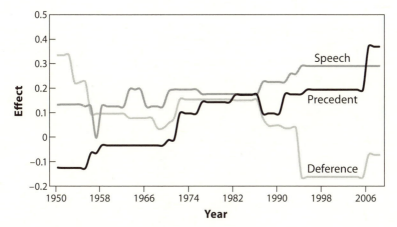

Figure 5.2. Average effects of different legal concepts

sitting members of the Court. Precedent mattered little in the 1950s and 1960s, became more important in the 1970s, and had its greatest impact in the 1990s. Deference, on the other hand, has been almost a mirror image of precedent: it was high in the 1950s but declined over time and is now a thing of the past. The median effect of speech has held relatively steady over the postwar era. Because we have not measured all important legal values this schematic cannot be treated as a comprehensive inventory of the doctrines justices employ; rather, it is a demonstration of the changing nature of the doctrines that constrain the Court.

Judicial regime theory provides a useful perspective on these changes. Studies in this tradition view "political time in terms of fluid eras or periods in American history characterized by shifting coalitions that seek to advance their agendas instrumentally under evolving understandings of the meaning of preferences and the rules of the game" (J. Barnes 2007, 31). The clear variation over time in the relevance of the three legal factors suggests that there may be more than idiosyncrasy behind the manner in which legal values rear their head in the Supreme Court.

Policy preferences may influence the legal values of justices at a meta-level; justices may "choose" the judicial values that most advance their broad policy goals. For example, during his service in the Nixon administration future Chief Justice Rehnquist wrote that a "judge who is a 'strict constructionist' in constitutional matters will generally not be favorably inclined toward claims of either criminal defendants or civil rights plaintiffs" (quoted in Dean 2001, 16). This kind of thinking may have made strict construction attractive to a young conservative lawyer such as Rehnquist. And whatever deviations from the conservative line that may later be called for due to adherence to this approach may simply be outweighed by the advantages of having a general theory upon which to base generally conservative action.

Justices' respect for stare decisis seems to respond to political context. As discussed above, New Dealers came to the Court with rather hostile feelings toward what the Court was doing. It was natural for them to be averse to precedent as they wanted to change the Court's direction. Frankfurter, for example, expressed opposition to being bound too closely to precedent before joining the Court (Gerhardt 2008, 56). His fellow New Dealers Black and Douglas showed clear antipathy toward stare decisis throughout their careers (Gerhardt 2008, 52).

Over time, however, new justices placed greater value on precedent. Part of this may be in response to choruses of concern about activist judges that arose in response to the Warren Court. Part of it may be that for many justices, the precedents became, on balance, more appealing. It is possible, for example, that Justice Souter valued precedent in part because precedents were generally liberal; he may have had to support some precedents he did not like, but on net adhering to stare decisis when possible may have led to outcomes closer to his policy preferences.

While most justices on recent Courts have valued precedent, Justices Thomas and Scalia have resisted this tendency. After decades of blockbuster liberal decisions, adherence to precedent can have a liberal patina and it is no surprise that Thomas and Scalia, like their New Dealer forebears, wanted little part of it. They have not simply opposed precedent, however. They have advocated originalism as an alternative, arguing that the Constitution should be interpreted as closely as possible to the intentions of its authors. While originalism is a complex and multifaceted approach to constitutional interpretation, the political logic of it for conservatives is clear as it solves "the problem of stare decisis by providing a justification for a jurist committed to judicial restraint to engage nonetheless in aggressive overruling" (Friedman 2009, 312). Supreme Court nominee Robert Bork is another advocate of originalism and his rejection by the Senate in 1987 was in part due to fears that he would use originalism to undo popular precedents (Gerhardt 2008, 54).

Interestingly, conservative justices Alito and Roberts come out as being very pro-precedent in our estimates. Our data stop in 2008, so these estimates are based on rather limited data for these two justices and the standard errors on the estimated effects for them are correspondingly large. Therefore, we should take the placement of these two at the high end of the precedent scale with a grain of salt. As time passes it will become clearer how solid their commitment to precedent is. The fact that both justices voted in *Citizens United v. F.E.C* (2010) to overturn longstanding precedent was viewed by many as a sign that Alito and Roberts are not strong defenders of stare decisis. On the other hand, Justice Roberts wrote a concurrence defending the overturning of precedent in a defensive tone. Perhaps this concurrence (which was joined only by Alito) is a sign that the two treat overturning precedent as a sensitive topic.

Judicial restraint also has an understandable historical arc. The emphasis on judicial restraint by justices such as Frankfurter, Reed, and others makes sense in light of the historical context we discussed with regard to Frankfurter. More recently, though, deference to Congress has not been a particularly constraining force. There are a number of possible factors. One is that public approval of Congress has plummeted while approval of the Court has held relatively steadily, creating an ironic situation where the unelected Court is more popular than the elected Congress (Friedman 2009, 372). Another factor is that other legal values have simply displaced deference to Congress. In various combinations, contemporary justices tend to value precedent, originalism, a states' rights view of federalism, and protection of free speech. By the time these values are satisfied, there may not be much room for deference to Congress, however much the justices state their fealty to this principle in their confirmation appearances.

The speech variable has been stronger in recent times. One aspect of this has been the embrace of free speech by conservatives such as Thomas and Scalia.[3] Epstein and Segal probe a modern argument about the changing political context of jurisprudential values. They argue that liberals have come to be less supportive of free speech than conservatives and that this may mean "First Amendment values are merely instrumental of more basic ideological concerns, with equality the number one suspect. If support for the First Amendment favors equality, then liberals will support it; if not, First Amendment values may be little more than an impediment toward their desired goals" (2006, 110). Our evidence does not lend itself to such a strong interpretation. Not only are some contemporary liberals as pro–free speech as conservatives (e.g., Justices Souter and Ginsburg), but it is important to note that we do not simply find that the pro-speech justices (conservative or not) favor free speech but that they are more willing to vote for free speech positions than are their co-ideologues in Congress.

Nonetheless, our findings are broadly supportive of regime theory. And our findings support the argument made by Epstein and Segal. Something has changed. What about the current regime has increased the proportion and ideological range of justices who are distinctively pro–free speech? Perhaps the simplest answer is that business has become more interested in free speech, but that leaves unanswered why justices across the ideological spectrum are more pro–free speech than are their co-ideologues in Congress. It is clear that a number of justices view the Constitution as providing clear guidance on issues of free speech.

In sum, legal values are not independent of politics. As legal regimes evolve, so too do the patterns of legal values that justices hold. Adhering to these legal values may lead justices to vote against their immediate policy preferences. Once a justice subscribes to a doctrine, it does indeed act as a constraint. But justices typically associate themselves with legal values that tend to promote their favored outcomes (Posner 2005, 50).

EXPERIENCE AND JUDICIAL VALUES

The sources of the legal values need not be exclusively political, however. Personal experiences may also shape justices' legal values. Justices have been judges, bureaucrats, corporate lawyers, activists, and politicians before joining the Court. Certainly it is plausible that such life experiences affected the way justices have approached their jobs.

Because of the relatively small number of justices in our study, we are generally unable to quantitatively test for the effect of specific life experiences on legal values. The major exception is experience on the bench. Enough justices served as judges before their rise to the Supreme Court that we can reasonably test whether such prior experience is associated with any particular set of values. Chief Justice Roberts maintained in a 2009 speech that former judges are more likely to take into account legal factors such as stare decisis than the politicians, law professors, and practicing attorneys who were routinely appointed in earlier eras. Roberts claimed that when the bench was dominated by individuals without judicial experience, "the practice of constitutional law—how constitutional law was made—was more fluid and wide ranging than it is today, more in the realm of political science" (quoted in Liptak 2009).

Although we obviously take great offense at the implicit slap at political science (perhaps the Chief Justice should read this book), Roberts raised an interesting empirical question: are former judges more likely to take into account legal factors than are justices without such experience? Political scientists and empirically oriented law professors have asked similar questions. In a recent study, Epstein et al. (2009, 833) find that "former appellate court judges are no more likely to follow precedent or to put aside their policy preferences than are justices lacking judicial experience."

Although the Epstein et al. finding contradicts Roberts's claims, it is not decisive as it is based on a much less precise approach to measuring deference to precedent than we have offered and is based only on a simple dummy variable to denote service on a federal appellate court. They conclude that ideology appears to have "far more to do" with a justice's decision to adhere to precedent than does prior federal appellate experience. Of course, the "far more to do" standard does not mean one should reject the importance of prior experience.

TABLE 5.1
Explaining Legal values for Individual Justices

	Precedent		Deference		Speech	
	Federal	All	Federal	All	Federal	All
Previous judicial	0.02	0.02	−0.01	−0.01	0.01	0.01
experience	(2.20)	(3.32)	(0.55)	(0.81)	(0.57)	(1.31)
Ideology	0.08	0.08	0.03	0.02	−0.02	−0.02
	(1.77)	(2.03)	(0.39)	(0.31)	(0.51)	(0.48)
Intercept	0.08	0.04	0.09	0.11	0.15	0.12
	(1.59)	(0.76)	(1.28)	(1.42)	(2.92)	(2.27)
N	26	26	24	24	30	30
R^2	0.31	0.43	0.02	0.04	0.02	0.07

Note: Each column presents OLS estimation in which the dependent variable is the legal value indicated, t-statistics are in parantheses.

To test the Roberts hypothesis that judicial experience matters, we modeled for each justice the average effects of stare decisis, deference to Congress, and strict interpretation of the Constitution's free speech clause plotted in Figures 4.2–4.4. From each model, we excluded justices if they did not vote on at least fifteen cases where the legal variable in question was coded as non-zero. As explanatory variables, we included both the ideology of each justice and the number of years they served on a bench prior to being promoted to the Supreme Court.

These results are presented in Table 5.1. The column headed by "Federal" counts only years on the federal lower courts; the column headed by "All" counts all previous judicial experience. We find ample support for Roberts's claim that experience shapes a justice's support for stare decisis, as the t-statistics are above 2, which is the conventional standard for statistical significance. Whether previous experience is measured in federal or total terms, justices who had more experience as a judge before coming to the Court show higher levels of influence by precedent. On the other hand, the table indicates little support for the hypothesis that prior judicial experience influences the extent a justice is constrained by a value of judicial restraint or strictly interpreting the First Amendment as the t-statistics on the judicial experience variables are well below 2.

IDIOSYNCRATIC COURT

Even though the political system induces fairly consistent temporal patterns in the association between legal values and ideology, we should be careful not to overstate the strength of the relationship. The lack of electoral connections or scheduled membership turnover of the Court induces definite idiosyncrasy. This can merely lead to unpredictability or, at times, create a disconnect between the Court and the rest of the political system.

The legal values of justices are part of their individual belief systems about policy and the policymaking process. Frequently these differ from the ideological systems that dominate the elected branches. A political ideology is a shared set of political preferences (Noel 2009). For elected officials, liberal and conservative ideologies provide fairly well-accepted packages of policy preferences. Members of Congress who want to fight global warming usually support affirmative action. Members who like guns typically do not want policies that mandate universal health care. And those who favored the war in Iraq probably support prayer in schools. And, members who accept or even welcome torture by the CIA hate intrusive IRS audits. Even when the connections between these issues are not obvious, a predictable ideology guides congressional behavior. Poole and Rosenthal (1997) provide systematic evidence of how remarkably predictable congressional behavior is across a wide range of issues once one identifies the ideological leanings of a member. Of course, one reason members of Congress are ideologically consistent is that they are judged on a routine basis by an electorate that has relatively stable views. In contrast, justices do not have the electoral or career-advancement constraints that elected and appointed officials have (Cross 1997, 279).

There are many examples of the belief systems of justices not mapping easily into conventional political ideologies. Even though, as discussed above, Frankfurter's commitment to deferring to legislative majorities often led him to vote with conservatives, his votes on separation of church and state (Dunne 1977, 267) and search and seizure (Dunne 1977, 270) were consistently liberal. This meant that his legal views held together in a way that, whatever its intellectual logic, was disconnected from the dominant political logic of the time. Similarly, Justice Scalia's hard line on Sixth Amendment requirements for jury deliberations (see, e.g., *U.S. v. Booker* [2005]) may follow directly from his originalist legal philosophy but leads him to vote with liberals in ways that do not correspond to conventional political cleavages.

Even when justices have policy preferences, they can transcend the traditional liberal-conservative dimension. For example, in *Granholm v. Heald* (2005) the Court ruled on state laws that allowed in-state wineries to ship their wine directly to consumers but forced out-of-state wineries to work through wholesalers. At one level, these laws seem to violate longstanding interpretations of the commerce clause of the Constitution that prohibit states from discriminating against out-of-state businesses. But the situation was complicated by the Twenty-first Amendment, which in the course of ending prohibition stated that "The transportation or importation into any State, Territory, or possession of the United States for delivery or use therein of intoxicating liquors, in violation of the laws thereof, is hereby prohibited." Some states argued that this meant that state laws regulating alcohol sales could survive commerce clause–based appeals. Justices Kennedy, Scalia, Souter, Ginsburg, and Breyer voted in favor of the small wineries that opposed the laws; Justices O'Connor, Rehnquist, Stevens, and Thomas voted to uphold the laws. What held the ideologically disparate coalitions together? Toobin (2007, 355) presents an oenological theory, as the five justices in the majority were reputed to be the Court's leading wine aficionados.

And, more generally, justices' values can evolve in unpredictable ways. When President Franklin Roosevelt's nominees went to the Court during the New Deal they were clearly expected to support government involvement in the economy. As issues moved from economics to social issues, the behavior of these justices would have been fairly predictable if belief systems were the same in Congress and the Court. Liberal justices would continue to be liberal even as the case mix changed; conservatives would be conservative. In reality, justices were quite unpredictable. Justice Black began his public life as a senator from Alabama. On the Court, he went far to the left in a way that would be unimaginable from a southern politician of the time; later he disappointed liberals by becoming quite conservative. However we explain his evolution, whether it was the result of a complicated mix of fiercely held views about the Constitution or a response to a rapidly changing society, it would have been difficult to sustain for an elected member of Congress.

One of the implications of the idiosyncratic nature of judicial belief systems is that the Court can get out of sync with the rest of the political system in a way that aggravates both sides of the political spectrum. The recent Court has been dominated by Republican appointees (twelve of the last sixteen have been nominated by a Republican president) and has generally moved to the right, disappointing many liberals. The movement to the right has been rather moderate, however (Baum 1997, ix; Kahn 1999; Toobin 2007, 160). This has led conservatives to be as upset with the Court as the left, if not more so (e.g., Bork 1990, 120; Levin 2005). Friedman (2009, 323) notes this state of affairs can take a surreal twist: within two years of each other critics from the left and right published anti-Court polemics with identical titles, *Courting Disaster* (Garbus 2002; Robertson 2004).

How has the Court managed to displease elites on both sides of the spectrum? One possibility is that pursuit of legal values has created a disconnect between the generally conservative justices and conservatives outside the Court. Specifically, when certain legal values are in play, the

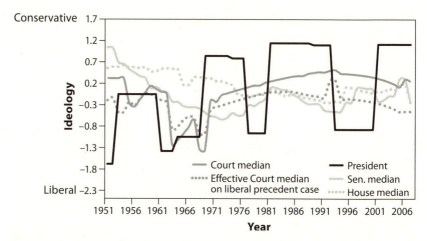

Figure 5.3. Court median on liberal precedent compared to Congress and president

Court may not have moved right very much at all (Lindquist and Cross 2009, 6). Figure 5.3 plots the preferences over time of the president, House median, Senate median, and Supreme Court median. We also add the effective Court median when precedent is liberal, which is calculated by setting the precedent variable to –1 and calculating net preferences ($\theta_{it} - \pi_i$ for each justice). We see that even though the Court is often ideologically situated within the political pareto set, adherence to precedent frequently pushes the Court median to be more liberal than the president, House median, and Senate median. (A pareto set in this context refers to the set of points from which deviation will make at least one of the elected branches worse off. It is the line segment connecting the most liberal of the president, House median, and Senate median to the most conservative of the three.) Across the time period, the ideology of the Court median is largely in the political pareto set (or to the right of it as in the Carter and Clinton years). However, the net location of the Court on liberal precedent cases is to the left. In the Reagan era the Court would be skating at the left edge of the political pareto set on liberal precedent cases; during the George W. Bush years the Court was well beyond the left edge of the political pareto set on liberal precedent cases. A corresponding figure with a conservative precedent would put the Court to the right of the political branches, but we suspect that after thirty-three years of the Warren and Burger Courts, precedents tended to be liberal rather than conservative, making the simulation of liberal precedent more relevant.[4]

Figure 5.4 shows a similar dynamic on speech. We again plot the president and institutional medians across time, but this time we add the effec-

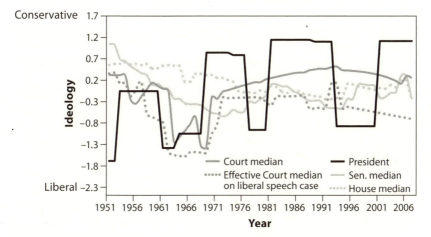

Figure 5.4. Court median on liberal speech case compared to Congress and president

tive Supreme Court median when speech implied a liberal vote (such that each justice's effective preference becomes $\theta_{it} - \sigma_i$). The Court on non-speech cases is the same as above—riding largely in the political pareto set. But on speech cases, the Court is considerably to the left of the political pareto set. In the 1950s and 1960s the Court was substantially out of the range of the elected branches at times; after that the Court settled in on the left edge of the political pareto set on speech cases until the 2000s when it again was far to the left of the congressional medians and president on cases where free speech implied a liberal vote.

CONCLUSION

Law matters to justices but in diverse ways. Some of the differences result from a political logic. In any given period, liberals and conservatives have policy positions that are important to them, and legal doctrines emerge that best comport with these goals (Friedman 2009, 281). Many liberals during the New Deal who were upset with Court invalidations of social and economic regulation had an affinity for judicial restraint; they were not particularly attracted to stare decisis. After decades of liberal dominance on the Court, liberals became more sympathetic toward stare decisis and conservatives became more hostile to the doctrine. Such processes ensure a rough correspondence between political goals and judicial values.

Justices' life experiences also help explain judicial values: by our measures justices with substantial experience on lower courts before joining the Supreme Court have been much more influenced by precedent. This is consistent with legalist claims that preferences are shaped by one's organizational experience.

But the correspondence between judicial values, political environment, and life experiences is imperfect. Justices are life tenured. They do not face election and they generally do not have career aspirations beyond the Court. This liberates justices to define what is important to them in ways that are hard to predict. Sometimes the policy preferences of justices appear to evolve; other times the firmly held legal values of justices express themselves differently depending on political context. This leads to unpredictability about the Court, raising the possibility that it falls out of sync with the rest of the political system at least for some issues or some time periods.

PART 2

Political Constraints

SEPARATION OF POWERS AND THE STRATEGIC CONSTRAINT

JUDICIAL REVIEW WAS BORN of a conflict between the courts, Congress, and the president. After Thomas Jefferson and the National-Republicans won the election of 1800, the lame-duck Federalists expanded the jurisdiction of federal circuit courts with the 1801 Judiciary Act (Turner 1961). Seeing this act as a Federalist effort to thwart the newly elected National-Republicans, they repealed it by passing the 1802 Judiciary Act. However, National-Republicans feared that the 1802 act would be declared unconstitutional by a Supreme Court led by Federalist Chief Justice John Marshall. Therefore, they abolished the Supreme Court's June and December terms and established a February term for the Court, effectively precluding the Court from reviewing the constitutionality of the 1802 act for almost a year. Jeffersonians in Congress also impeached and removed Judge John Pickering and delivered numerous speeches critical of the Court to signal to the Court the danger of infringing upon the will of the elected branches.

In this context, William Marbury asked the Court to issue an order (writ of mandamus) instructing President Jefferson to appoint him as Justice of the Peace for the District of Columbia. Although the Senate had confirmed Marbury and President Adams had signed the appointment the night before his term ended, Marbury had not received the appointment. Upon assuming office, Jefferson instructed his secretary of state, James Madison, to withhold the final appointment.

Marbury v. Madison (1803) put the Supreme Court in a delicate situation. The justices almost certainly wanted to grant the writ given that every justice on the Court was a Federalist (J. Smith 1996; Epstein and Knight 1998). And if they did not grant the writ—which was explicitly provided for by statute—they would call the rule of law into question (J. Smith 1996, 318). At the same time, Chief Justice Marshall knew that if the Court issued the writ, Secretary of State Madison would likely ignore it, exposing the Court as powerless.

Marshall solved the dilemma by recasting the choice before the Court (Knight and Epstein 1996; O'Brien 2000; Breyer 2010). Marshall's opinion declared that even though Marbury was entitled to his appointment, the provision of the 1789 Judiciary Act that authorized one to seek relief from the Supreme Court was unconstitutional. Marshall argued that the 1789 law expanded the Court's original jurisdiction in violation of the Constitution's express limitation of original jurisdiction to cases "affecting ambassadors, other public ministers and consuls, and those in which a state shall be a party." In short, Marshall ruled that even though Marbury was entitled to his appointment, there was nothing the Court could do.

The opinion simultaneously established the power of judicial review and secured the approval of the Jefferson administration by denying Marbury the appointment. By sacrificing the relatively inconsequential goal of completing Marbury's appointment and by taking into consideration the likely response of the legislative and executive branches, Marshall secured a broader role for the bench. After *Marbury*, "it would be the great task of the Supreme Court to weave recurring popular mandates, claimed by victorious presidents and their political parties, into the preexisting constitutional traditions of the American people" (Ackerman 2005, 243).

Marbury was not the last time the Court had to maneuver in the face of political opposition. In 1866, the Supreme Court ruled in *Ex parte Milligan* that citizens could not be tried by military tribunals and that constitutional protections applied "equally in war and peace." Shortly thereafter, journalist William McCardle was jailed by a military commander for publishing "incendiary" newspaper articles that opposed the Reconstruction laws being passed by Congress. After the Court heard oral arguments in McCardle's case, Congress stripped the Court of its jurisdiction in such Reconstruction cases. The Court re-docked the case and found itself in a precarious political situation: the Court's sympathies clearly lay with McCardle (Epstein and Knight 1998, 153), but it seemed likely that Congress would punish the Court if it ruled in favor of McCardle. The Court backed down. Chief Justice Salmon Chase announced a unanimous opinion that accepted that the Court did not have jurisdiction and thus could not provide McCardle relief.

In the 1930s, the Court again faced a hostile political environment (Rehnquist 1987; Caldeira and Wright 1988). It repeatedly struck down key elements of the New Deal, overturning New Deal legislation that limited the ability of lenders to foreclose on farms in *Louisville Joint Stock Land Bank v. Radford* (1935), declaring the National Industrial Recovery Act unconstitutional in *Schechter Poultry v. United States* (1935), and limiting the president's ability to remove Federal Trade Commissioners in *Humphrey's Executor v. United States* (1935). President Roosevelt responded in 1937 by asking Congress to allow the president to nominate a new justice for every justice over the age of seventy. If successful, Roosevelt's "Court packing" plan would allow him to appoint six additional justices to the Court.

While the plan was being debated, the Court retreated by narrowly upholding a Washington state minimum wage law (*West Coast Hotel Company v. Parrish* [1937]) and the National Labor Relations Act (*National Labor Relations Board v. Jones & Laughlin* [1937]). The decisions suggested that "much territory in the way of reform legislation desired by the New Deal that had previously seemed out of bounds to Congress was now within reach" (Rehnquist 1987, 129). And both decisions appear to have convinced several members of the Senate that the president's Court-packing plan was not necessary.[1]

These examples are well-known to judicial scholars, but are they celebrated anomalies or illustrations of routine constraints on the Court? To date, the academic literature is divided. Many analyses find no effect (Segal 1997; Hansford and Damore 2000; Spriggs and Hansford 2001; Sala and Spriggs 2004), although several more recent analyses do find effects (Clark 2009; Harvey and Friedman 2006, 2009; Harvey and Woodruff 2011).

The outcome of the debate is important. As we have discussed, there is considerable latitude for justices to pursue either their personal preferences (as in the attitudinal model) or their personal visions of the law (as in chapter 4). The danger is that the Court gets so far out of line from the rest of the political system that we see fundamental institutional showdowns that threaten the independence of the judiciary such as the Court-packing controversy in the 1930s. If the elected branches influence justices, however, they can keep the Court in check, thereby attenuating such risks.

In this chapter, we test whether the Court systematically yields to the elected branches. In particular, we examine whether individual justices vote differently when the constraints imposed by the executive and legislative branches are likely to be at their strongest. We focus on the two versions in the literature: one in which the Court is constrained only on statutory cases and the other in which the constraint extends to all cases, including constitutional cases.

SEPARATION-OF-POWERS MODELS

The notion that the Court is constrained by external political factors is an old one. An 1892 article stated that "whenever there is any departure by the Court from the popular opinion it will meet with successful opposition" (quoted in Tamanaha 2010, 24). Legal realist Roscoe Pound wrote in 1907 that judges decide cases "in the long run so as to accord with the moral sense of the community" (quoted in Tamanaha 2010, 40), and his realist contemporary Karl Llewellyn argued in 1930 that if judges do not "reshape the law to conform to current social commands it will be accomplished through legislation" (quoted Tamanaha 2010, 85).

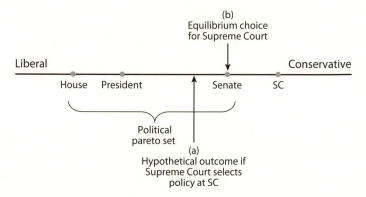

Figure 6.1. Separation-of-powers model

In this perspective, fear motivates justices to pay attention to external actors. When the Court interprets statutes, justices fear that Congress and the president will simply change the relevant statute if they oppose the Court decision. When the Court makes constitutional decisions, justices fear disobedience, constitutional amendments, changes to Court jurisdiction, Court budget changes, changes to the size of the Court, and impeachment of individual justices (W. Murphy 1964; Toma 1991; Peretti 1999; Clark 2009; Rosenberg 1991). In anticipation of such political responses, justices strategically hedge their position so as to avoid being overturned or otherwise rebuked, yielding better outcomes for the justices than if they had not done so (Ferejohn and Shipan 1990; Ferejohn and Weingast 1992; Epstein and Knight 1998; Gely and Spiller 1990).

Separation-of-powers models formalize the mechanism whereby the threat of unfavorable reaction by the elected branches can induce justices to act differently than they would otherwise. Figure 6.1 develops this logic. In the basic version of these models, actors have preferences that fall on a single dimension with the chamber medians representing the House and Senate. The median of the Court is indicated by SC and in this example is to the right of all the other actors. This means the Court in this example is outside the elected branches' "pareto set." If the Court were to rule in a manner that set policy at their ideal point, SC, all three elected branch actors would be united in wanting to push policy to the left. If it were a statutory case, Congress and the president could simply pass legislation that would produce a policy at some other point. The exact location of the resulting policy would depend on the location of the status quo and the relative power of the elected branches, but it could be quite far from the Court's preferred policy. In the figure, the location is at (a), a point relatively far from the desired policy of the Supreme Court median.

The Court achieves a better outcome for itself by setting policy at the right edge of the elected branches' pareto set. In Figure 6.1, this would be at the policy preferred by the Senate median.[2] Once the Court does this, the Senate would block any efforts by the president and House to move policy to the left, thereby guaranteeing a reasonably conservative decision. If the Court had chosen an outcome at SC (or some other point to the right of the Senate median), the final outcome would have been at (a); clearly the Court does better by choosing (b) in this context even though this outcome is more liberal than the policy the Court median prefers.

The constraints on the Court disappear if the Court's ideal point is in the pareto set defined by the elected branches. In this situation, the Court could set policy at its own ideal point without fear of being overturned. An example of this is the Court's 5–4 decision in *Ledbetter v. Goodyear Tire & Rubber Company* (2007). Goodyear had been paying Lilly Ledbetter substantially less than men doing the same work in the same plant—many of whom had less experience. It had been going on for years, but Ledbetter only found out about it when she received an anonymous note with her colleagues' salary information shortly before she was planning to retire. Ledbetter sued but was thwarted by a provision of the 1964 Civil Rights Act that the Supreme Court read to require Ledbetter to file a complaint within 180 days from the time the discrimination first occurred (rather than from the time it was first discovered).

Subsequently, Democrats in the House and Senate introduced a statutory fix to restore a discriminated against employee's legal recourse if the discrimination is ongoing. Although the bill was adopted by the House on a 225–199 vote and even though 56 senators voted to end a filibuster of the measure, the bill did not pass the Senate. The failed cloture vote occurred a day after the Bush administration reiterated its pledge to veto the act. Even though the House opposed the Court, the Senate and president "protected" the Court such that it could rule conservatively.[3]

Skeptics of separation-of-powers models argue that the models fail to explain Supreme Court behavior. Elected officials may complain, but the Court need not worry. Or, as the *New York Times* put it in 1923, "the old chorus rises, as it is rising now. It will die into silence, as it has died before . . . Congresses have their little hour of strut and rave. The Court stays" (Friedman 2009, 168).

Skeptics base their argument on several factors. First, the Supreme Court is often within the pareto set of the elected branches. This is particularly true if one characterizes the legislative process as involving numerous pivotal actors who effectively possess the ability to block legislative action. These would include chamber medians, committee chairs and medians, and, in the case of the Senate, filibuster pivots (see, e.g., Krehbiel 1998; Ferejohn and Shipan 1990; Tsebelis 2002).

Second, skeptics argue that even if the Court were to occasionally fall outside the elected branches' pareto set, Congress and the president are unlikely to find the benefits of overturning the Court greater than the transaction costs of legislating (Segal 1997, 42). These costs include the time and effort that go into crafting legislation and shepherding a bill through the legislative process but also the opportunity costs. How often would we expect Congress to drop what it is doing on national security and the economy in order to rebuke the judiciary on something like the Mushroom Promotion, Research and Consumer Information Act of 1990, which was overturned by *United States v. U.S. Food* (2001)?

In addition to the costs associated with building a winning coalition, elected officials may fear an unfavorable public response if they overturn a Court decision. The American public views the judiciary favorably and often opposes congressional intervention into judicial affairs. For example, a 2005 *Time* magazine poll found that 75 percent of survey respondents opposed congressional intervention in the Schiavo case (a dispute about who had the right to decide whether to disconnect life support for Terri Schiavo), and 54 percent of respondents indicated that they would be less likely to vote for their member of Congress if he or she voted to move the Schiavo case to the federal courts (pollingpoint.com). As a result, politicians may hesitate to incur the electoral costs of overturning the Court.

Although the traditional separation-of-powers model is built upon a rational choice framework where the bench majority strategically takes the preferences of elected officials into account, justices might respond to the preferences of elected officials for non-strategic reasons. Most important, justices may be conflict averse or they may simply value the personal relationships they have with other Washington elites. Although the importance of such relationships is difficult to quantify, their existence has been documented extensively.[4] As Justice Scalia explained, "the well-known and constant practice of justices' enjoying friendship and social intercourse with members of Congress and officers of the Executive Branch has not been abandoned, and ought not to be" (2004, 17–18).

Whether a justice's decision to take into account the preferences of elected officials stems from a fear of retribution or from a preference for interbranch comity influences how the justices respond to elected officials. The strategic separation-of-powers model is based upon the notion that elected officials retaliate against the Court when it promulgates an outcome outside the elected branches' pareto set. Such a perspective suggests that only the pivotal justices who make up the majority need to switch. An extreme justice who supports a position that is antithetical to the position preferred by elected officials would not need to act strategically if her position left her in the minority. In contrast, a comity of branches version suggests that the justices do not want to challenge the elected branches for the sake of comity. As such, one might expect every justice, even one whose position was not pivotal, to respond to elected officials.

Previous Empirical Tests

Segal (1997) established the general strategy for testing separation-of-powers models for statutory decisions. First, he created preference measures designed to be comparable across Congress, the Supreme Court, and the presidency and independent of any potential strategic deference to the political branches on the part of the Court. Then he used those measures to assess whether justices changed their positions when they were outside the elected branches' pareto set. He concluded that "the empirical results cast serious doubt on whether the justices vote other than sincerely with regard to congressional preferences" (Segal 1997, 42).

Although many scholars have reacted to Segal, no consensus has emerged. Segal, Westerland, and Lindquist (2007) followed Segal's general approach and found no evidence of a constrained Court, similar to the findings of Hansford and Damore (2000), Spriggs and Hansford (2001), and Sala and Spriggs (2004). Spiller and Gely (1992), however, found Congress constrains the Court on labor rulings and Harvey and Friedman (2006, 2009), Harvey and Woodruff (2011), Clark (2009), and Martin (2006) argue that the Supreme Court has been deferential on constitutional cases (see also Meernik and Ignagni 1997; Rogers 2001).

Part of the reason for the disparate findings is that the various works have approached three methodological challenges in different ways. The first challenge is one we discussed at length in chapter 2: creating preference measures that are comparable across institutions. These are necessary in order to identify when the Court is outside the elected branches' pareto set. Segal used existing measures of preferences for justices (Segal-Cover scores and percent-liberal voting scores) and members of Congress (ADA scores) and compared them directly. The problems with such an approach have been widely remarked upon, beginning with Segal himself in the original article (1997, 36; see also Bailey 2007). As we detailed in chapter 2, the problem is that the scores are based on completely different sets of votes, making it impossible to say, for example, what ADA score should correspond to a 50 percent liberal Supreme Court voting record in 1978. Other efforts to create cross-institutionally comparable preference measures are also problematic. Spiller and Gely (1992) use ADA scores for legislators and imputed the ADA scores for the justices based upon whether they were appointed by Democratic or Republican presidents. Many scholars are uncomfortable with such a procedure as it implies all Republican-appointed justices are the same (e.g., Warren had the same preferences as Scalia) and all Democratic-appointed justices are the same (e.g., Clark had the same preferences as Marshall; see Moraski and Shipan 1999; Krehbiel 2007; Shepsle and Rohde 2007; Nemachek 2008).

A second major challenge facing the separation-of-powers literature is ensuring that the judicial preference estimates are uncontaminated by possible strategic behavior by the justices. As Segal (1997) points out, if justices act as predicted by separation-of-powers models then we should never observe the Court outside the pareto set. When their true preferences would place them outside the elected branches' pareto set, strategic justices would adjust their behavior either by not hearing such cases (Harvey and Friedman 2009) or by ruling in a manner such that their observed choices would place them within the pareto set.

For empirical tests to even get off the ground, one needs some way to calculate the location of the Court median's "true" preferences relative to the elected branches' pareto set. Segal's (1997) innovation was to use the behavior of justices on constitutional cases to identify "true" preferences of justices. The logic is that the justices have more discretion on constitutional issues given that the probability of being overturned is very small. Based on judicial preferences on constitutional cases, he identifies individual justices who were outside the elected branches' pareto set and investigates whether justices strategically adjusted their behavior on statutory cases—those cases most directly subject to threats of being overruled.

Harvey and Friedman (2006) deal with the challenge that the Court may respond to political pressure by not hearing problematic cases by looking at the probability of a law being declared unconstitutional by the Court as a function of the Court's being located inside or outside the elected branches' pareto set. They used modified Bailey and Chang (2001) scores to generate comparable preference estimates for justices and members of Congress. These scores are similar to those discussed in chapter 2, relying on bridge observations to provide inter-institutional comparability. However, these scores—and those in chapter 2—are based on revealed behavior (see, e.g., Bailey 2007, 439) and therefore do not net out possible strategic anticipation; even though this should bias against finding evidence of constraint, Harvey and Friedman (2006, 2009) find such evidence.

A third challenge is accounting for what we discovered in chapter 4: justices' preferences frequently involve more than just policy outcomes. In particular, we have seen that many justices value stare decisis, judicial restraint, and protecting speech. When these values are implicated, justices are apt to part ways with their ideological compatriots in Congress. Failure to take this into account leads to puzzling inferences. For example, most measures of the Court in 1989 place the Court median to the right of the Democratic House and Senate (see, e.g., Bailey 2007; Harvey and Friedman 2006). However, in *U.S. v. Eichman* (1990), the Court struck down from the left the conservative Flag Protection Act that banned flag burning. This outcome is unsurprising in light of our chapter 4 finding that most justices are more pro–free speech than their co-ideologues in Congress. But if we were to simply use a traditional single dimension measure of Court preferences, it would appear that a conservative Court struck down a liberal Congress even though, in fact, the exact opposite occurred.

Test 1: Constraint on Statutory Cases

We first test separation-of-power theory by assessing the version in which justices are constrained by elected officials on statutory cases. We proceed in three steps. First, we create judicial, congressional, and presidential preference measures that are comparable across institutions and time. We follow the approach described in chapter 2 but now limit Court cases to only constitutional cases. Doing so allows us to follow Segal's (1997) prescription for identifying the unconstrained or "true" preferences of justices relative to members of Congress. The logic is that strategic constraints on the Court will be less on constitutional cases because overriding a constitutional decision is clearly more complicated than overriding a statutory decision (Segal 1997, 35).

Second, we use these preference estimates to identify cases where the Court may be constrained. Separation-of-power theory predicts that the Court may strategically acquiesce to elected branches when the Court median is outside the pareto set of the elected branches—the set of points that connects the president, Senate median, and House median. Therefore, we identify for each case whether the Court median is within the pareto set established by the House, Senate, and president. We do this by taking the estimated policy preference of a justice at the time of the case and adjusting it based on the individual justice's value for any of the legal concepts that are in play for that particular case. We do not wish to ignore the differences on cases where speech, for example, pushes the Court to the left and those where precedent pushes it to the right. Our approach allows us to control for situations where the support of specific justices for specific legal concepts alters expected outcomes. For example, we know that on cases such as the *Eichman* flag-burning, normally conservative justices who value free speech were more liberal.[5]

Third, we create a Separation-of-Powers (hereafter *SOP*) variable. If the Court is left of the elected branches' pareto set, we code the *SOP* variable for each justice on the case as a +1, indicating that separation-of-powers effects should make justices more conservative. If the Court median falls to the right of the elected branches' pareto set, we code the *SOP* variable as a −1. In these instances, we expect each justice to act in a more liberal manner than we would expect based upon preferences and the law. If the Court median falls within the elected branches' pareto set, the *SOP* variable is 0 for all justices. Table 6.1 shows the frequency distribution of the *SOP* variable for each justice. *SOP* is −1 when the Court is to the right of the elected branches' pareto set (and hence separation-of-power effects should move justices to the left), and it is +1 when the Court is to the left of the elected branches' pareto set (and hence separation-of-power effects should move justices to the right).[6]

We then re-estimate the ideal point model but this time limit Supreme Court cases to statutory interpretation cases, cases where separation-of-power theory suggests the Court will be influenced by the elected branches.[7] The model is similar to that used in chapter 4:

$$Pr(y_{itv} = 1) = \Phi(\alpha_v(\theta_{it} - \kappa_v) + \rho_i SOP_v + \pi_i Precedent_v)$$

where y_{itv} is 1 if individual i takes a conservative position at time t on vote v, α_v is the vote discrimination parameter, θ_{it} is the policy preference of individual i at time t, κ_v is the vote cutpoint, ρ_i is the weight on the separation-of-powers variable, and π_i is the weight justice i places on precedent. The primary differences between this model and the model in the previous chapter are that we now include the SOP_v variable and limit the Supreme Court cases to those involving statutory interpretation (we exclude the deference to Congress and First Amendment variables from chapter 4 because they are zero by definition for all statutory cases). As in previous chapters, the model is estimated using a Bayesian Markov Chain Monte Carlo (MCMC) algorithm. The data set is similar to that used in the previous chapter; it includes Supreme Court cases, congressional roll-call votes, and congressional and presidential bridge observations on cases and votes that involved criminal procedure, civil rights, due process, and privacy from 1950 to 2008.[8]

The statutory version of separation-of-power theory suggests that ρ is greater than zero for at least some justices. This would indicate that justices are more likely to vote conservatively when the Court's true preferences are to the left of the pareto set (when *SOP* = +1) and less likely to vote conservatively when the Court median is right of the pareto set (when *SOP* = −1).

Table 6.2 reports the estimated separation-of-powers parameters for all justices who served since 1950. The p-values are below the parameter

TABLE 6.1
Distribution of *SOP* Variable for Justices

	Value of SOP *constraint variable*		
	−1	0	1
Black	0	212	73
Reed	0	85	12
Frankfurter	0	148	32
Douglas	0	279	74
Jackson	0	62	0
Burton	0	101	26
Vinson	0	57	0
Clark	0	170	46
Minton	0	82	9
Warren	0	129	70
Harlan	0	133	69
Brennan	65	434	73
Whittaker	0	61	16
Stewart	68	230	48
White	86	412	49
Goldberg	0	19	8
Fortas	0	14	24
Marshall	65	348	31
Burger	68	260	7
Blackmun	100	369	7
Powell	64	227	3
Rehnquist	219	421	16
Stevens	217	390	18
O'Connor	152	317	16
Scalia	152	252	15
Kennedy	151	219	13
Souter	152	168	11
Thomas	152	148	11
Ginsburg	133	134	11
Breyer	114	125	11
Roberts	0	50	0
Alito	0	46	0
Total	804	29,309	2,242

Note: Values indicate how many times each justice voted on cases with each possible value of the *SOP* constraint variable. For example, Brennan voted on 65 cases where the *SOP* constraint was −1 (the Court median was to the right of the elected branches' pareto set), 434 cases where the *SOP* constraint was 0 (the Court median was within the elected branches' pareto set), and 73 cases where the *SOP* constraint variable was +1 (the Court median was to the left of the elected branches' pareto set).

TABLE 6.2
Separation-of-Powers Constraints for Statutory Model

Justice	SOP (ρ)	Justice	SOP (ρ)
Black	0.30 (p = 0.14)	Burger	0.28 (p = 0.11)
Frankfurter	−0.40 (p = 0.89)	Blackmun	0.21 (p = 0.11)
Douglas	0.52 (p = 0.05)	Powell	0.29 (p = 0.10)
Burton	0.06 (p = 0.43)	Rehnquist	0.002 (p = 0.49)
Clark	−0.34 (p = 0.88)	Stevens	0.31 (p = 0.02)
Warren	0.78 (p = 0.00)	O'Connor	0.66 (p = 0.00)
Harlan	−0.27 (p = 0.85)	Scalia	0.50 (p = 0.00)
Brennan	0.36 (p = 0.02)	Kennedy	0.70 (p = 0.00)
Whittaker	0.10 (p = 0.39)	Souter	0.45 (p = 0.01)
Stewart	0.28 (p = 0.07)	Thomas	0.41 (p = 0.04)
White	0.06 (p = 0.34)	Ginsburg	0.003 (p = 0.48)
Fortas	1.08 (p = 0.04)	Breyer	0.02 (p = 0.45)
Marshall	0.23 (p = 0.15)		

estimates. The first thing to note is that separation-of-power considerations appear to affect a number of justices after controlling for their
ideology and the legal factors we discussed in the previous chapter. The
parameter is significant at the $p = .10$ level for twelve justices, at the $p = .05$ level for ten justices, and at the $p = .01$ level for five justices. The justices with significant effects span the ideological spectrum, from Warren,
Brennan, Fortas, Douglas, and Stevens on the left to Souter, Stewart,
Powell, and O'Connor in the middle, and Kennedy, Scalia, and Thomas
on the right.

We cannot directly interpret or compare parameter magnitudes because they are generated in a non-linear model similar to a probit model.
Therefore, to provide a sense of the relative importance of separation-of-
power constraints across justices we use the estimated parameters to
simulate justices' probabilities of voting conservatively. For each justice
we calculated his or her average policy preference over the time period in
the sample and calculated the probability of voting conservatively given
that the separation-of-power variable implied a liberal vote and that the
separation-of-power variable implied a conservative vote. The simulated
effect of the SOP variable is the difference between those two values.
Because the difference depends on the simulated cutpoint of the vote, we
conducted simulations for three different policy cutpoints (−0.5, 0.0, and
0.5) and averaged across them.

Figure 6.2 presents these results. The heterogeneity is clear; not all justices appear affected equally. This is consistent with the pattern found in
chapter 4 and with common sense: justices are influenced in different
ways by any given factor. Relatively large separation-of-power effects are

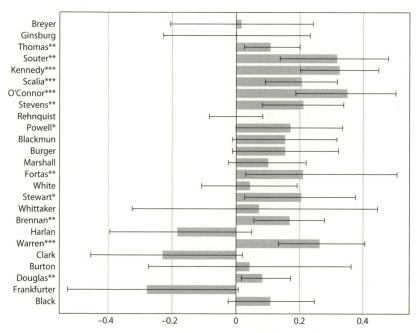

Figure 6.2. Separation-of-powers constraints for statutory model. The shaded bar indicates average change in probability of a conservative vote when moving from $SOP = -1$ to $SOP = 1$. The line indicates a simulated 90 percent Bayesian confidence interval. ***change significantly > 0 at $p = .01$; **change significantly > 0 at $p = .05$; *change significantly > 0 at $p = .1$.

apparent for some justices with reputations for being political (e.g., Brennan, Warren, Fortas, and O'Connor). Frankfurter, Harlan, and Clark are the only justices who seem to go against the separation-of-power current, but there is considerable uncertainty about their parameter estimates. Blackmun, Burger, and Marshall also exhibit positive separation-of-power effects, but there is enough uncertainty that we cannot rule out zero effects at conventional levels.

When we modeled judicial restraint in chapter 4, justices deferred to Congress out of principle. Here justices defer to Congress out of fear. The judicial restraint in chapter 4 was measured by looking at whether justices' ideal points moved in the direction of the congressional statute when considering congressional laws; this is equivalent to giving Congress the benefit of the doubt as deferential normative legal theories suggest. Here, justices move in the direction of Congress and the president only when Congress and the president are unified against the justices. This is deference from necessity, a much different phenomenon. This distinction makes sense of the historical patterns we observe here. Normative

deference thrived in the early period of our study as a natural response to
the aggressively interventionist Court of the early twentieth century. In
more recent times, justices have moved away from normative deference
toward other legal theories, but these results indicate that they make up
for it with strategic deference. Justices from the contemporary Court are
less inclined to defer to Congress for principled reasons but more likely
to defer for practical ones.

TEST 2: CONSTRAINT ON ALL CASES

Political constraints on the Court may not be limited to statutory cases.
Several scholars argue that potential congressional action on constitutional amendments, Court jurisdiction, and the judiciary's budget encour-
age the justices to be strategic on constitutional cases too (Harvey and
Friedman 2006; Epstein, Knight, and Martin 2004; Meernik and Ignagni
1997; W. Murphy 1964; Rosenberg 1992, 377). Their logic is that even
though the costs to Congress of overturning (or at least affecting) constitutional decisions are higher than they are for statutory cases, the benefits
to Congress of affecting these decisions is also higher. For the Court the
cost of being overturned on an important constitutional case may mean
loss of authority within a broad class of cases either because of constitutional amendment, loss of jurisdiction, or open defiance. Epstein, Knight,
and Martin (2004, 177) go so far as to argue that the costs to the Court
of being overturned on constitutional cases are "infinite."

   If one hypothesizes that justices are constrained on all cases, any test
needs to overcome additional methodological obstacles that did not exist
when we were testing constraint on statutory cases. Recall that when testing statutory constraint we used constitutional cases to ascertain whether
the "true" preferences of justices were in the elected branches' pareto set.

   Thus, we use a different approach. In particular, we assess whether
justices change along with shifts in the preferences of the political pareto
set. Even if we cannot precisely identify shifts in this set's true preferences,
we do know when the political pareto set shifts decisively, as we can identify elections that lead to a clear shift in the pareto set. For example, an
election that removed a conservative constraint on the Court would
allow justices to shift left as they would no longer need to shade their
decisions in a conservative direction to forestall a negative reaction from
the elected branches. In other words, after a liberal electoral win a liberal
justice who had been moderating her positions could vote more in line
with her underlying liberal views.

   Identifying preference shifts is not simple, however. As we have discussed, it is hard to distinguish preference change from agenda change.

The analogy to test scores that we first developed in chapter 2 is useful here. Suppose that we tested a class of students at the beginning and end of the year and found that students scored higher at the end of the year. One could not interpret the finding without knowing whether the difficulty of the tests was comparable. If they were, then the increased scores are impressive; if the second test was easier, the higher scores mean little.

For our purposes, we need some way of calibrating our preference measure across the pre- and post-election periods. If the Court voted on identical cases before and after the election then comparisons would be easy. Of course, this never happens. Therefore, we compare justices to non-justices to calibrate preference changes over time.

Going back to the educational testing example, suppose we are interested in whether one teaching environment is better than another and that we cannot give students the same test at the start and end of the year (perhaps we worry that they would remember the questions or we want to test them on new material they have learned over the course of the year). How could we assess whether a certain educational innovation worked? One option is to give comparable tests to two groups at the beginning and end of the year. One group is our students who were subject to some innovation. The control group is another class of students who were not subject to the innovation. If students who were exposed to the innovation did better relative to students in the control group, we would have evidence that the innovation worked.

We use a comparison set of actors who are not subject to separation-of-power constraints as our control group. We then create preference measures across institutions to assess whether justices' preferences shifted in the predicted direction relative to this comparison set. For example, if justices' preferences shifted left relative to these actors after a liberal electoral victory that shifted the elected branches' pareto set to the left, this would support separation-of-power theory. Our control group is comprised of members of Congress and presidents over a four-year time period covering two years before and two years after a clear pareto-shifting election as our baseline. The clear pareto-shifting elections occurred when the party in control of the presidency shifted: 1960, 1968, 1976, 1980, 1992, and 2000.

Using our bridging data we generate preference estimates for members of Congress across the entire time frame before and after a major election. We create separate preference estimates for each justice in the pre- and post-election periods and can then see if justices moved relative to the members of Congress. Figure 6.3 depicts the logic. We plot each justice's ideology before and after the electoral shift. In the example, Democrats win such that we expect a liberal separation-of-power constraint in the post-election period. We also plot the estimated preferences of six

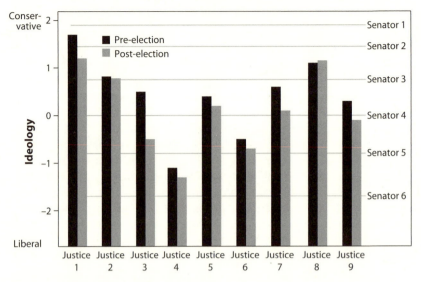

Figure 6.3. Electoral discontinuity model

senators to highlight the fact that members of Congress are the comparison baseline. Senator 1 is the most conservative and Senator 6 is the most liberal. Justice 1 shifts to the left as predicted by separation-of-power theory, going from being more conservative than Senator 2 to being more liberal than Senator 2. Justice 3 also behaves consistently with separation-of-power theory, going from being more conservative than Senator 4 to being more liberal. Justice 2 acts as if there were no constraint, as she has essentially the same preferences relative to the senators before and after the election.

Separation-of-power theory is indeterminate about who on the bench should move. The theory simply says that the Court's rulings should shift to within the political pareto set when constrained. The most natural place to look for movement would be around the Court median, perhaps with the minimal number of justices shifting the minimal amount to move the Court within the political pareto set. However, the Court could achieve this result with many possible changes in the configurations of preferences. Given our findings so far that different justices put different weights on different factors, we therefore look for all justices to move.[9]

This identification strategy cannot reveal all conceivable types of preference shifts. If all members of Congress shifted in response to an election (as they probably do in at least some cases), then they would maintain the same preference ordering. If justices also shifted the same amount, their ranking relative to each other and to members of Congress would be the

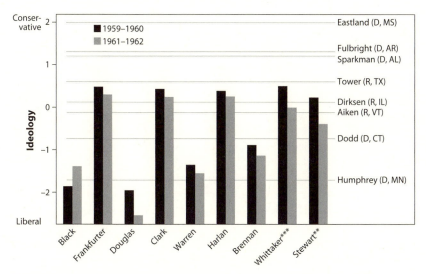

Figure 6.4. Results for justices and selected members of Congress, 1960;
***change significant at $p = .01$; **change significant at $p = .05$.

same and we would have no observable change in measured preferences. But note that separation-of-power theory is about a constraint that affects justices but not members of Congress; if justices and members of Congress move in tandem after an election, some other theory is required to explain justices' behavior.

Hence, the way to think about what we are doing is as looking for relative change on the Court. If justices are constrained by elected officials, their ranking compared to members of Congress should disproportionately shift when the constraints defined by the legislative and executive branches change. For example, the preferences of a given justice may correspond to congressional moderates when the Court is not constrained but may shift to correspond to more conservative members of Congress when the elected branch constraint moves to the right.

We should also note that failure to find evidence for separation-of-power theory using this method could arise from one of two reasons. First, the theory may be false. Second, it could be that the conditions for separation-of-power constraints to affect Court behavior were not satisfied. This could be the case because we are not directly measuring whether the Court moves in or out of the political pareto set but instead assuming presidential party shifts are instances where the Court was more likely to have moved in or out of the political pareto set.

Figure 6.4 shows results for 1960. In 1960, the observed Court behavior put it at the liberal edge of the political space (see Figure 2.13). The more liberal President Kennedy replaced the relatively moderate President Eisenhower. If justices had been conservatively constrained before Kennedy took office, we would expect these justices to move to the left after Kennedy was sworn in since this constraint would no longer hold.

Ideology is on the vertical axis and across the horizontal axis we plot pre- and post-election preferences for each justice. The pre-election preferences are based on votes in the two years before President Kennedy replaced President Eisenhower (1959–60); they are indicated with darker shading. The post-election preferences are based on votes in the first two years of the Kennedy administration (1961–62); they are indicated with lighter shading. As reference points we also plot the ideal points of selected senators. Thus, one can see that Senators James Eastland (D, Mississippi), William Fulbright (D, Arkansas), and John Sparkman (D, Alabama) were extremely conservative and Senator Hubert Humphrey (D, Minnesota) was quite liberal. Two Republican senators—Everett Dirksen (R, Illinois) and George Aiken (R, Vermont)—were in the ideological middle. Although we display only eight senators, our model estimates the preferences of every member of Congress in the four-year window around the election.

The figure shows some evidence for the separation-of-power model. The model predicts that if the Court was in fact constrained before 1960 there should be a shift downward (in a liberal direction) for justices relative to members of Congress and the president. In other words, their post-election light bars should be lower than their pre-election dark bars. For every justice, except Hugo Black, this is the pattern we see. And two of the justices, Charles Whittaker and Potter Stewart, changed significantly. Stewart was more conservative than Senators Dirksen and Aiken before the 1960 election and more liberal than those senators afterward. Whittaker was more conservative than Dirksen before 1961 and more liberal afterward. We should note that the significant movement of only two justices is actually consistent with the separation-of-power perspective in this case as the Court median (Stewart) and the justice immediately to the right of the median after the election (Whittaker) are the ones who moved significantly, implying an overall shift in the Court following Kennedy's election.

Justices also behaved consistently with separation-of-power theory in 1968. Figure 6.5 shows the results for the period prior to and following the 1968 political alignment shift that occurred with Nixon's election. Before 1968 President Johnson protected a liberal Court from a relatively conservative Congress. With Nixon's election, all political actors were more conservative than the Court and separation-of-power theory would predict at least some justices would move right. We display estimated preferences for all justices and selected members of Congress.

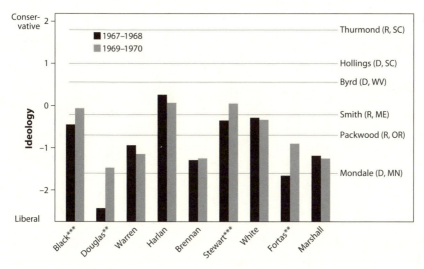

Figure 6.5. Results for justices and selected members of Congress, 1968;
***change significant at $p = .01$; **change significant at $p = .05$.

Four justices—Black, Douglas, Stewart, and Fortas—became significantly
more conservative after the election. For example, Black and Stewart
went from being more liberal than Senator Margaret Smith (R, Maine) to
being more conservative. Fortas and Douglas leapfrogged Senator Walter
Mondale (D, Minnesota). Although the pre-election Court median (Chief
Justice Warren) does not himself become significantly more conservative,
the identity of the Court median shifts to Fortas, who has shifted significantly to the right after the election. The expected median also clearly
shifts right as the average preferences shifted to the right.

In 1976, the election of Jimmy Carter brought the Democrats unified
control of government and the observed behavior of the Court left it on
the conservative edge of the political pareto set (see Figure 2.13). Before
the election, the Republicans controlled the presidency, providing a reasonably large interval in which the Supreme Court could operate without the threat of being overturned or otherwise punished by the elected
branches of government. After that election, however, Democrats controlled all elected branches of government, raising the possibility of a
liberal constraint on the Court. Figure 6.6 shows that the preferences of
several justices moved significantly to the left as predicted by separation-
of-power theory: Justices Blackmun, Powell, White, and Marshall all became significantly ($p < .1$) more liberal. For example, Blackmun went from
being more conservative than Senator Robert Dole (R, Kansas) before
Carter came to office to being more liberal than Dole; Powell went from

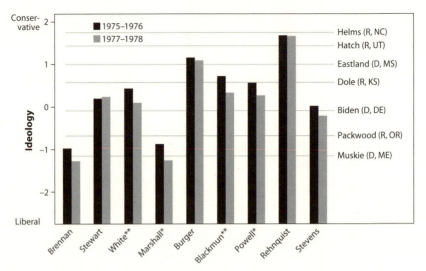

Figure 6.6. Results for justices and selected members of Congress, 1976;
**change significant at *p* = .05; *change significant at *p* = .1.

being very close to Dole to being more liberal; Marshall leaped to Senator
Edmund Muskie's (D, Maine) left. The median shifted to the left and the
expected median shifted even more.

Results for 1980 provide even stronger support for separation-of-
power theory. In 1980, Reagan's election removed any possible liberal
constraint. Unlike the 1960, 1968, and 1976 elections, the 1980 shift in
the executive branch was accompanied by large congressional coattails
as Republicans gained twelve seats and control of the Senate and thirty-
four seats in the House of Representatives. This returned the Court to its
position in the middle of the political pareto set, which likely removed
separation-of-power constraints and freed justices to vote more sincerely.
Figure 6.7 shows that every single member of the Court moved right relative to members of Congress (who themselves may have moved right,
too). Rehnquist shifted from being near Senator John Stennis (D, Mississippi) to being near Senator Jesse Helms (R, North Carolina). Burger
shifted from being near Senator William Roth (R, Delaware) to being
near Representative Dick Cheney (R, Wyoming). Stevens jumped Senator
Frank Church (D, Idaho). And Marshall and Brennan became more conservative than Senator Chris Dodd (D, Connecticut). Again, the results
suggest separation-of-power constraint with the Court median shifting to
the right after Republican success at the ballot box.

The results continue to be consistent with the separation-of-powers
model in 1992, although not as strongly. With Clinton's election the rela-

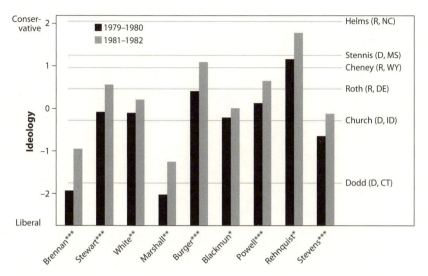

Figure 6.7. Results for justices and selected members of Congress, 1980; ***change significant at $p = .01$; **change significant at $p = .05$; *change significant at $p = .1$.

tively conservative Supreme Court lost the protection of having a conservative president. Separation-of-power theory therefore predicts that justices should move to the left. Figure 6.8 shows that after 1992 two justices—Blackmun and Souter—moved significantly to the left. Souter moved to the left of Senator Arlen Specter (R, Pennsylvania); Blackmun moved left of Senator Leahy (D, Vermont). However, the overall effect is less clear as Justices Kennedy, O'Connor, and Thomas shifted to the right (albeit insignificantly). It is possible that either separation-of-power theory did not apply or the election did not shift the Court out of the political pareto set.

In 2000 Bush's ascension to the presidency brought back a conservative protector to a moderately conservative Court. While it is possible that the Republican House and Senate before the election provided enough cover for the Court to be unconstrained, having a Republican president ensured that the political pareto set covered the Court median's right flank. In this instance, separation-of-power theory predicts that if there were a shift, it would be to the right as justices were no longer constrained by liberal elected branches. In Figure 6.9 Justices Rehnquist, Stevens, and Scalia moved significantly to the right after 2000. The median (O'Connor) does not shift much, but the expected median shifts to the right. Since we do not directly observe whether the "true" preferences of the Court were inside or outside the political pareto set, we again cannot be sure whether these relatively weak results for separation-of-power

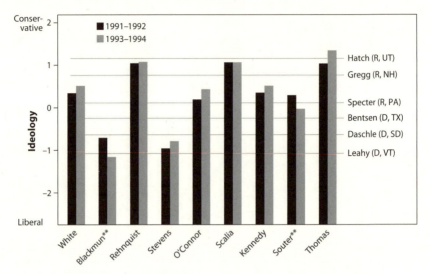

Figure 6.8. Results for justices and selected members of Congress, 1992;
**change significant at $p = .05$.

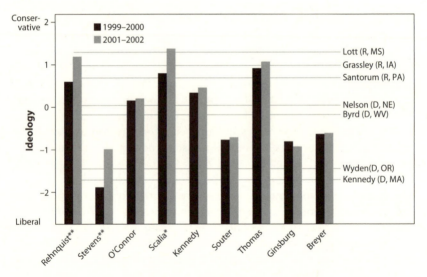

Figure 6.9. Results for justices and selected members of Congress, 2000;
**change significant at $p = .05$; *change significant at $p = .1$.

theory are due to a failure to explain behavior or due to the possibility that the theory's conditions for constraint were not satisfied.

TEST 3: SALIENCE AND CONSTRAINT

Standard separation-of-power models make extremely crisp predictions: if the Court is outside the political pareto set, it is constrained; otherwise it is not. Of course, not all Supreme Court cases are created equal. Some matter more to elected officials and others involve arcane issues that may be legally, but not politically, salient.[10] An (unnamed) justice told political scientist Tom Clark recently that "we read the newspapers and see what is being said—probably more than most people do. . . . We know if there is a lot of public interest; we have to be careful not to reach too far" (2009, 973). This would imply that separation-of-power constraints are more binding on politically salient issues.

To test this expectation, we employ a similar strategy as in the previous section, but we change how we measure constraint. In the previous section, only the timing of a case relative to a major election determined how we coded it for separation-of-power constraint. In this section, the timing *and* the salience of a case determine its coding for separation-of-power constraint. We assume no constraint if either (a) the Court was clearly within the political pareto set or (b) the case was not salient, meaning that Congress and the president would be unlikely to punish the Court even if the Court's decision wandered outside the political pareto set. We consider a case to be salient if it was mentioned on the front page of the *New York Times* (Epstein and Segal 2000).

Figure 6.10 provides an example. Recall from Figure 2.13 that the Court in 1999 and 2000 was at the conservative end of the political pareto set, implying a possible liberal separation-of-power constraint. With the election of President Bush, the Court was comfortably within the political pareto set and therefore subject to no constraint. The salience version of separation-of-power theory would predict that justices would be significantly more liberal on salient cases in 1999–2000 (when constraint was plausible) than on either low salient cases or on high salient cases in 2001 and 2002. The darker bars in Figure 6.10 report the estimated ideology of justices on high salience cases in 1999–2000. The lighter bars report the estimated ideology of justices on all other cases that came up in the 1999–2002 time period. We expect the darker bars (labeled "constrained" in the figure) to be shorter (more liberal) than the lighter bars (labeled "unconstrained" in the figure) as the dark bars reflect preferences on cases in which we expect justices to be constrained by a liberal pareto set.

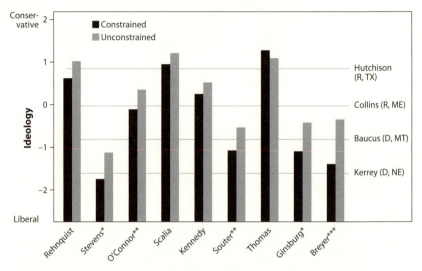

Figure 6.10. Salience model results for justices and selected members of Congress, 2000; ***change significant at $p = .01$; **change significant at $p = .05$; *change significant at $p = .1$.

The figure shows that O'Connor shifted significantly in the direction predicted by the salience version of separation-of-power theory. In 1999–2000 she was more liberal on salient cases than was Senator Susan Collins (R, Maine). On cases that were either low salience or arose when Bush was in office, she was more conservative than Collins. Four other justices—Souter, Ginsburg, Breyer, and Stevens—moved in the manner predicted by this version of separation-of-power theory as they were all significantly more liberal on salient cases before Bush took over than they were on the combined pool of non-salient cases in both periods and salient cases post-Bush. (In addition, the preference changes of Justices Rehnquist and Kennedy were nearly significant with p-values of .11 and .13, respectively.) In this case, the weak evidence of constraint in Figure 6.9 is now bolstered by the additional evidence of constraint on salient cases in Figure 6.10.

We summarize the results for the other periods in Table 6.3. As we mentioned earlier, when we compare the behavior of justices before and after the 1960 elections, we expect justices to shift toward the left on salient cases when Kennedy replaced Eisenhower. Contrary to expectations, none of the justices significantly changed after Kennedy came into office.[11] In 1968, however, Justices Black, Stewart, and Fortas were all more conservative on salient cases after Nixon took office, as predicted by the *SOP*-salience theory. In 1976, the number of justices for whom there is statistical evidence consistent with the theory jumped to five as Justices

TABLE 6.3
Summary of Salience Model Results

Year	SOP-*Salience Prediction*	*Justices with statistically significant shifts consistent with* SOP-*salience prediction*
1960	More conservative on salient cases before 1961	None
1968	More conservative on salient cases after 1968	Black, Stewart, Fortas
1976	More liberal on salient cases after 1976	Brennan, White, Marshall, Blackmun, Powell
1980	More liberal on salient cases before 1981	Brennan, Stewart, White, Burger, Blackmun, Stevens
1992	More liberal on salient cases after 1992	Souter
2000	More liberal on salient cases before 2001	O'Connor, Souter, Ginsburg, Breyer, Stevens

Brennan, White, Marshall, Blackmun, and Powell were more liberal on salient cases after Carter took office. The 1980 election led six justices to significantly shift to the right on the subset of salient cases. In 1992, only Justice Souter shifted significantly to the left on salient cases (although Justices Blackmun and Ginsburg had p-values of .13 on the difference in estimated preferences on salient post-Clinton cases versus the other cases). In none of the periods did justices have statistically significant shifts counter to the predictions of *SOP*-salience theory.

CONCLUSION

The attitudinal and legal models hold that justices are immune from the influence of the elected branches. Separation-of-power models challenge this claim by hypothesizing that justices sometimes hedge their positions in light of the preferences of Congress and the president. Prior empirical work has provided mixed support for separation-of-power models. One reason for the lack of scholarly consensus has been that existing tests have been hindered by methodological challenges associated with measurement and identification.

In this chapter we present methods and data that allow us to address these challenges. We find evidence that many justices are constrained by the president and Congress on statutory cases. Our evidence indicates that many justices moderate their revealed preferences during periods when the Court median's preferences are more likely to be overturned by the elected branches. Unlike the normatively motivated deference we found in chapter 3, this strategically motivated deference is common among contemporary justices and rare among justices from the earlier period of our study.

We also find that many justices are constrained on all cases, including constitutional ones. Across our entire time period, but particularly from 1968 to 1980, justices responded to changes in presidential party by moving in the direction of the newly elected president's party. These effects are often strongest on politically salient cases. Such a pattern is what we would expect if justices are trying to preempt legislative retribution of some sort.

We also again find considerable diversity across justices. Many, but not all, justices responded to the elected branches. Likewise, we do not find evidence that only the median justice responds. Numerous justices across the ideological spectrum showed evidence of responding to elected branch preferences. This raises the possibility that factors beyond those in separation-of-power models may also be at work, including a desire for cross-institutional comity. But even with this diversity, the evidence makes clear that although *Marbury v. Madison* may have been the first instance in which justices acted strategically, it is unlikely to have been the last.

Chapter 7

SIGNALS FROM THE EXECUTIVE

Two of the most important Supreme Court cases in recent years stem from the University of Michigan's decision to deny admission to two white applicants, Jennifer Gratz and Barbara Grutter. After their rejection, both women sued the university, claiming that the university's affirmative action policies unconstitutionally denied them admission. Ms. Gratz objected to a point system that automatically gave applicants to the undergraduate program from under-represented groups 20 extra points (out of 100 needed to be admitted). Ms. Grutter objected to the law school's policy of taking race into account, although less formally.

The cases put the Bush administration in a difficult position. While President Bush tended to support conservative policies, he had made numerous efforts to reach out to minorities. His main political advisor, Karl Rove, often spoke of building a long-lasting conservative majority by reaching out to African Americans and Hispanics. Opposing affirmative action could endanger such efforts.

The first question for Bush was whether his administration should even take a position on the cases. They did not need to, as the cases were between private citizens and a state university. However, many saw this as a chance for President Bush to take a stand on affirmative action. Conservative columnist Diana West (2003) wrote, "What the administration chooses to do—the likely choice being either taking a stand opposing race-based admissions, or taking no stand—will reveal more than just the outcome of a power struggle within White House circles. . . . George W. Bush must decide between setting off an electrifying jolt of principle by opposing affirmative action, or yielding to heavy political pressure." Other newspapers including the *Washington Times*, the *Wall Street Journal*, the *New York Times*, the *Seattle Post-Intelligencer*, and even the British *Manchester Guardian* published editorials encouraging the administration to, in the words of the *Michigan Daily* (2003), "Get off the Fence."

If the Bush administration were to weigh in on the cases, it would need to decide what its position should be. Conservatives wanted a brief that opposed all affirmative action policies (Biskupic 2003; J. Lewis 2003; Murray 2003; Sammon 2003). Roger Clegg, general counsel for the conservative group Center for Equal Opportunity, argued that "a brief that said Michigan should lose but that in principle, diversity justifies the practice of taking race into account, regarding who gets in and who doesn't get in . . . would be a disaster" (Murray 2003; Sammon 2003). Ward Connerly and Edward Blum, the chairman and director of legal affairs, respectively, of the American Civil Rights Institute, expressed a widely held view on the right that it would be a shame if the Bush administration "split-the-baby" by submitting an amicus brief that claimed "discrimination is permissible so long as it is narrowly tailored" (2002). They were bolstered by the fact that Solicitor General Ted Olsen sent the White House a draft brief that strongly opposed Michigan's efforts to "discriminate" in order to achieve racial diversity.

But not all Bush advisors shared these views. Some felt that the Michigan cases provided a unique opportunity "to reach out to minority groups" by siding with the university (Biskupic 2003, 4A). And Bush's longtime confidant and White House Counsel, Alberto Gonzales, urged the president to refrain from participating (Novak 2003).

In the end, the administration hedged in exactly the way that Blum, Clegg, and Connerly feared. The solicitor general's amicus brief insisted that Michigan's program unconstitutionally contained quotas but also argued that

> In the final analysis, this case does not require the Court to break any new ground to hold that race-based admissions is unconstitutional. . . . Ensuring that public institutions, especially educational institutions, are open and accessible to a broad and diverse array of individuals, including individuals of all races and ethnicities, is an important and entirely legitimate government objective. Measures that ensure diversity . . . are important components of government's responsibility to its citizens.

Outside the Court, the brief had predictable effects. Conservatives condemned the brief and supporters of affirmative action praised it. For example, even as she criticized the Bush administration for not understanding the University of Michigan's admissions systems, University of Michigan president Mary Sue Coleman stated that she was "pleased to hear President Bush say that diversity, and explicitly racial diversity, in our student bodies is very important for America's colleges and universities" (quoted in Gnagey 2003).

Despite all the attention the brief generated, one wonders whether it really mattered. Did the brief actually affect the Court? Or was the back and forth over the amicus filing part of a political game that had a great deal to do with electoral politics and nothing to do with the legal outcome? In other words, was the Supreme Court more than an incidental backdrop?

Some have argued that the result itself answers these questions as the majority opinions in *Grutter v. Bollinger* and *Gratz v. Bollinger* were quite consistent with the language in the administration's brief. The Court struck down Michigan's undergraduate (*Gratz*) and upheld the law school (*Grutter*) admissions policies. Observers reinforced this view. Thomas W. Merrill, deputy solicitor general from 1987 to 1990, insisted the amicus brief was important because on high-profile cases the justices "look to the Solicitor General for guidance . . . for signals about the political atmosphere, 'for what's do-able'" (Greenhouse 2003).

How much of a role did the administration's brief really play? How much do these briefs play in general? There are many possible explanations for the Supreme Court's ruling other than deference to the administration. We can easily imagine, for example, that a conservative-leaning Supreme Court that also understood how entrenched affirmative action was in society would come to the same conclusion as the Bush administration, brief or no brief.

In this chapter, we provide general answers to questions about executive influence on the Court, which will help us understand decision-making on the Court—what matters and when. They will also help us think about the Supreme Court in a broader political context. One of our core interests is whether the Court is beyond democratic control. If the solicitor general's briefs influence justices, this could provide at least some measure of democratically accountable influence on Court decision-making.

Motivated by such questions, we focus on whether the solicitor general and the executive branch she represents shape judicial decision-making. In particular, we ask whether justices defer to the solicitor general. If so, is it non-ideological deference or does ideology condition the nature of deference? We develop and test a signaling model of deference, allowing us to show that non-legal and non-attitudinal forces influence the Court. But we also show that the nature of the deference depends on ideological factors as well.

THE SOLICITOR GENERAL AND THE COURT

While much about the relations between the Supreme Court and other branches is contested, there is little doubt about one thing: the solicitor general does well before the Court (Kearney and Merrill, 2000). This success occurs at every stage of the process. The Supreme Court is more likely to grant certiorari when the solicitor general requests it (Tanenhaus et al. 1963; Ulmer 1984; Provine 1980; Caldeira and Wright 1988) and disproportionately sides with the solicitor general's position when she represents a party to the case or files an amicus brief (Johnson 2003; McGuire 1998; Salokar 1992; Segal 1988; Segal and Reedy 1988; O'Connor 1983; Puro 1981). In addition, the Court disproportionately incorporates the solicitors' general amicus briefs arguments into its opinions (Spriggs and Wahlbeck 1997). Such success has given rise to the widely held view that the solicitor general is the "tenth justice" (Caplan 1987).

Many believe solicitors general are successful because they work "almost as a surrogate for the Court rather than as an unrestrained advocate for the government" (Perry 1991, 130; see also Scigliano 1971; Caldeira and Wright 1988; Caplan 1987; Segal 1988; and Ulmer and Willison 1985). In this view, the solicitors general have a "loyalty to the Court, and a personal dedication to the development of law" (Salokar 1992, 2) that gives them special credibility before the Court. If this is the primary mechanism of influence, judicial deference to the solicitors general should not depend on ideological factors.

Some also argue that the success of solicitors general stems from their legal skills. As "repeat players," solicitors general benefit from the reputations they establish in the legal profession and the experience they gain (McGuire 1998; Galanter 1974; Segal 1988; Caldeira and Wright 1988; Spriggs and Wahlbeck 1997). Perry discovered the importance of being a repeat player when a former clerk told him that the solicitor general was successful because "the Solicitor General also knows all the catchwords and they just know how to write them in a brief" (1991, 132).

Another possibility is that solicitors general succeed because justices do not want to cross them and the administration they represent. As we have seen, Merrill suggests that the solicitor general's participation signals to the Court what is "do-able." While one could conceive of "do-ability" as a legal concept, this is more likely a political concept. Following the logic of the previous chapter, justices may wish to avoid alienating the president in order to avoid having him endorse legislation unappealing to the Court. Likewise, justices may defer to the president to prevent him from unilaterally deciding not to enforce Supreme Court decisions.

Justices may also defer to solicitors general because of a social desire by justices to be liked by others (Baum 2006; Burbank and Friedman 2002, 5; Geyh 2006, 15). While such a motivation—to the extent it exists—would almost certainly vary across justices, there is ample evidence of friendships that span the judicial and executive branches. Justice Scalia escaped unharmed from a hunting trip with Vice President Cheney only to find himself in a firestorm of controversy when he refused to recuse himself from a case involving Cheney (Cohen 2006). The business of the Court can affect these friendships; for example, after the Court struck President Truman's action in the Youngstown case in 1952, Justice Black threw Truman a party to soften the blow (Dunne 1977, 240).[1]

The attitudinal model rejects the idea that justices defer to the solicitor general for any reason, whether it is fear of the executive branch's reaction, a desire to maintain personal relationships, or because of the solicitor general's litigation skills. One way to reconcile the attitudinal model with the disproportionate success of solicitors general is to argue that the success of the solicitor general is due to ideological compatibility between the solicitor general and justices. If true, solicitors general win because of ideology, not because of non-attitudinal deference by justices. As Segal and Spaeth (2002, 412) put it:

> [O]ur research has shown that virtually every justice serving between 1953 and 1982 supported the party favored by the Solicitor General in amicus curiae briefs over half the time. This, of course, suggests some degree of nonattitudinal influence. Nevertheless, such support was largely conditioned on the ideological position of the party being supported. Fifteen of the twenty justices examined demonstrated significantly different levels of support when the Solicitor General favored the liberal side than when he favored the conservative side. Rehnquist, for example, supported the Solicitor General 77 percent of the time in conservative briefs but only 39 percent of the time in liberal ones, the largest difference among the Court's conservatives.

Bailey, Kamoie, and Maltzman (2005; hereafter BKM) provide a hybrid explanation of solicitor general influence that depends on both expertise and ideology. They argue that it is not in the interest of justices to uncritically accept solicitor general arguments even if the solicitor general has valuable expertise about the legal or political implications of a case. If all justices did this, the solicitor general would be able to lead naive justices to vote against their interests, making them worse off than not listening to the solicitor general at all.

BKM present a model in which justices take into account the solicitor general's preferences when they read the solicitor general's amicus briefs. Such a model is consistent with the fact that justices have demonstrated a clear concern with the preferences of amicus writers. Justice Scalia, for example, noted bitingly in *Jaffee v. Redmond* (1996) that "not a single amicus brief was filed in support of petitioner. That is no surprise. There is no self-interested organization out there devoted to pursuit of the truth in the federal courts" (Kearney and Merrill, 2000, 745). The next year the Court required those who filed amicus briefs to disclose who financed the production of the brief (Kearney and Merrill, 2000, 766).

BKM developed a signaling model in which justices appreciate both that the solicitor general has potentially useful information and that the solicitor general does not necessarily share the justices' ideological predispositions. In the model, justices assess the credibility of the solicitor general's recommendation in light of what the justices know about the solicitor general's ideology in general. If the justice and solicitor general are very close ideologically, then the information from the solicitor general is likely to be quite useful to a justice. But information can also be credibly transmitted if the solicitor general is far from the justice ideologically but goes against expectations. For example, if a liberal solicitor general advocates a conservative position this will be credible, as the liberal solicitor general's only incentive to mislead is to try to trick conservatives into voting liberally.[2]

THE SOLICITOR GENERAL AS AN IDEOLOGICAL SIGNAL

Signaling theory explores the conditions under which information can be credibly transmitted from one actor to another (Crawford and Sobel 1982; Li and Wing 2004). Signaling models build from two premises. First, the models assume that an information asymmetry exists among different actors: a "sender" (who in our case corresponds to the solicitor general) possesses some privately observed information and transmits a "message" to a "receiver" (who in our case is a Supreme Court justice).

Second, the models assume that the receiver recognizes that the sender's signal may be inaccurate. This may occur because the sender has different preferences than the recipient and thus has an incentive to intentionally distort the message he or she is sending. Receivers therefore strategically take into account the sender's preferences when processing the sender's message. In the case of the Court, justices interact repeatedly with the solicitor general and thus are likely to possess a great deal of information about the solicitor general's preferences.

The heuristic example depicted in Figure 7.1 applies the theory to relations between the solicitor general and the Court. Policy space is one-dimensional and preferences are single-peaked. We look at a single justice who is ideologically located at the point marked "Justice" and a solicitor general who is more conservative than the justice, with his ideal point marked "Solicitor General." For simplicity, we refer to the justice as male and the solicitor general as female.

On any given case there will be a policy outcome associated with voting liberally and a policy outcome associated with voting conservatively. The solicitor general and justice do not know the exact location of these policy outcomes, so they have to make informed estimates about them. If, based on his best estimate of the policy locations, the justice believes the conservative outcome is closer to his ideal point, he will favor the conservative outcome; if the justice believes the liberal outcome is closer, he will favor the liberal outcome. Hence, the decision calculus of the justice reduces to calculating whether his ideal point is to the left or the right of the case cutpoint (the midpoint between the liberal and conservative policy outcomes for the case). The amicus brief filed by the solicitor general can

Figure 7.1. Hypothetical Court and signals about cutpoint

be taken as relaying the solicitor general's understanding of where the cutpoint resides and a recommendation of how the justice should vote.

The solicitor general has private information about where the true cutpoint is located. This comes in part from her organizational advantages. She heads a large office that is well connected to the legal, administrative, and political worlds. In addition, the solicitor general has private information based on personal judgment, on how she integrates all the facts and what weight each element deserves.

For simplicity, we assume that the solicitor general learns that the cutpoint is one of three possible locations: S_1, S_2, or S_3. If the solicitor general were somehow forced to fully and truthfully reveal her private information, this information would prove very helpful to the justice. Information from the solicitor general that the cutpoint is at S_1 would lead the moderate justice to opt for a conservative outcome. If the solicitor general revealed that the true cutpoint is at S_2 or S_3, the justice would vote liberally.

The problem, of course, is that the solicitor general may not wish to truthfully reveal what she knows. A strategic solicitor general who knows that the cutpoint is S_2 and that a fully informed justice would prefer the liberal outcome might wish to deceive the justice into voting conservatively by claiming the cutpoint was S_1. Hence, a wise justice would be uncertain whether the solicitor general was accurately passing on information.

The ability of a sender such as the solicitor general to distort information inhibits transmission of information but does not rule it out. There are, generally speaking, two conditions that facilitate information transmission. In the first, the sender and receiver are ideologically closer to each other (Crawford and Sobel 1982). In this case, the receiver has good reason to trust the signal sent by the sender. For example, if the ideal point of the solicitor general in Figure 7.1 were between S_1 and S_2 (as is the justice), then for none of the three possible states of the world would the solicitor general and justice have divergent preferences. Under this scenario, the solicitor general has no incentive to mislead the justice. This is why a universal theme in signaling models is that information transmission is more precise the closer the preferences of the sender and receiver.

Information transmission is also easier when the sender sends a signal that is counter to his ideological predisposition. As Calvert (1985, 552) has argued, "a biased advisor recommending the alternative he was supposed to have been biased against is likely thereby to prevent the decision maker from making a relatively large error." For example, in Figure 7.1, if the relatively conservative solicitor general suggests that a liberal outcome is desirable since the cutpoint is S_3, the justice would be wise to accept the position embraced by the solicitor general. After all, there is no strategic reason for a conservative solicitor general to say this unless the state of the world really were S_3. On the other hand, if the relatively conservative solicitor general suggests that the liberal justice should prefer a conservative outcome since the cutpoint is S_1, the justice should be skeptical of the solicitor general's signal. In this case, the justice has no way of knowing whether the solicitor general is being truthful or whether the solicitor general is misrepresenting the case when the true cutpoint is S_2. If the solicitor general is being truthful, the justice and the solicitor general will prefer a conservative outcome. But if the solicitor general is misrepresenting the cutpoint, the justice will prefer a liberal outcome.

More generally, the value of the signal sent to a justice depends upon the position taken by the solicitor general and the preference of the solicitor general relative to the preferences of the justice. When a solicitor general who is more conservative than the justice takes a liberal position, the justice can infer that if the information were compelling enough to make the conservative take a liberal position, the information should be even more compelling to someone who is more liberal in the first place. The logic works equally well (in reverse) when a more liberal solicitor general takes a conservative position (see Cameron, Songer, and Segal 2000 for related arguments).

We can translate these themes from signaling theory into specific hypotheses about how Supreme Court justices will respond to messages from the solicitor general. The first important conjecture is that the credibility of the message decreases as the solicitor general and a Supreme Court justice become more ideologically distant. In other words, we expect that a justice whose policy views are similar to those of the solicitor general is more likely to support the position advocated by the solicitor general and that a justice with views that are ideologically distinct from those of the executive to be less likely to support the positions advocated by the solicitor general.

The credibility of a signal also increases when the sender of the message takes a position against his or her policy predisposition and in favor of the justice's predisposition. For the reasons outlined above, moderate and liberal members of the Court may be duly skeptical of claims by a conservative solicitor general about the legal merits of the conservative position. But these same members may be much more open to claims by a liberal solicitor general that the conservative position is legally meritorious. This is particularly the case if the solicitor general and the justice have distinct policy preferences. Even after controlling for each justice's policy predispositions, a justice who is extremely conservative is likely to take the information conveyed by a liberal solicitor general embracing a conservative position more seriously than would a moderate justice. As a result, we expect a justice will be more likely to support the solicitor general when the solicitor general is more liberal than the justice and takes a conservative position or when the solicitor general is more conservative than the justice and takes a liberal position.

Exploring the Solicitor General's Relationship with the Justices

Two fundamental questions remain unanswered in the literature. First, can we definitively say that the solicitor general has influence even after controlling for ideological and other factors? Second, if the solicitor general does influence the Court, does the influence depend on ideology? Answering these questions helps us shed light on how justices make decisions and if they are constrained by external factors. If a justice defers to any solicitor general regardless of ideological compatibility this implies the justice either values deference to the executive branch or is typically persuaded by the legal arguments put together by the office. If there is an ideological component to the deference to the solicitor general, we have to ask whether it is due to a simple coincidence of ideological values or the result of information transmission as in signaling models.

Case selection by the solicitor general complicates matters. It is quite plausible that the solicitor general selects cases in part based upon her expectation of what justices will do on the case. In particular, solicitors general may be more likely to file briefs on cases they expect to win in order to compile a high winning percentage that would impress future employers and clients. Hence Nicholson and Collins (2008, 383) argue that "if the Solicitor General selects cases based in part on his estimate of whether the Court will endorse his position, this suggests that scholars have likely overstated the influence of the Solicitor General on the Court." The concern is that the solicitor general would win at a high rate but that the success would be due to selection bias rather than the influence of the solicitor general. Therefore one of our challenges is to distinguish such cherry-picking (where the solicitor general wins with big majorities) from influence (where—again—the solicitor general wins with big majorities).

To understand the role of the solicitor general, we employ a statistical model that resembles the model used in earlier chapters. In particular, we model the probability that a justice, member of Congress, or president takes a conservative stance on cases and votes that involved criminal procedure, civil rights, the First Amendment, due process, privacy, or federalism from 1950 to 2008.[3]

Our focus here is an additional variable, the position of the solicitor general. This variable plays a role in three independent variables. The first is simply a dummy variable, *SG*, indicating the position of the solicitor general in an amicus brief (−1 for liberal, 0 for no position, and +1 for conservative). We will be controlling for the ideology of justices, so a positive and significant coefficient on this parameter indicates influence.[4]

Once again, we employ non-Court actors to identify κ, the ideological cutpoint of cases. As in chapter 4, we need to assume that non-Court actors are not affected by the legal consideration. This is important for two reasons. First, we simply cannot identify the effect of a dummy variable if the dummy variable affects all actors comparably. This is an application of what we showed in chapter 3 (where the solicitor general position is analogous to the "law" variable). Second, identifying the ideological cutpoint helps us distinguish solicitor general influence from possible cherry-picking of winnable cases by the solicitor general. If solicitors general filed conservative briefs only when most justices were conservative ($\theta_i > \kappa_v$) or filed liberal briefs only when most justices were liberal ($\theta_i < \kappa_v$) and we did not identify and control for κ_v, we would observe the solicitor general dummy variable as having a value of +1 on conservative votes by justices and −1 on liberal votes by justices. This would induce a spurious relationship between the solicitor general dummy variable and voting.

We also include other variables connected to the solicitor general's position on a case. One, *SGDistance*, is an interaction of *SG* (which is −1, 0, or +1) and the absolute value of the ideological distance between the justice and the solicitor general.[5] We expect the coefficient on this variable to be negative: when *SG* indicates that the solicitor general is taking a conservative position, the further the solicitor general is from a justice, the less likely the justice will vote conservatively.[6]

SGOutlier captures the situation in which informational credibility increases with the distance between a justice and the solicitor general. The variable is *SGDistance* times a dummy indicating that either the solicitor general is more liberal than the justice and advocates a conservative position or the solicitor general is more conservative than the justice and advocates a liberal position. The variable is zero when the solicitor general takes no position. It is also coded as zero when a solicitor general more liberal than the justice files a liberal brief or a solicitor general more conservative than the justice files a conservative brief. Signaling theory suggests a positive coefficient because a liberal solicitor general taking a conservative position and a conservative solicitor general taking a liberal position are each sending a particularly credible signal about the best non-ideologically driven outcome.

The equation we estimate is

$$Pr(y_{itv} = 1) = \Phi(\alpha_v(\theta_{it} - \kappa_v) + \lambda_{1i}SG_v + \lambda_{2i}SGDistance_v + \lambda_{3i}SGOutlier_v$$
$$+ \pi_i Precedent_v + \delta_i Deference_v + \sigma_i Speech_v)$$

where y_{itv} is 1 if individual i takes a conservative position at time t on vote v, α_v is the vote discrimination parameter, θ_{it} is the policy preference of individual i at time t, κ_v is the vote cutpoint, and the λ parameters capture the effect of the solicitor general variables discussed above. The rest of the variables (*Precedent_v*, *Deference_v*, and *Speech_v*) are controls for the precedent, deference, and speech variables described in chapter 3. In order to identify the κ, λ, π, δ, and σ parameters, we assume they are zero for non-justices. As in previous chapters, we estimate the model using a Bayesian Markov Chain Monte Carlo (MCMC) algorithm.

We proceed in two steps in order to ensure that our estimates of ideological distance between justices and solicitors general are not contaminated by deference to the solicitor general. First, we estimate preferences based on a model where we exclude cases where the solicitor general filed a brief. This is the model from chapter 3 where we control for legal values associated with precedent, deference, and free speech. This allows us to calculate justices' and presidents' preferences based on cases where there was no solicitor general brief, meaning that solicitor general influence was impossible. In the second stage, we use the calculated distances from the first stage as the variables in the above model.

The expectations for the λ variables follow from our theory above. The coefficient on SG (λ_1) should be positive as a conservative solicitor general amicus brief (SG = +1) should make a justice more conservative and a liberal solicitor general amicus brief (SG = −1) should make a justice less conservative. The coefficient on SGDistance (λ_2) should be negative as the influence of a solicitor general on an individual justice should decline as the distance between the solicitor general and the justice increases; this captures the idea that signals are less effective as the signaler's and receiver's preferences diverge. The coefficient on SGOutlier should be positive; this captures the idea that signals are more effective when they are contrary to type—a firm conservative advocating a liberal position is quite convincing, especially if you are more liberal than the conservative.

As in the previous chapters, we do not have sufficient data for all justices to estimate all parameters. Some justices participated in very few cases in which the solicitor general filed an amicus brief; for other justices, we have very little variance in who was president. In these instances, there is little or no variance in the SGDistance and SGOutlier variables, making them highly collinear with the SG variable. Thus, we dropped the justices who did not leave with us enough observations. Table 7.1

TABLE 7.1
Solicitor General Observations by Justice

	SG			Outlier Signal	
	-1	*0*	*1*	*< 0*	*> 0*
Black	44	922	7	22	5
Reed	4	202	1	0	1
Frankfurter	10	422	1	3	0
Douglas	50	1,188	17	49	0
Jackson	3	126	0	1	0
Burton	5	283	1	0	1
Vinson	1	112	0	0	0
Clark	38	646	4	0	4
Minton	4	183	1	0	1
Warren	43	668	6	43	0
Harlan	41	726	4	3	2
Brennan	97	1,941	161	97	0
Whittaker	5	208	0	0	0
Stewart	71	1,327	39	15	18
White	99	1,823	193	48	19
Goldberg	22	122	0	22	0
Fortas	12	203	5	12	1
Marshall	67	1,461	170	67	0
Burger	50	1,136	100	22	24
Blackmun	74	1,438	193	48	19
Powell	51	1,012	113	34	12
Rehnquist	114	1,714	270	37	94
Stevens	109	1,460	294	79	28
O'Connor	84	1,074	242	44	39
Scalia	70	847	209	29	44
Kennedy	65	746	184	25	39
Souter	63	595	148	25	38
Thomas	58	587	134	3	116
Ginsburg	55	474	121	16	37
Breyer	45	441	115	15	32
Roberts	5	82	32	5	0
Alito	5	71	24	5	0
Total	1,464	24,240	2,789	769	574

displays the number of non-zero *SG* observations for each justice. We have very few observations on cases where the solicitor general filed an amicus brief for Justices Reed, Frankfurter, Jackson, Burton, Vinson, Minton, and Whittaker. For Justice Goldberg, we have twenty-two observations, but they are all on cases where the solicitor general filed a liberal brief. For an additional four justices (Clark, Harlan, Roberts, and Alito), we have very little variation on our other solicitor general variables. For example, the only observations for Justice Alito in our data set (which ends in 2008) occurred under President Bush, meaning that the distance between Alito and Bush was the same for all cases where none of the legal variables was implicated, making the distance variable almost perfectly correlated with the *SG* variable.[7]

RESULTS

Table 7.2 shows the results from the test of our claims about the nature of the solicitor general's influence while controlling for ideology. The column headed by *SG* reports λ_1 for each justice; the column headed by *SGDistance* reports λ_2 for each justice, and so forth. The "p" values are the Bayesian analogs to conventional *p*-values.[8] The coefficients are significant for many justices: the coefficient on *SG* is significant at the .10 level for 12 of the 23 justices for whom it was estimated. The coefficient on *SGDistance* is significantly less than zero (as predicted) at the .10 level for 7 of the 19 justices for whom it was estimated. And the coefficient on *SGOutlier* is significant at the .10 level for 10 of the 19 justices for whom it was estimated (and there are five other justices who are relatively close to being significant at the .10 level).[9]

As in previous chapters, the non-linear structure of the model precludes the parameters from being directly interpretable. Therefore, we used the estimated parameters to simulate justices' probabilities of voting conservatively for various configurations of the independent variables. For the first simulation, we assume that the effect of deference is unconditional. In other words, we simulate the effect of solicitor general amicus briefs on a justice who has the same ideology as the solicitor general. Following the general approach used in previous chapters, we simulate the probability of a conservative vote when the solicitor general is liberal and when the solicitor general is conservative, with the difference being an estimate of the effect of the solicitor general's amicus brief.

The bars in Figure 7.2 indicate the average simulated percentage change in the probability of supporting a conservative outcome that occurs when a solicitor general switches from a liberal amicus to a conservative amicus, with the average across three values of κ. The lines connect the 10th and 90th percentiles of the posterior distribution; if the line is completely above zero this indicates that the parameter was above zero for more than 90 percent of the posterior simulations. Twelve of twenty-three justices have positive predicted effects and many are estimated precisely enough to be confident that the effect is larger than zero.

TABLE 7.2
Solicitor General Parameter Estimates

Justice	SG variable		
	SG	SGDistance	SGOutlier
Expected sign	> 0	< 0	> 0
Black	−0.37 (p = 0.81)	0.00 (p = 0.47)	−0.44 (p = 0.76)
Douglas	−0.31 (p = 0.61)	−0.21 (p = 0.68)	0.86 (p = 0.05)
Clark	0.51 (p = 0.03)	—	—
Warren	0.58 (p = 0.22)	−0.35 (p = 0.41)	1.15 (p = 0.14)
Harlan	−0.39 (p = 0.94)	—	—
Brennan	0.75 (p = 0.00)	−0.22 (p = 0.03)	−0.04 (p = 0.59)
Stewart	0.15 (p = 0.41)	−0.001 (p = 0.51)	0.30 (p = 0.16)
White	0.19 (p = 0.36)	0.46 (p = 0.93)	−0.08 (p = 0.62)
Marshall	0.82 (p = 0.02)	−0.42 (p = 0.00)	0.41 (p = 0.01)
Burger	0.49 (p = 0.03)	−0.27 (p = 0.15)	0.88 (p = 0.00)
Blackmun	0.16 (p = 0.30)	0.07 (p = 0.69)	0.46 (p = 0.01)
Powell	0.28 (p = 0.30)	−0.10 (p = 0.38)	0.52 (p = 0.03)

Note: The "*p*" values are the Bayesian analogs to conventional *p*-values (indicating percentage of posterior distribution inconsistent with alternative hypothesis): — indicates insufficient data.

The results suggest that Justices Alito, Kennedy, and O'Connor stand out as being particularly swayed by the positions of the solicitor general. For example, the simulation suggests that all else equal, if a solicitor general were to shift from a liberal to conservative brief, Justice Kennedy's probability of voting conservatively would go up by 76 percentage points. In other words, across the three κ values we simulated, Kennedy had an average simulated probability of voting liberally of about 20 percent when the solicitor general filed a liberal brief; the average simulated probability of voting conservatively shot up to almost 96 percent when we simulated a conservative solicitor general brief. The estimated effects on Alito were nearly as large and even for O'Connor the net simulated effect was around 60 percent. That Court medians such as Kennedy and O'Connor appear so strongly influenced by the solicitor general raises the possibility of inter-institutional influence on the Court by the executive branch.

Others with clear positive effects include Chief Justices Roberts and Rehnquist. Justices Souter, Stevens, Harlan, Douglas, and Black have negative estimated effects, but only Harlan's effect is significantly different from 0. This implies that Harlan was a solicitor general contrarian who was pushed in the opposite direction of what the solicitor general recommended.

TABLE 7.2
(continued)

Justice	SG variable		
	SG	SGDistance	SGOutlier
Expected sign	> 0	< 0	> 0
Rehnquist	0.70 (p = 0.00)	−0.37 (p = 0.00)	0.65 (p = 0.00)
Stevens	−0.11 (p = 0.69)	0.04 (p = 0.66)	0.56 (p = 0.00)
O'Connor	0.98 (p = 0.01)	−0.71 (p = 0.00)	0.30 (p = 0.04)
Scalia	0.47 (p = 0.01)	−0.26 (p = 0.04)	0.0005 (p = 0.50)
Kennedy	1.37 (p = 0.00)	−0.89 (p = 0.00)	0.19 (p = 0.15)
Souter	−0.34 (p = 0.88)	0.46 (p = 0.99)	0.28 (p = 0.12)
Thomas	0.36 (p = 0.04)	−0.30 (p = 0.04)	0.24 (p = 0.08)
Ginsburg	0.01 (p = 0.48)	0.15 (p = 0.85)	0.38 (p = 0.08)
Breyer	0.69 (p = 0.05)	−0.07 (p = 0.35)	0.31 (p = 0.14)
Roberts	1.03 (p = 0.00)	—	—
Alito	1.46 (p = 0.00)	—	—

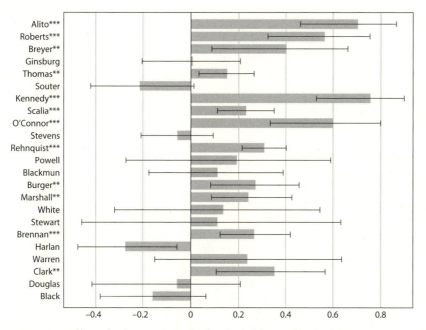

Figure 7.2. Effect of solicitor general. The shaded bar indicates the change in probability of a conservative vote when moving from $SG = -1$ to $SG = 1$. The line indicates a simulated 90 percent Bayesian confidence interval; ***change significantly > 0 at $p = .01$; **change significantly > 0 at $p = .05$.

There are several suggestive patterns in the results but little that is definitive. More recent justices have tended to be more deferential to the solicitor general than were earlier justices. Since Rehnquist, eight of thirteen justices exhibited significant deference in contrast to only four of twelve justices before Rehnquist. This is likely due at least in part to data limitations, as Table 7.1 shows that the amount and variation of data were much more limited for earlier justices. This could also be due to an increasing comfort with executive power among many in the legal community. It is also possible that the office of the solicitor general has become more professional over time, leading to more effective legal arguments. However, this is speculation as so much in the American legal world has become more, not less, political. It is also interesting that three of four chief justices in the sample deferred significantly to the solicitor general; perhaps they are more attuned to the institutional standing of the Court, although the small sample size limits our ability to come to firm conclusions.

The signaling model suggested that the effectiveness of the solicitor general briefs systematically varies depending on the ideological compatibility of a justice and solicitor general. In Figure 7.2, we assumed that the solicitor general and the justice had identical preferences. In Figure 7.3, we simulate what happens when the ideological distance between each justice and the solicitor general goes from zero (as in Figure 7.2) to one. Whereas Figure 7.2 showed that a solicitor general brief going from liberal to conservative moved Justice Kennedy 76 percentage points when the solicitor general was simulated to have identical preferences as Justice Kennedy, in Figure 7.3 we learn that if the solicitor general and Kennedy had ideological preferences that were one unit away from each other, the effect of the solicitor general brief is only 32 percentage points. This 44-percentage-point decline in potency of the solicitor general brief is plotted in Figure 7.3 next to Justice Kennedy's name. Twelve of the seventeen justices for whom we have sufficient data become less responsive to the solicitor general when they become more ideologically distant; the effect is statistically significant at conventional levels for seven justices.

The patterns in Figure 7.3 indicate that conservatives on recent Courts have been selective in which solicitors general they defer to. Kennedy defers a lot to solicitors general near him ideologically but does not defer much to those far from him. This is also true of O'Connor and, to a lesser extent, of Thomas, Scalia, and Rehnquist. Among earlier justices, only two liberals—Marshall and Brennan—made such distinctions in their deference. Two interesting results are for Justices Souter and White. The estimates indicate that they found solicitors general who were ideologically distant to be more persuasive. They could be contrarian toward their ideological allies in the executive branch or they could have a sense of

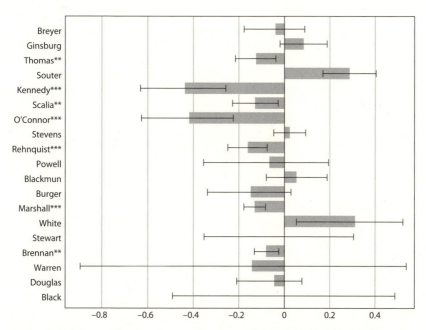

Figure 7.3. Effect of distance from solicitor general. The shaded bar indicates the change in probability of a conservative vote when moving from *SGDistance* = 0 to *SGDistance* = 1. The line indicates a simulated 90 percent Bayesian confidence interval; ***change significantly > 0 at $p = .01$; **change significantly > 0 at $p = .05$. The informational model predicts a negative coefficient on distance on $SG \times Distance$. The estimated coefficients for Stewart and Black are near zero.

bending over backward to defer to the executive branch when they differed on policy.

The signaling model also suggests that ideological distance can actually boost the solicitor general's influence in cases where the solicitor general takes an unexpected position. The results in Table 7.2 provide evidence of this dynamic for more than half of the justices, and Figure 7.4 illustrates the magnitude of the effects graphically. The figure shows the change in the effectiveness of a solicitor general's brief when the ideological distance between the solicitor general and justice is 1 and when the solicitor general's position switches from being ideologically expected (a solicitor general more liberal than the justice filing a liberal brief or vice versa) to being an outlier signal (a solicitor general more liberal than the justice filing a conservative brief or vice versa). For example, whereas the predicted influence on Justice Kennedy with an ideologically expected brief is 32 percentage points if the solicitor general is one unit away from Kennedy, the predicted influence on Kennedy is 43 points if the same solicitor general

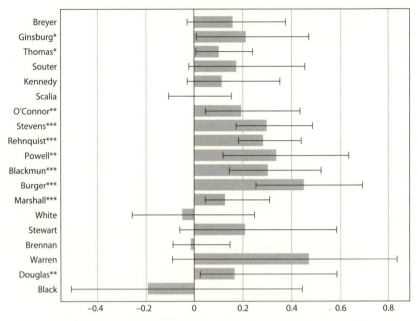

Figure 7.4. Effect of outlier signals. The shaded bar indicates the change in probability of a conservative vote when moving from *SGOutlier* = 0 to *SGOutlier* = 1. The line indicates a simulated 90 percent Bayesian confidence interval; ***change significantly > 0 at p = .01; **change significantly > 0 at p = .05; *change significantly > 0 at p = .1.

takes an ideologically unexpected position. We plot this 11-percentage-point increase and its standard errors in the figure.

There are few clear patterns here. Chief Justices Warren and Burger both had high levels of responsiveness to outlier signals (although Warren's is not statistically significant at the .10 level). The influence of the solicitor general on both changed more than 40 percentage points when the solicitor general went from an ideologically expected signal to a signal counter to ideological expectations. Others with statistically significant levels of responsiveness to these signals ranged the ideological spectrum and spanned the time period in our analysis. They are Justices Douglas, Marshall, Blackmun, Powell, Rehnquist, Stevens, O'Connor, Thomas, and Ginsburg.

CONCLUSION

The solicitor general influences justices. Some of the influence is direct; even after controlling for ideology and possible cherry-picking by solicitors general, we find that many justices move toward the position advocated by the solicitor general regardless of the ideological position of the solicitor general. This finding comports well both with perspectives that emphasize the solicitor general's legal skill and with perspectives in which justices defer to the executive branch.

We also find ideological components to solicitor general influence. Consistent with signaling theory, solicitors general exert more influence on justices who are ideologically sympathetic to the president being served by the solicitor general. And, again consistent with signaling models, the solicitor general's influence on many justices is even larger when she takes an unexpectedly liberal or conservative position relative to her political predispositions.

These findings provide a window into the role of the Supreme Court in the constitutional system of shared powers. The attitudinal model implies that the Court's nine unelected, life-tenured justices simply do what they want. These results imply a different relationship. Certainly the Court is not under the thumb of the president. The executive branch is, however, an important part of the conversation, adding an additional level of interbranch influence and even constraint on the decision-making of justices.

Chapter 8

CONCLUSION

FEW CASES BETTER DEMONSTRATE the limits of the attitudinal model than *Texas v. Johnson* (1989). The case originated when Gregory Lee Johnson burned an American flag outside the 1984 Republican National Convention in Dallas. He was arrested and convicted for vandalizing a respected object, but the Texas Court of Criminal Appeals overturned the conviction on First Amendment grounds. The case went to the U.S. Supreme Court where Justice Brennan wrote a majority opinion that upheld the lower court's decision, thereby freeing Johnson.

The outcome was not what was puzzling from the attitudinal model perspective; the voting alignment of the justices was. Justices on the left (Blackmun and Marshall), middle (Kennedy), and right (Scalia) supported Brennan's majority opinion, while justices on the left (Stevens), middle (O'Connor and White), and right (Rehnquist) dissented. How can we explain such a breakdown in standard ideological voting? Why, on a 5–4 vote, would the winning coalition be made up of individuals from across the bench's ideological spectrum?

One clue is from the justices themselves. In his concurrence with the Brennan opinion, Justice Kennedy wrote:

> For we are presented with a clear and simple statute to be judged against a pure command of the Constitution. The outcome can be laid at no door but ours. The hard fact is that sometimes we must make decisions we do not like. We make them because they are right, right in the sense that the law and the Constitution, as we see them, compel the result. And so great is our commitment to the process that, except in the rare case, we do not pause to express distaste for the result, perhaps for fear of undermining a valued principle that dictates the decision. This is one of those rare cases.

Our findings reinforce Kennedy's position. As anomalous as *Texas v. Johnson* is for the attitudinal model, it is completely consistent with a legal values story. In particular, a model in which justices vote in accord with their legal attachment to the First Amendment can explain the voting very well. Table 8.1 shows this by sorting the justices who participated in *Texas v. Johnson* by the extent that we reported they were constrained by "free speech" in Figure 4.4. We have shaded the five justices.

TABLE 8.1

Free Speech Support, Ideology, and *Texas v. Johnson*

Justice	Vote *in* Texas v. Johnson *(1989)*	*Effect of Free Speech[1]*	Ideology in 1989[2]	
			Bailey (2007)	*Martin-Quinn (2002)*
Kennedy	Concurrence	0.62	0.47	1.32
Scalia	Majority	0.32	0.58	1.90
Blackmun	Majority	0.26	−0.52	−0.88
Brennan	Majority	0.24	−1.06	−3.73
O'Connor	Dissent	0.23	0.22	1.36
Stevens	Dissent	0.17	−0.77	−1.06
Marshall	Majority	0.13	−1.40	−4.48
Rehnquist	Dissent	0.06	0.71	2.49
White	Dissent	0.04	0.37	0.79

[1] Using data from Figure 4.4. Large values signal greater restraint based upon a strict reading of the First Amendment.

[2] Higher values are assigned to more conservative justices.

Four of the justices who voted with the majority (Kennedy, Brennan, Scalia, and Blackmun) constitute the top four justices who participated in *Texas v. Johnson* in terms of the estimated effect of free speech values. A fifth member of the majority, Marshall, has a statistically significant coefficient on speech (see Table 4.1) and, as a staunch liberal, would have been expected to support the liberal ruling anyway. The four justices who opposed the decision had four of the five lowest estimated effects of the First Amendment parameters. And only two justices (O'Connor and Stevens) interrupt the continuity of the winning coalition.

To compare our results to models that suggest justices are unconstrained, we provide purely ideological measures from Bailey 2007 and Martin and Quinn 2002. Clearly, the connection between the final vote and these ideological scores is tenuous. Neither the Bailey nor the Martin-Quinn ideology measures do a good job explaining the vote on this case. In fact, with both measures the five most liberal justices split 3–2 in favor of Johnson. The free speech parameters estimated in chapter 4 do a much better job of explaining the vote than does a purely ideological model.

Models that assume ideology accounts for all behavior on the Court also lack the capacity to explain cases where a single left-right dimension fails to account for the complexities of a case. *Virginia v. Black* (2003) is one such case. In it, the Court considered a Virginia law banning all cross-burnings. The law had been supported by political liberals who were concerned about protecting minority rights (Gerhardt 2008, 79), but it was

TABLE 8.2
Free Speech Support, Ideology, and *Virginia v. Black*

Justice	*Vote in* Virginia v. Black *(2003)*	*Effect of Free Speech*[1]	Ideology in 2003[2] Bailey *(2007)*	Ideology in 2003[2] Martin-Quinn *(2002; updated)*
Kennedy	Dissent	0.62	0.38	0.74
Souter	Dissent	0.43	−0.88	−1.73
Ginsburg	Dissent	0.34	−0.89	−1.80
Scalia	Majority	0.32	1.07	2.93
Thomas	Majority	0.29	1.14	4.11
O'Connor	Majority	0.23	0.24	0.18
Stevens	Majority	0.17	−1.14	−2.60
Rehnquist	Majority	0.06	0.95	1.38
Breyer	Majority	−0.03	−0.65	−1.30

[1] Using data from Figure 4.4. Large values signal greater restraint based upon a strict reading of the First Amendment.
[2] Higher values are assigned to more conservative justices.

challenged on First Amendment grounds. In a plurality opinion, the Court held that the law was unconstitutional because it did not clearly distinguish between cross-burnings that were intended to intimidate and those that were merely expressions of support for a particular group. Instead the law assumed that the burning of a cross was prima facie evidence of intent to intimidate.

Table 8.2 provides a breakdown of the voting, free speech, and ideological values of justices on *Virginia v. Black*. The coalition on the Court is hard to reconcile with a simple attitudinal approach. While liberals in the Virginia legislature supported the law, two liberals on the Court (Souter and Ginsburg) joined with a moderate (Kennedy) to argue that the law should be struck and that Virginia could not even ban cross-burning conducted with an intent to intimidate. Their behavior is hard to explain with traditional left-right ideology. However, Table 8.2 suggests that there is indeed a unifying characteristic that led these three justices to sign the same opinion: Kennedy, Souter, and Ginsburg are the three justices with the highest estimated effect of free speech.

The case also makes clear that even as legal values matter they do not matter in the same way for all justices. While Justice Kennedy stated that his decision in *Texas v. Johnson* was constrained by the "pure command of the Constitution," Justice Stevens saw things in a completely different light, arguing in his dissent that "the case has nothing to do with 'disagreeable ideas.' It involves disagreeable conduct that, in my opinion, diminishes the value of an important national asset."

These patterns reflect three themes of this book. First, justices are influenced by more than just the policy preferences emphasized by the attitudinal model. Second, law matters for justices. Third, the influence of specific legal doctrines varies across justices.

We also found other constraints. In chapter 6, we showed that the elected branches influence justices. This, too, is something routinely denied by the attitudinal model. But here again some justices were more responsive than others. In chapter 7 we demonstrated that the solicitor general influenced the Court; here the influence varied by justice, not only idiosyncratically but also systematically in accord with the ideological congruence of justices and solicitors general.

Our findings mesh well with other parts of the literature. For example, scholars have made a convincing case that justices are affected by their colleagues when signing a particular opinion (see W. Murphy 1964; Epstein and Knight 1998; Maltzman, Spriggs, and Wahlbeck 2000; Hammond, Bonneau, and Sheehan 2005). Scholars have also found that American public opinion affects the Court (e.g., McGuire and Stimson 2004). Much of the influence is indirect, as public opinion influences presidential elections that in turn affect who is nominated to the Court. However, Mishler and Sheehan (1993, 1996) also find that public opinion directly affects the Court, although the effects are modest and inconsistent.

Our findings have important implications for understanding the political context of the Court. What does it mean for the legitimacy of the Court that both law and policy influence justices? What do the existence and patterns of these non-policy influences mean for the Court in it relations with the rest of the political system? We devote the rest of this conclusion to exploring such questions.

WHY FIDELITY TO THE LAW?

The finding that the law matters contradicts the attitudinal model but is consistent with the public pronouncements of justices. In fact, justices tend to go further, articulating strong forms of a legalism that Posner (2008, 41) calls the "official" theory of judicial behavior. Chief Justice John Roberts famously argued in his opening statement to the judiciary committee hearings on his confirmation that

> Judges and justices are servants of the law, not the other way around. Judges are like umpires. Umpires don't make the rules; they apply them. The role of an umpire and a judge is critical. They make sure everybody plays by the rules. But it is a limited role. Nobody ever went to a ball game to see the umpire. Judges have to have the humility to

recognize that they operate within a system of precedent, shaped by other judges equally striving to live up to the judicial oath. (2003)

Roberts's nomination faced little serious challenge, in part perhaps because his statements reassured lawmakers that he believed that the policy spotlight belonged to elected officials.

The path to confirmation becomes bumpier when nominees talk like attitudinalists. Supreme Court nominee Sonia Sotomayor is a perfect example. She was an accomplished judge with academic accolades. A graduate of Princeton (summa cum laude) and Yale Law School, she heard more than three thousand cases and wrote almost four hundred opinions in her ten years on the Second Circuit Court (Stolberg 2009). Her rise from a modest background to become the first Latina woman nominated to the bench gave her nomination added appeal.

However, some of Sotomayor's statements stirred controversy. In a 2001 speech, she said, "I would hope that a wise Latina woman with the richness of her experiences would more often than not reach a better conclusion than a white male who hasn't lived that life" (Sotomayor 2001). Senator Jon Kyl (R, Arizona), a senior Republican on the Senate Judiciary Committee, took that speech to mean that Sotomayor does not believe that "judges should set aside biases, including those based on race and gender, and render the law impartially and neutrally" (2009). Columnist Charles Krauthammer took her statements to mean that she favors "a judicially mandated racial spoils system and a jurisprudence of empathy that hinges on which litigant is less `advantaged'" (2009).

In response, Sotomayor backtracked substantially, describing her judicial philosophy to the Judiciary Committee in starkly legalist terms:

> It is simple: fidelity to the law. The task of a judge is not to make law, it is to apply the law. And it is clear, I believe, that my record . . . reflects my rigorous commitment to interpreting the Constitution according to its terms, interpreting statutes according to their terms and Congress's intent and hewing faithfully to precedents established by the Supreme Court and by my Circuit Court. In each case I have heard, I have applied the law to the facts at hand. (2009)

Senator Patrick Leahy (D, Vermont), chairman of the Senate Judiciary Committee, helped push Sotomayor away from the taint of attitudinalism:

> When I met with Judge Sotomayor last week I asked her about her approach to the law. She answered that of course one's life experience shapes who you are, but "ultimately and completely"—and she used those words—as a judge you follow the law. There is not one law for one race or another, there is not one law for one color or another, there is not one law for rich and a different one for poor.

There is only one law. She said ultimately and completely a judge has to follow the law no matter what their upbringing has been. That is the kind of fair and impartial judging that the American people expect. That is respect for the rule of law. That is the kind of judge she has been. (2009)

The politics of this episode raise questions about how central the legalist view of the Court is to its legitimacy. Does the American public care whether Supreme Court decisions uphold (or appear to uphold) the Constitution and the law? Or do they care only about the policy implications of Supreme Court decisions, regardless of their apparent constitutional or legal validity? Do they trust the Court as a policy actor? If voters care only about policy and trust the Court in that domain, Supreme Court justices will have little incentive to attempt to impress the public with constitutional arguments. In fact, justices might be better off arguing for their favored policies on the merits of the policy outcome if they hope to curry public favor. On the other hand, if voters want the Court to shy away from policy, constitutional and legal arguments may prove to be valuable tools for justices seeking to increase the legitimacy of their rulings.[1] Indeed, Justice Breyer recently argued that "the Court should interpret written words, whether in the Constitution or a statute, using traditional legal tools, such as text, history, tradition, precedent, and particularly, purposes and related consequences, to help make the law effective. In this way, the Court can help maintain the public's confidence in the legitimacy of its interpretative role" (2010, 74).

Gash and Murakami (2009) provide some initial answers to these questions. They investigated the relative public support for policies that emanate from the courts and other sources such as legislatures and ballot initiatives. To figure this out, they conducted a survey experiment about equalizing education spending across a state. In their experiment, they provided respondents with an overview of a plan to equalize spending throughout a state. Three randomly selected treatment groups were then given differing information about the source of the plan. One group was informed that the equalization plan originated in the courts. Another group was informed that the plan originated in the legislature. And a third group read that the plan came from a ballot initiative. A control group was given no information about the origins of the plan.

The results indicated public skepticism of court-led policy change. Fifty-three percent of respondents in the control group who were given no sourcing information supported the plan. This number went up to 57 percent and then 63 percent for the groups who were told the plan originated with the legislative and ballot initiative processes, respectively. The group that was told that the plan originated with the courts, however,

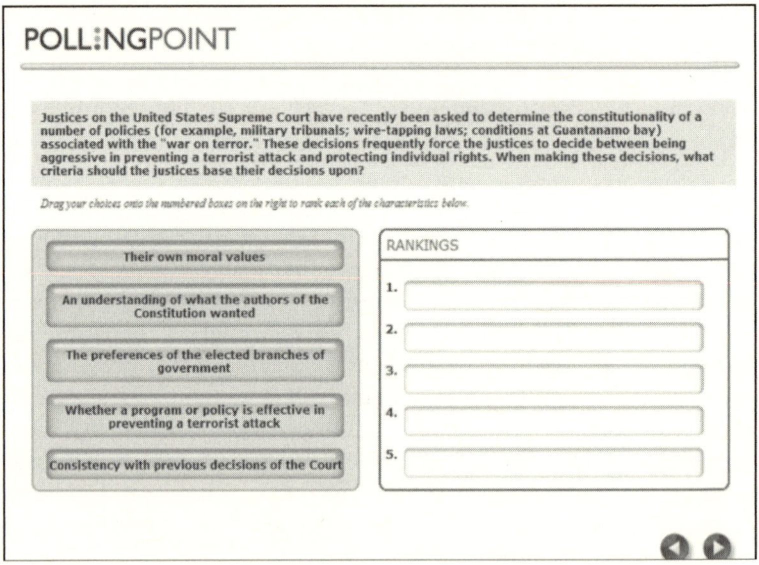

Figure 8.1. What criteria should justices base their decisions on?

was least supportive, with only 48 percent supporting the plan. The effect was even stronger among self-identified partisans (people identifying with either Democrats or Republicans). For them, the difference between the control respondents and the group who were told that policy came from the courts was almost 12 percentage points.

Interestingly, the skepticism of court-led policy change did not extend to self-identified independents. For them, the above pattern was reversed. The highest support for the policy came from the group given the court-prompt. It seems that for part of the population, the judicial branch is more trusted on policy grounds, perhaps due to an even deeper distrust of politicians and partisan voters.

To further probe the role of legal values in public legitimacy, we used George Washington University's participation in the 2008 Cooperative Congressional Election Study (CCES) to conduct two experiments. First, we asked respondents to rank five criteria for making decisions in terrorism-related Supreme Court cases. We show the options and inter-face in Figure 8.1.

Respondents were clear in their preferences: justices should base deci-sions on the Constitution. The criterion "An understanding of what the authors of the Constitution wanted" was ranked most important by 631 of the 1,000 respondents—nearly three times the amount that ranked any other criteria number one. Constitutional interpretation was ranked as the second-most important criterion by 193 respondents. There can be little doubt that Americans profess to want Supreme Court decisions to reflect the Constitution and what the authors of the Constitution wanted.

But how deeply held are these views? What happens when voters are faced with a tradeoff between their preferences for legalist judges and their desires for outcomes they like? Will Americans stick to their desire for legalist judges or will they be more influenced by their own policy preferences? To get at this, we conducted a survey experiment using the 2008 CCES. We designed the experiment to assess the impact of constitutional arguments and policy-based arguments on respondents' assessments of a specific Court decision and a specific justice. As we explain below, the experiment was facilitated by the fact that the CCES instrument had a panel design where the same respondents were surveyed twice with approximately a month intervening (before and after the election).

Respondents for this experiment were randomly assigned into three treatment groups. All groups were provided a description of a Supreme Court decision overturning a handgun ban, with Justice Antonin Scalia identified as the author. We presented respondents in treatment group A with the following constitutional justification for the decision:

> The Supreme Court recently ruled that the government cannot ban all citizens from keeping a handgun at home. In the Court's opinion, Justice Scalia recognized that the Court was overturning the policy enacted by a legislative body. But Scalia argued that the "enshrinement of constitutional rights necessarily takes certain policy choices off the table," which includes measures such as a "prohibition of handguns." Both Senator Obama and Senator McCain released statements supporting the Court decision.

We presented respondents in treatment group B with the following policy-based explanation of the case:

> The Supreme Court recently ruled that the government cannot ban all citizens from keeping a handgun at home. In the Court's opinion, Justice Scalia recognized that the Court was overturning the policy enacted by a legislative body. But Scalia argued that "there were more effective mechanisms for curbing violence than a ban on handguns." Both Senator Obama and Senator McCain released statements supporting the Court decision.

Respondents in treatment group C were our control group and offered the following relatively sparse description of the case:

> The Supreme Court recently ruled that the government cannot ban all citizens from keeping a handgun at home. In the Court's opinion,

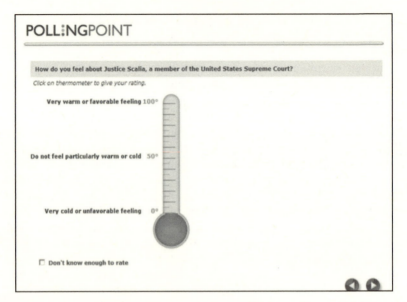

Figure 8.2. Feeling thermometer about Justice Scalia

Justice Scalia recognized that the Court was overturning the policy enacted by a legislative body. Both Senator Obama and Senator Mc-Cain released statements supporting the Court decision.

Approximately a month prior to exposing the respondents to the experimental condition, respondents were asked to describe their feelings about Justice Scalia through use of a thermometer widget (see Figure 8.2), with higher values representing a "warm or favorable feeling." To ascertain the change in each respondent's attitude toward Scalia immediately following exposure to the experimental conditions, this question was posed again after respondents had been exposed to the experimental condition.[2] In addition, following exposure to the experiment and the rating of Scalia, we asked respondents whether they agreed "with the Court's ruling regarding the regulation of handguns." For our analysis, a 1 meant "I strongly disapprove" and a 5 meant "I strongly approve."[3]

Of course, respondents' views of both Justice Scalia and a handgun ban might also stem from their ideological orientations. Fortunately, the common content portion of the CCES survey asked respondents to rate their own ideology on a 100-point scale, with 100 being the most conservative (*Ideology*). One would expect conservatives to respond more positively than liberals to a Supreme Court decision upholding handgun rights. Furthermore, we can use this variable to assess how the effect of the

TABLE 8.3
Effect of Treatments on Evaluation of Justice Scalia

Variable	Coefficient/Standard error
Treatment A (legal justification)	5.68*
	(3.38)
Treatment B (policy justification)	10.07***
	(3.31)
Ideology	0.03
	(0.05)
Education	−1.34
	(0.95)
Intercept	5.68
	(5.58)

$N = 265$
Adjusted $R^2 = .03$
$* p \leq .05$ $*** p \leq .01$, one-tailed tests

treatments varies across the ideological spectrum. Other control variables include respondents' prior levels of trust in the Court (*Trust*) and education level (*Education*).[4] Both of these variables allow us to control for deference that may be given to the Supreme Court because of faith in the institution or a particular understanding of the role of the Court.

In Table 8.3, we model the change in the feeling thermometer rating each respondent gave Scalia before and after the experiment. Independent variables include Treatment A (legal justification), Treatment B (policy justification), Ideology, and Education. The coefficients for both Treatments A and B are positive and statistically significant, indicating that respondents were more favorably disposed toward Scalia when given some explanation of the decision as opposed to none at all. (The excluded reference category is Treatment C, the respondents who received no additional justification of the decision.) Interestingly, and contrary to the conclusion one would draw based upon the answers respondents gave when directly asked about the criteria justices should employ, the coefficient for the policy-based explanation (Treatment B) is roughly twice the magnitude of that for the constitutional explanation (Treatment A). This means respondents seemed to prefer the policy justifications.

Table 8.3 does not distinguish whether support for Scalia improves when given the policy-based explanation because his natural conservative constituency appreciates his willingness to uphold their principles regardless of the law or because the public in general does not appreciate the importance of legal considerations. Therefore we also interact respondent ideology with treatment groups A and B in Table 8.4. Here, we can begin

TABLE 8.4
Effect of Treatments on Evaluation of Justice Scalia Conditioned on
Respondent's Ideology

Variable	Coefficient/Standard error
Treatment A (legal justification)	16.60**
	(7.41)
Treatment B (policy justification)	7.19
	(7.50)
Ideology	0.08
	(0.09)
Ideology × Treatment A (legal justification)	−0.20*
	(0.12)
Ideology × Treatment B (policy justification)	0.06
	(0.11)
Education	−1.23
	(0.94)
Intercept	2.11
	(7.05)

$N = 265$
Adjusted $R^2 = .04$
* $p \leq .05$ ** $p \leq .025$, one-tailed tests

to see the patterns of how the constitutional explanation impacts people of different ideological persuasions. The coefficient on Treatment A is positive, statistically significant, and substantively large (representing an increase of about 16.6 "degrees" in Scalia's thermometer ranking). With the presence of the Ideology × Treatment A interaction term, the coefficient on Treatment A represents the impact of the constitutional explanation treatment on respondents with an ideology score of zero (i.e., liberals, those least likely to agree with Scalia's opinion on its policy merits). Meanwhile, the negative and statistically significant coefficient on the interaction term indicates that as respondents grow more conservative, Treatment A has less and less of an impact on the favorability rating of Scalia. Likewise, legal justifications produce more support for Justice Scalia for liberals who have been faced with an undesired Court ruling. At the same time, conservatives who would naturally support Scalia appreciate it when he deviates from the law. In short, legal justifications build support where it does not already exist.

A similar pattern is apparent when respondents' trust in the Court (*Trust*) is included in the analysis and interacted with the treatments. Table 8.5 displays the results of this model. While the Trust × Treatment A interaction term fails to achieve statistical significance in this analysis, the coefficient for Treatment A is once again positive, large, and statistically

TABLE 8.5

Effect of Treatments on Evaluation of Justice Scalia Conditioned on
Respondent's Trust in the Supreme Court

Variable	Coefficient/Standard error
Treatment A (legal justification)	16.37*
	(9.55)
Treatment B (policy justification)	12.38
	(10.06)
Ideology	0.04
	(0.05)
Trust	0.67
	(2.20)
Trust × Treatment A (legal justification)	−3.68
	(3.13)
Trust × Treatment B (policy justification)	−0.73
	(3.27)
Education	−1.23
	(0.96)
Intercept	2.49
	(8.47)

$N = 261$
Adjusted $R^2 = .02$
* $p \leq .05$, one-tailed tests

significant. For those with low levels of trust, the legal justification increases respondents' evaluations of Scalia. For people with higher levels
of trust in the courts, however, exposure to the legal justification made
people less (albeit not significantly less) favorable toward Scalia across
the two sessions of questioning.

The data are clear. Those who are not already supportive of Justice
Scalia or the institution are more likely to embrace the justice when they
learn that the decisions he makes are based upon legal reasoning rather
than his policy preferences. For this reason, a justice who wanted to
broaden public support for the Court would be wise to rely upon legal
reasoning.

This pattern persists in a somewhat different way when we turn to an
analysis of respondents' agreement with the actual decision (as opposed
to approval or disapproval of Justice Scalia). In Table 8.6, we examine
how our experimental conditions and their interaction with a respondent's preconceived trust of the Court influence the public's support for
the actual decision. We see from the negative and statistically insignificant
coefficient on Treatment B that respondents who came in with low levels
of trust in the Court were not pleased with a policy-based explanation of

TABLE 8.6
Effect of Treatments on Evaluation of Decision Conditioned on
Respondent's Trust in the Supreme Court

Variable	Coefficient/Standard error
Treatment A (legal justification)	−0.08
	(0.48)
Treatment B (policy justification)	−0.88*
	(0.49)
Ideology	0.01***
	(0.002)
Trust	0.08
	(0.11)
Trust × Treatment A (legal justification)	0.03
	(0.16)
Trust × Treatment B (policy justification)	0.27*
	(0.16)
Education	0.02
	(0.05)
Intercept	2.38***
	(0.42)

$N = 397$
Adjusted $R^2 = .10$
* $p \leq .05$ *** $p \leq .01$, one-tailed tests

the decision. The positive and statistically significant coefficient on Trust ×
Treatment B indicates that this effect is mitigated for respondents who
trusted the Court. For respondents who rate their trust in the Court at
three or higher on the five-point scale, the policy-based explanation increased approval of the Court's decision.[5]

Once again, we see that the nature of the arguments made by a justice
will have a different impact on individuals' opinions toward the Court's
decisions depending on whether they are favorably disposed toward the
Court (whether via ideological affinity or diffuse "trust" in the institution
and its members). In our experiment, it appears that an explanation of a
pro-gun decision based on policy merits would only win favor among the
converted: conservatives who naturally support such a decision and those
disposed to trust the current Supreme Court. Meanwhile, it would appear
that such arguments further alienate those who are not as disposed to
approve of the decision or the Court. A constitutionally based argument
may not impress the already converted, but it has the power to placate (if
not win over) those who are not likely to support the decision in the first
place (liberals, those who distrust the Court).

The Court in Context

To say that justices are fundamentally different from elected politicians is not to say that they are deaf to politics. Indeed, we have shown that the Court is influenced by external actors, whether via principle (as in chapter 4), fear (chapter 6), or information (chapter 7). The elected branches do appear to systematically influence the Court. Justices take a more liberal stance on statutory cases when the Court median is even more conservative than the most conservative of the elected branches. Likewise, justices are more likely to embrace a conservative position on statutory cases when the Court median naturally falls to the left of the elected branches. On constitutional cases, we have seen that justices move relative to members of Congress toward whichever party takes over the presidency, something predicted by theories of inter-institutional influence on the Court.

These results are helpful in thinking about how the Court addresses the "countermajoritarian difficulty." This is the fundamental dilemma of the Court: we want the Court to stand up to popular majorities when they violate constitutional rights, but we worry about the non-majoritarian basis of the Court's decisions (Bickel 1962). Depending on your nature, our results offer grounds for either optimism or pessimism about how it can address this difficulty. On the positive side, we find the Court is distinctive from the elected branches, providing at least hope that it will see things differently than elected branches when constitutional rights have been violated. We also find that the Court is not necessarily beyond control as it seems to respond to some extent to elected branches. On the more pessimistic side, the specifics of how distinctive the Court is (in the degree to which various legal factors matter) fluctuate over time, perhaps due in a complex way to the interests of powerful political actors so there is no guarantee that the Court will consistently stand up for any given legal principle. And the fact that we find some responsiveness of the Court to elected branches does not quantify the responsiveness relative to the liberties the Court may be taking; a half-glass type might worry that the Court merely scales back its flaunting of majority will when the political branches are united against it.

Our findings also have some bearing on how we view the "coordinate construction" of the Constitution. This occurs when the Court jointly interprets the Constitution with the president, Congress, and, conceivably, the states and public (Whittington 1999; Devins and Fisher 2004; Fisher 1988; Ackerman 1991). Our findings imply a Court that is consistently distinctive, possibly idiosyncratic, and not beyond the influence of elected branches. This is not necessarily a high-minded dialogue among branches of government about constitutional theory. It is more of a practical give-and-take among actors with diverse interests. We have shown that the Court trims its sails when political winds are too rough; the other side of this result is that the Court may proceed apace when it is within the elected branches' pareto set.

Perhaps the right way to think of the Court is as an agent of democratic experimentation. It is not a dictator or even a final arbiter of legal questions (Starr 2002 and Alexander and Schauer 1997 notwithstanding). Justices who are constrained by both legal doctrines and the other branches are unlikely to radically impose new policies. Instead, the policies promulgated by the Court are likely to reflect what was done in the past (e.g., precedent) and to fall within boundaries defined by the political pareto set. But this does not mean that the Court cannot change policy. Nor does it mean justices don't want to change policy.

Instead, the Court can induce change in two important ways. First, it can change the legal status quo. Perhaps the Court's movement of the status quo could reveal information about what the actual effects of a policy are and, like the Life cereal commercial, the country may like it (Rogers 2001). Or a new status quo could activate interests to protect policies that could not have passed on their own. Second, the Court can move policy within the pareto set—and need not even have widespread public acquiescence, as long as the policy choice it makes is acceptable to at least one veto player. From a democratic theory perspective, the downside is relatively small: it is not obvious that changing policy from one defended by one veto player to a different policy defended by another veto player is that problematic. And the upside could be substantial as such behavior could shake up potentially unhealthy democratic scleroses that build up around well-entrenched interests. Without the distinctiveness of the Court, it would be harder for the Court to offer such positive benefits to the political system (Page 2007).

Understanding the Court and Political Science

Many political scientists share the conventional wisdom that justices simply pursue policy goals on the bench. This is not always viewed as a good thing. As mentioned in chapter 5, Chief Justice Roberts recently equated policy-motivated judges with a "political science" perspective and then praised the contemporary Court (and Chief Justice Rehnquist in particular) for utilizing "a more legal perspective and less of a policy perspective" (Liptak 2009).

Political scientists do not need to be so equated with the attitudinal model. While we recognize that policy preferences matter, we also have demonstrated that there is much more to judicial behavior than narrow pursuit of policy preferences. Justices act in an environment shaped by constraints. Some constraints, such as the law, are not binding. But they are influential and often separate justices from their co-ideologues in the elected branches. Other constraints, like the strategic influence of Congress and the president or the direct and signaling influence of the solicitor general, push justices in different directions as well. A complete understanding of the Court and its role in the U.S. political system recognizes these and other ways in which the Court is not simply a powerful little legislature composed of politicians who are pursuing at any cost their policy preferences. Instead, the Court is an institution controlled by nine individuals who recognize both the opportunities and limits associated with their position.

Appendix

STATISTICAL DETAILS

THROUGHOUT THE BOOK, we estimate models to test whether the tendency of justices to support outcomes consistent with their policy preferences is constrained by either legal doctrines or a combination of doctrines and the legislative and executive branches. Here we describe the latent variable specification employed to test whether non-ideological factors affect justice behavior. Generalizing the model to include multiple non-ideological factors is straightforward. Let $i = 1, \ldots , N$ index individuals and $v = 1, \ldots , V$ index votes. The utility of actor i of voting for the conservative alternative is

$$u_i(\lambda_t^C) = -(\theta_{it} - \lambda_v^C)^2 + \delta_i \hat{D}_v^C + \eta_{iv}^C$$

where λ_v^C is the spatial location of the conservative alternative, θ_{it} is the ideal point of the actor at the time of proposal t, $\hat{D}_v^C$ is the non-policy value of voting for the conservative alternative, δ_i is the weight placed by i on non-policy values, and η_{iv}^C is a random shock. The utility of voting for the liberal alternative with spatial location of λ_v^L is analogous.

Let $\tilde{y}_{itv}^*$ be the utility difference between the conservative and liberal alternatives. It is

$$
\begin{aligned}
y_{itv}^* &= -(\theta_{it} - \lambda_v^C)^2 + \delta_i \hat{D}_v^C + \eta_{iv}^C + (\theta_{it} - \lambda_v^L)^2 + \delta_i \hat{D}_v^L + \eta_{iv}^L \\
&= 2\theta_{it}(\lambda_v^C - \lambda_v^L) + \lambda_v^{L2} - \lambda_v^{C2} + \delta_i(\hat{D}_v^C - \hat{D}_v^L) + \eta_{iv}^C - \eta_{iv}^L \\
&= (\lambda_v^C - \lambda_v^L)(2\theta_{it} - (\lambda_v^L + \lambda_v^C)) + \delta_i(\hat{D}_v^C - \hat{D}_v^L) + \eta_{iv}^C - \eta_{iv}^L.
\end{aligned}
$$

Let $\kappa_v = \frac{\lambda_v^L + \lambda_v^C}{2}$ be the vote cutpoint, $\alpha_v = 2(\lambda_v^C - \lambda_v^L)$ be the vote "discrimination parameter,"[1] $D_v = (\hat{D}_v^C - \hat{D}_v^L)$ be an observed non-ideological deference variable, and $\varepsilon_{iv} = \eta_{iv}^C - \eta_{iv}^L$ be a N(0, 1) random variable; then

$$y_{itv}^* = \alpha_v(\theta_{it} - \kappa_v) + \delta_i D_v + \varepsilon_{iv}. \tag{A.1}$$

Observed votes (as opposed to unobserved latent values above) are denoted by y_{itv}. To address rotational identification (e.g., liberals can have high values or low values), conservative votes are coded as $y_{itv} = 1$. The location and scale of ideal points are identified by assuming they have mean 0 and variance 1; this is equivalent to fixing two individuals at arbitrary points (see, e.g., Bafumi et al. 2005).

The estimation process uses a Gibbs sampler algorithm. This algorithm allows us to draw samples from the posterior distribution of the parameters (Gelman et al. 1995, 326; see also Johnson and Albert 1999, 194–97). After a "burn in" period, the following iterative procedure will produce random samples from the underlying posterior distribution.

1. Equation A.1 implies that y_{itv}^* (where i indicates individual, t indicates term, and v indicates vote) will be distributed according to one of the two truncated distributions (see, e.g., Jackman 2000, 387):

$$y_{itv}^* \mid y_{itv} = 1 \sim N(\alpha_v(\theta_{it} - \kappa_v) + \delta_i D_v, 1) I(y_{itv}^* > 0)$$
$$y_{itv}^* \mid y_{itv} = 0 \sim N(\alpha_v(\theta_{it} - \kappa_v) + \delta_i D_v, 1) I(y_{itv}^* \leq 0)$$

where I is an indicator function that serves to truncate distributions above or below zero.

2. Generate individual-specific preference parameters on an individual-by-individual basis. Let $\theta_{it} = T_{it}' \rho_i$ and substitute the equation for the time-path of policy preferences into Equation A.1. This yields

$$y_{itv}^* + \alpha_v \kappa_v = \sum_{p=0}^{3} \alpha_v \rho_{pi} T_{it}^p + \sum_{m=1}^{M} \delta_{im} D_{mv} + \varepsilon_{itv}$$
$$= X_i' \gamma_i + \varepsilon_{itv}$$

where X_i is a $V_i \times M$ matrix of covariates for individual i (based on M non-policy variables) and V_i is the number of observations for individual i. The first column of X_i is a column of α_v for the votes for individual i. The second column of X_i is α_v multiplied by the time variable for individual i for each vote and so on for the third through fifth columns. The last three columns of X are the deference variables for each of the votes for individual i. For chapters 4 and 5 these are deference to precedent, Congress, and strict interpretation of the free speech clause. For chapter 6 these are precedent and separation of powers. For chapter 7 these are the three solicitor general variables used to test the signaling model articulated in the chapter. This is only relevant for justices as the δ parameters for non-justices are constrained to zero.

The distribution of γ is therefore

$$\gamma_i \sim N((X_i'X_i)^{-1} X_i' \tilde{y}, (X_i'X_i)^{-1})$$

where $\tilde{y} = y_{itv}^* + \alpha_v \kappa_v$. A $N(0, \Omega)$ prior on γ identifies the preferences of individuals who vote conservatively or liberally all the time. Without this prior, their estimated ideal points could become unbounded. The implementation of the prior follows Gelman et al. (1995, 260). The coefficients on the higher order elements of time (e.g., the coefficient on T^3) are restricted to 0 for individuals who served relatively short periods of time. Specifically, $\rho_3 = \rho_4 = 0$ for all individuals who served 24 or fewer years, $\rho_2 = 0$ for all individuals who served 16 or fewer years, and $\rho_1 = 0$ for all individuals who served 8 or fewer years.

3. Generate α, $\alpha\kappa$ on a vote-by-vote basis. If we let $\beta_v = [\alpha_v, \alpha_v\kappa_v]'$ and $\theta_{it} = [\theta_{it}, -1]$ (indicating the preference parameter of individual i for vote v, which occurred during term t), we can rewrite Equation A.1 as

$$y^*_{itv} - \delta_i D_v = \Theta_v \beta_v + \varepsilon_{iv}.$$

By standard GLS results,

$$\beta_v \sim N((\Theta'_{it}\Theta_v)^{-1} \Theta'_v \, y^{**}_v, (\Theta'_v\Theta_v)^{-1})$$

where $y^{**}_v = y^*_{itv} - \delta_i D_v$ for all individuals who voted on vote v, Θ_v is a $N_v \times 2$ matrix of Θ_{it}, and N_v is the number of votes cast on vote v.

The discrimination parameter is, in part, a measure of vote-specific variance and as a variance parameter is subject to becoming unbounded as discussed above (see also Baker 1992, 97–98; Mislevy and Bock 1990, 8). Therefore there are normal priors and maximum values for α and κ (the priors follow Gelman et al. 1995, 254, 260; see also Johnson and Albert 1999, 192).

A model is unidentified "if the same likelihood function is obtained for more than one choice of the model parameters" (Gelman et al. 1995, 422). For fixed preference one-dimensional models, identification can be achieved by fixing the polarity (meaning, for example, conservative preferences are high values and liberal preferences are low values) and two observations (which is equivalent to setting the mean $\theta = 0$ and variance of $\theta = 1$) (see discussions in Clinton, Jackman, and Rivers 2004, 356 and Bafumi et al. 2005).

DATA

Central to our analysis are both position-taking and case-differentiation variables. Bridge observations enable us to ascertain the positions embraced by individuals who are not on the bench but who take positions on Supreme Court cases. Case-differentiation variables enable us to distinguish those cases where doctrines of stare decisis, judicial restraint, and a strict reading of the First Amendment are most likely to shape the decisions justices make.

Bridge Observations

Bailey (2007) provides us with bridge observations for 1950 through 2002. We have updated the data through 2008 following the same strategies.

1. Amicus briefs. Filings by the solicitor general are from Gibson 1997 for the period 1953–87 and from Lexis-Nexis Academic Universe and the solicitor general's website thereafter. Amicus filings for members of Congress are identified in Epstein, Segal, Spaeth, and Walker 2007 and from Lexis-Nexis Academic Universe. Only amicus filings on merit are included.

2. Comments by members of Congress. These were primarily taken from the *Congressional Record*. For 1989 to the present, the Thomas.gov database was searched for entries with "Supreme Court." For years before that every entry under "Supreme Court" in the annual indices was researched. Some observations were found in other sources such as Eskridge 1991 and the *Congressional Almanac*.

3. Roll-call votes. One must be careful when using roll-call votes to ascertain the positions of members of Congress on Supreme Court cases. First, provisions that address Court cases are often embedded in broader legislation. This makes it impossible to know if the vote indicates an opinion on the Court case or some other matter. An example is *Denver Area Educational Telecommunications Consortium v. Federal Communications Commission* (1996), which struck some elements and upheld other elements of the Cable Television Consumer Protection and Competition Act of 1992. This act was passed over the veto of President Bush with nearly universal support of Democrats and substantial support of Republicans (although 85 of the 114 votes against it in the House on October 5, 1992, came from Republicans). The Court ruled only on one small part of the bill, a part that put various restraints on cable operators in the interest of controlling "indecent" programming. Using a vote on the overall bill as an indicator of congressional positions on the issue addressed by the Supreme Court would not be reasonable. However, it turns out that the Court explicitly addressed Sections 10(a) and (b) of the law (upholding the first and striking the second) and that these were added in an amendment by Senator Helms (R, North Carolina) that passed 95–0. We use the vote on the amendment but not

a vote on passage. Section 10(c) of the law was also explicitly addressed by the Court. There was no roll-call vote on this, but the legislative history reveals that Senator Wyche Fowler (D, Georgia) and Senator Tim Wirth (D, Colorado) sponsored this language, meaning that the position of these two on this section is clear.

4. Co-sponsorship. We used Thomas.gov to search for bills that had "Supreme Court" in their text and assessed whether these bills directly related to a Supreme Court case. Data are less comprehensive for periods predating Thomas.gov coverage.

We exclude repeat bridge observations (e.g., a senator taking the same position on the same case) that are within five years of an observation already in the data set. We provide additional examples of all categories of bridge observations in Tables A.1–A.4.

As described in chapter 2, we also used information on the relative position of case cutpoints to help identify preference differences across chambers and over time. As discussed in that chapter, much of our relative cutpoint information was related to abortion, the death penalty, and civil rights legislation. In Table A.5 we provide additional examples of relative cutpoint information.

Selection of Supreme Court Cases

We use the Spaeth (2009) database and limit cases to those VALUE < 6 (criminal procedure, civil rights, the First Amendment, due process, and privacy). Citations are the unit of analysis (ANALU = 0 in Spaeth's data set) and add split-vote decisions (ANALU = 4) when there are bridging observations. *Bakke* is a prominent example of a case with a split vote and many members of Congress taking positions on one or the other (or both) of the main holdings. We do not include memorandum cases and decrees (DEC TYPE = 3 or 4).

Selected cases are those for which at least one of the following is true: discussed directly in the *Harvard Law Review*'s annual Supreme Court review, included as a landmark case in the Legal Information Institute's database of cases (see supct.law.cornell.edu/supct/cases/name.htm), coded as a salient case in Epstein and Segal 2000, included in the Congressional Quarterly's key cases list, a president or member of Congress or non-contemporaneous justice took a position on the case, the case has clear cutpoint relation to another case, the case implicates precedent, deference, or speech as coded.

There are a few instances where we do not use Spaeth's coding of the liberal/conservative directionality of a decision because it does not comport with the underlying politics of the case. This occurs in ten campaign

TABLE A.1
Selected Presidential Comments on Supreme Court Cases

President	Case	Date of comment	Comment	Source
Kennedy	*Baker v. Carr*	3/29/1962	Q: Would you comment on Supreme Court reapportionment decision? A: The administration made clear its endorsement of the principles implicit in the Court decision.	*Public Papers*, 1962, 274
Nixon	*Brown v. Board of Education*	3/24/1970	To reaffirm my personal belief that the 1954 decision of the Supreme Court in *Brown v. Board of Education* was right in both constitutional and human terms.	*Public Papers*, 1970, 304
Nixon	*Swann v. Charlotte-Mecklenburg County Board of Education*	4/29/1971	Q: Ten days ago the Supreme Court approved the mandatory use of busing to overcome racial segregation. Do you endorse that decision? A: I expressed views with regard to my opposition to busing for the purpose of achieving racial balance and in support of the neighborhood school . . . last year.	*Public Papers*, 1971, 596
Carter	*Fullilove v. Klutznick*	7/2/1980	The President strongly applauds the Supreme Court's decisions upholding the constitutionality of the minority business set-aside provision . . .	*Public Papers*, 1980, 1280
Reagan	*Lynch v. Donnelly*	10/13/1983	We believe that the city of Pawtucket . . . has the right to include the Nativity scene as part of its annual Christmas performance.	*Public Papers*, 1983, 1451
Reagan	*Roe v. Wade*	1/22/1987	Together we can overturn *Roe v. Wade* and end this national tragedy.	*Public Papers*, 1987, 43

(*Continued*)

TABLE A.1
(Continued)

President	Case	Date of comment	Comment	Source
Bush, George H. W.	*Skinner v. Railway Labor Exec. Assoc.*	3/22/1989	I am very pleased that yesterday the Supreme Court validated drug testing.	Remarks to Law Enforcement, Wilmington, DE
Clinton	*U.S. v. Lopez*	4/29/1995	I was terribly disappointed that . . . the Supreme Court struck down a law . . . to keep guns away from schools.	*Public Papers*, 1995, 610
Clinton	*Shaw v. Hunt*	6/29/1995	I am disappointed by the Supreme Court decision in the Georgia congressional redistricting case.	*Public Papers*, 1995, 977
Bush, George W.	*Stone v. Graham*	1/16/2000	Districts ought to be allowed to post the Ten Commandments, no matter what a person's religion is.	GOP debate in Johnston, IA
Bush, George W.	*Zelman v. Simmons-Harris*	7/1/2002	The Supreme Court . . . gave a great victory to parents and students throughout the nation by upholding the decisions made by local folks here in . . . Cleveland.	*New York Times*, July 2, 2002

finance cases. For example, Spaeth codes the *Buckley v. Valeo* (1976) decision to strike a limit on campaign expenditures as a conservative decision, when it is clear by the coalition on the Court and in Congress that expenditure limits were a liberal reform targeting wealthy contributors. This also occurs in four agricultural advertising cases and eight other cases. For example, in *Hurley v. Irish American Gay, Lesbian and Bisexual Group of Boston* (1995) Spaeth coded as liberal the Court's decision to side with conservatives who argued that parade organizers did not have to allow a gay group in a St. Patrick's Day parade.

Coding of Precedent

To identify the cases where respect for a stare decisis doctrine was particularly likely to shape outcomes, we relied upon Segal and Howard's

TABLE A.2
Selected Senate Comments on Supreme Court Cases

Senator	State	Case	Date of comment	Comment	Source
Eastland	MS	*Brown v. Board of Education*	5/31/55	To resist them is our only answer. We must resist them in the courts, in our legislative halls, and by the ballots . . . Southern people will not be violating the Constitution or the law when they defy this monstrous proposition.	*Congressional Record, 7285*
McCarthy	WI	*Slochower v. Board of Education*	4/11/56	The Supreme Court has handed down another case that flagrantly violates States rights.... And it has handed another solid victory to the Communist Party.	*Congressional Record, 6063*
Kefauver	TN	*Cole v. Young*	7/3/56	Personally I happen to think that the Court was right in its security decision which was the occasion for most of the recent attacks.	*Congressional Record, 11686*
Javits	NY	*Mallory v. U.S.*	8/19/58	An intelligent rule. A forward looking rule. A modern rule.	*Congressional Record, 18490*
McGovern	SD	*Baker v. Carr*	9/16/64	Yet another proof that democracy acts to correct its own evils.	*Congressional Record, 22237*
Kennedy	MA	*Furman v. Georgia*	6/29/72	Today's decision by the Supreme Court—declaring that capital punishment is unconstitutional . . . will rank as one of the great judicial milestones in American history.	*Congressional Record, 23169*
Percy	IL	*Roe v. Wade*	4/10/74	I believe that the Supreme Court ruling on abortion is correct and proper.	*Congressional Record, 10471*

(Continued)

Table A.2
(Continued)

Senator	State	Case	Date of comment	Comment	Source
Laxalt	NV	*Engel v. Vitale*	3/20/84	Contrary to the Supreme Court's interpretation, the First Amendment establishment clause was never intended to render our public institutions hostile toward religion.	*Congressional Record*, 5910
Simpson	WY	*Griswold v. Connecticut*	9/15/87	I think it was nutty, too.	*Bork Hearings I*, 48
Lieberman	CT	*Lee v. Weisman*	1/24/92	I am surprised and disappointed by the Supreme Court's decision.	*Congressional Record*, S8771
Moseley-Braun	IL	*Adarand v. Pena*	6/14/95	The *Adarand* decision was bad law.	*Congressional Record*, S8376
Thurmond	SC	*Texas v. Johnson*	10/14/98	I have fought to achieve Constitutional protection for the flag ever since the Supreme Court first legitimized flag burning. . . . Have we focused so much on the rights of the individual that we have forgotten the rights of the people?	*Congressional Record*, S12574

(2005) identification of these cases for the 1984–95 period. For the other time periods, we relied upon a three-stage process. First, we identified phrases or words associated with overturning precedent based on reading the cases identified in Segal and Howard 2005. Second, we searched for all such phrases in petitioner and respondent briefs in the appropriate times. Third, we read and manually coded each identified case.

Deference to Congress

To identify the cases where a doctrine of deference to Congress is particularly applicable, we relied upon Spaeth's (2009) *authdec* variable. We also read each case identified in this manner to ensure that they involved the

TABLE A.3
Selected House Comments on Supreme Court Cases

Member of Congress	State	Case	Date of comment	Comment	Source
Ashbrook	OH	*Abington v. Schempp*	10/2/64	. . . the unfortunate Supreme Court decision which has had the effect of forcing our public schools to become materialistic and has reversed the historical religious tradition of our society.	*Congressional Record*, 572
Quillen	TN	*U.S. v. Robel*	12/13/67	I am outraged by the decision . . . which struck down the section of Federal law banning Communists and members of Communist-action groups from working in defense plants.	*Congressional Record*, 1400
Riegle	MI	*Alexander v. Holmes County*	10/30/69	I rise today to congratulate the Supreme Court.	*Congressional Record*, 32422
Rangel	NY	*Roe v. Wade*	1/22/74	[*Roe*] furthered the cause of freedom and dignity for American women.	*Congressional Record*, 1616
Mazzoli	KY	*Akron v. Akron Center for Reproductive Health*	6/21/83	I join all of those who support full protections for the unborn in expressing my disappointment over the Supreme Court's June 15 abortion ruling.	*Congressional Record*, 16684
Mikulski	MD	*Grove City College v. Bell*	2/29/84	I rise today in outrage about yesterday's decision by the Supreme Court in the *Grove City College* case.	*Congressional Record*, 3973
Coburn	OK	*Roe v. Wade*	8/6/97	What the Supreme Court has said is wrong. It is wrong morally, it will always be held wrong morally.	*Congressional Record*, 9048

(Continued)

TABLE A.3
(Continued)

Member of Congress	State	Case	Date of comment	Comment	Source
Ramstad	MN	*Phillips v. Washington Legal Foundation*	8/3/98	On top of this, a recent Supreme Court decision is further threatening re-sources for legal aid to the poor.	*Congressional Record*, 6982
Stearns	FL	*Kelo v. New London*	11/3/05	This ruling embodies ev-erything for which our Founding Fathers did not want this country to stand.	*Congressional Record*, E2253

constitutionality of a law enacted by Congress and the president. We use these cases as a vehicle for identifying differences in the behavior of Su-preme Court justices relative to that of members of Congress. Of course, it is possible that members of Congress may also share the concept of legislative deference; that is, it is possible that members who vote against a law would want the Supreme Court to uphold the law (despite their personal opposition to it) on the grounds that the issue is one for Con-gress, not the Court, to decide. As discussed in chapter 3, our approach is estimating any additional influence the logic of judicial restraint may have on justices. We suspect this issue may not arise very often. Indeed, members of Congress do not normally switch their views simply because of legal action. Senator Mitch McConnell (R, Kentucky) is a case in point. One could imagine that he would fight for the Court to uphold the McCain-Feingold campaign finance bill that he vigorously opposed in the Senate on the grounds that the Court should defer to Congress. In fact, however, he argued for the same substantive outcome before the Court as he did in the Senate, opposing the legislation in both venues.

Additional Data Description

Case and Roll-Call Data

Figure A.1 displays information about the number and type of congres-sional roll calls and Supreme Court cases in the database. There are 1,536 roll calls in the House and Senate and 3,239 cases in the Supreme Court.

TABLE A.4

Selected Justice Comments on Previous Supreme Court Cases

Justice	Case	Year of comment	Comment	Source
Brennan	*Lee v. U.S.* (1952)	1963	I believe that that decision was error, in reason and authority, at the time it was decided.	*Lopez v. U.S.* (1962)
Goldberg	*Kent v. Dulles* (1958)	1965	I would rule here, as this Court did in *Kent v. Dulles*, that passport restrictions may be imposed only when Congress makes provision therefor in explicit terms.	*Zemel v. Rusk* (1965)
Black	*Schwartz v. Texas* (1952)	1968	I thought the holding in *Schwartz* was correct then and still think so.	*Lee v. Florida* (1968)
Powell	*Kirkpatrick v. Preisler* (1969)	1973	Had I been a member of the Court when *Kirkpatrick* . . . [was] decided, I would not have thought that the Constitution . . . could be read to require a rule of mathematical exactitude in legislative reapportionment.	*White v. Weiser* (1973)
Blackmun	*Brown v. United States* (1959)	1975	I was not on the Court when *Brown* and *Harris* were decided. Had I been, I would have joined the Court in *Brown* and the dissenters in *Harris*.	*U.S. v. Wilson* (1975)
Marshall	*Food Employees v. Logan Valley Plaza* (1968)	1976	The *Logan Valley* decision should not be overruled, since it was reconcilable with the *Lloyd Corp.* case, and since its First Amendment principles were sound.	*Hudgens v. NLRB* (1976)
Stevens	*Baker v. Carr* (1962)	1983	Otherwise, the promise of *Baker v. Carr* . . .—that judicially manageable standards can assure [full] and effective participation by all citizens— may never be fulfilled.	*Karcher v. Daggett* (1983)
Kennedy	*Lynch v. Donnelly* (1984)	1989	I accept and indeed approve both the holding and the reasoning of Chief Justice Burger's opinion in *Lynch*.	*Allegheny v. ACLU* (1989)

(*Continued*)

TABLE A.4
(Continued)

Justice	Case	Year of comment	Comment	Source
Rehnquist	*Roe v. Wade* (1973)	1992	We believe that *Roe* was wrongly decided, and that it can and should be overruled.	*Planned Parenthood v. Casey* (1992)
Thomas	*Buckley v. Valeo* (1976)	2001	I continue to believe that *Buckley v. Valeo* should be overruled.	*FEC v. Colorado Republican Fed. Campaign Comm.* (2001)
Rehnquist	*Stanford v. Kentucky* (1989)	2002	*Stanford*'s reasoning makes perfectly good sense, and the Court offers no basis to question it.	*Atkins v. Virginia* (2002)
Scalia	*Austin v. Michigan Chamber of Commerce* (1990)	2007	*Austin* was a significant departure from ancient First Amendment principles. In my view, it was wrongly decided.	*FEC v. Wisconsin Right to Life* (2007)

Key to the method is use of actors not subject to the legal principle in question to pin down the policy cutpoints of Supreme Court cases. We have 1,039 Supreme Court cases with such observations; 908 of them have direct positions taken by members of Congress or presidents and 288 of them have positions taken by non-contemporaneous justices (there are some cases with both).

There are 399 cases in which precedent was non-zero for at least some observations; 227 had conservative codes and 193 had liberal outcomes.[2] There are 232 cases in which deference to Congress was coded as implying either a conservative (193 times) or liberal (39 times) vote on the Court. There are 509 cases in which deference to speech was coded as implying either a conservative (26 times) or a liberal (483 times) vote on the Court.

While the precedent cases are divided reasonably equally across cases that support liberal and conservative outcomes, the deference to Congress cases tend to disproportionately imply conservative outcomes and the speech cases tend to imply liberal outcomes. We do not believe these

TABLE A.5
Selected Cutpoint Linkages

Subject	Lower bound	Upper bound	Explanation
Minnesota v. Olson (495 U.S. 91)	Minnesota v. Carter (525 U.S. 83)	—	Olson was about privacy for an overnight guest; Carter about privacy for an afternoon guest. If liberal on afternoon guest (who is much less part of a home), then liberal on privacy for overnight guest.
Milliken v. Bradley (418 U.S. 717)	—	Swann v. Charlotte-Mecklenburg (402 U.S. 1)	In Swann, Court held that "it may be necessary for a district court to require busing in the achievement of racial balance among schools afflicted by de jure segregation" (Ducat, 2004, 1142). Liberals in Milliken wanted to extend to de facto segregation. If liberal on Milliken, liberal on Swann.
Drug testing for all federal employees (105th House #1063)	National Treasury Employees v. Von Raab (489 U.S. 656)	—	Von Raab about drug testing U.S. Customs employees; House vote was for all federal employees. If believe all federal employees should be subject to drug testing, then believe U.S. Customs employees should be subject to such testing.
Lee v. Weisman (505 U.S. 577)	—	Religious freedom amendment (105th House #829)	Amendment would give people right to pray and recognize religion on public property including schools; if conservative on this, then conservative on Lee v. Weisman.
African American contractors (101st House #170)	—	Civil Rights Act (88th Senate #409)	Left of Civil Rights Act—someone who favors affirmative action would be liberal on Civil Rights Act.
Women in military (105th Senate #478)	—	Women in military (94th House #167)	House bill banned women from the academies. Senate bill required separate platoons/housing for women. If liberal on Senate bill (meaning one favored shared housing), then liberal on House bill (meaning one opposes banning women from academies).

(Continued)

TABLE A.5
(Continued)

Subject	Lower bound	Upper bound	Explanation
Temporary assistance for needy families (108th House #29)	TANF (104th Senate #613)	—	Welfare legislation in 108th House pushed policy to the right—see 2008 *Congressional Quarterly Almanac*.
Civil Rights Act of 1960 (86th House #100)	Voting Rights Act (89th Senate #178)	—	Civil Rights Act of 1960 was less ambitious than 1965 Voting Rights Act. Liberal on 1965 Voting Rights Act would be liberal on less ambitious 1960 Civil Rights Act.
Voting Rights Act (91st Senate #342)	—	Voting Rights Act (89th Senate #178)	1970 Voting Rights Act expanded 1965 Voting Rights Act (see 1970 *Congressional Quarterly Almanac*). If favor 1970 version, implicitly favor 1965 version as well.

distributions exert undue influence on our results. First, note we are not simply looking for justices to be more or less liberal on these cases but to be more or less liberal in the direction predicted by the coding of the law variable conditional on what co-policy ideologues in Congress want. Second, our results work across three types of legal variables in a manner that defies simple categorization in terms of the model coding of the legal variable: some (but clearly not all) conservative justices are estimated to have low regard for precedent and deference even as the precedent cases tend to be liberal and deference cases tend to be conservative.

Bridging Observations

There are 17,882 bridge observations on Supreme Court cases; 16,669 of these are by members of Congress and presidents and 1,213 are by justices. These are non-voting observations of individuals taking positions on Supreme Court cases as described in the text and above.

Figure A.2 summarizes these data with respect to their support for the majority opinion on the Court case and characteristics of the commenter and case. The top bar shows that the positions are reasonably evenly distributed across comments that support the Court's majority opinion and those that oppose it. Figure A.3 summarizes these data with respect to whether the comment supported the liberal or conservative side. Again, we have a reasonably even distribution of comments on both sides.

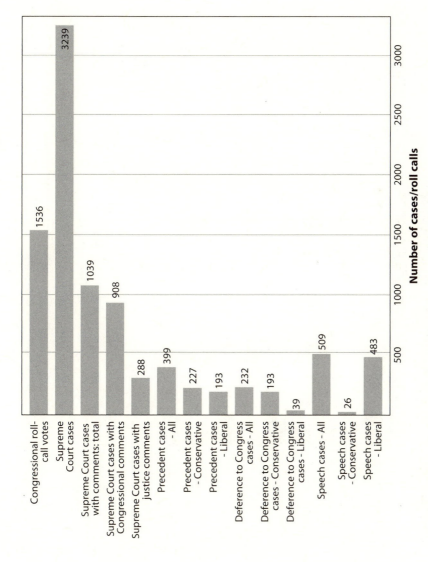

Figure A.1. Supreme Court cases and congressional roll calls by type

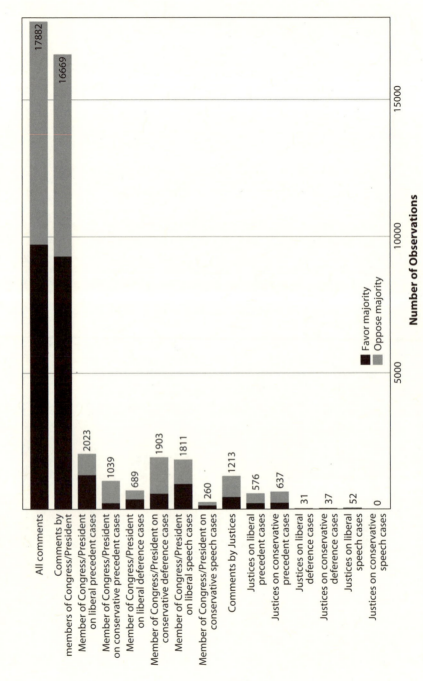

Figure A.2. Bridge observations on Supreme Court cases by support for Court majority

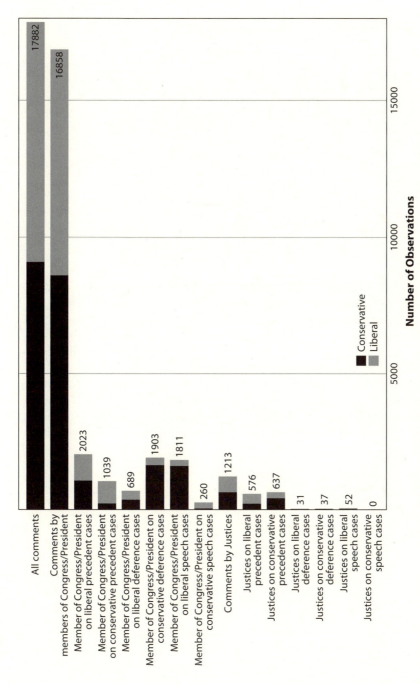

Figure A.3. Bridge observations on Supreme Court cases by support for liberal/conservative outcomes

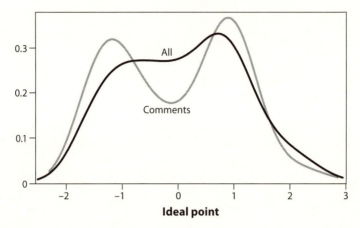

Figure A.4. Distributions of ideal points

Distributions of Ideal Points

Figure A.4 plots the distribution of ideal points for all members of Congress and those who provided either direct or implicit comments. The direct comment data have a skew toward the extremes as liberals and conservatives are more likely to provide direct comments. The implicit comment has a skew to the right, indicating that those providing comment data tended to be more conservative.

While skew one way or the other does not indicate bias, it does affect the efficiency of the estimation. In the limit, a distribution of all conservatives or all liberals would not allow us to make meaningful distinctions about locations of cutpoints, one of the central pieces of this research design.

NOTES

Chapter 1   Introduction

1. Note that some proponents of the attitudinal model believe solicitors general influence the Court, making the organization the only "non-attitudinal influence" on the Court (Segal and Spaeth 1993, 237–38).

2. See Lindquist and Cross 2009 for a discussion of the origins of judicial restraint and its opposite, judicial activism.

3. Baum (1997, 59) notes that judicial restraint is not a legal doctrine per se but rather a doctrine about the appropriate role of the Court vis-à-vis the other branches of government.

4. Separation-of-powers models focus on the influence of the other branches of government. There are other possible external influences on justices. Maltzman, Spriggs, and Wahlbeck (2000) and Epstein and Knight (1998) demonstrate that justices take positions that reflect their understanding of the need to build a majority coalition. Numerous scholars (e.g., Caldeira and Wright [1988] and Kearney and Merrill [2000]) argue that interest groups influence the justices. Claims about interest group influence are explicitly rejected by Segal and Spaeth (1993, 241). There is also a large literature on the influence of public opinion on the Court (e.g., Mishler and Sheehan 1993). For a critical critique of the claim that justices take into account the preferences of those who are not on the bench, see Brenner and Whitmeyer 2009.

Chapter 2   The Measure of Law: Estimating Preferences across Institutions and Time

1. The approach for measuring ideological preferences across institutions was originally detailed in Bailey 2007. The models presented throughout this book employ a similar approach for measuring ideology. They also employ a data set that is expanded beyond Bailey 2007 to include the Court appointments of John Roberts and Samuel Alito. Preference estimates and a methodological appendix are available at http://press.princeton.edu/titles/9598.html.

2. An exception is Epstein, Martin, Segal, and Westerland 2007, which re-scales Poole-Rosenthal Common Space scores and Martin and Quinn (2002) scores. Because their approach uses both Poole-Rosenthal and Martin-Quinn scores, it inherits the concerns we discuss below about both methods.

3. Segal's use of the approach is understandable given the fact his work appeared prior to more recent breakthroughs in ideal point estimation.

4. This approach to inter-institutional preference measurement is *not* endorsed by Poole, Rosenthal, Martin, or Quinn; we present it simply as an example of assuming direct comparability across institutions.

5. The ADA and percent-liberal measures have been subtracted from 1 in order to give them the same ideological polarity as the Poole-Rosenthal and Martin-Quinn measures.

6. It is also interesting to note that Hollings's views changed over time. Hollings portrayed *Brown v. Board of Education* (1954) as "the most significant judicial decision of that century." And he elaborated that "there is no question in my mind that it was for the good. I had my doubts at that particular time. . . . [The plaintiffs] understood the Constitution in America better than this particular Senator" (*Congressional Record*, 108th Cong., May 13, 2004, p. S5457).

7. Although Martin and Quinn allow individual judicial preferences to vary from term to term, they constrain preferences from moving too much from one term to the next by constraining justices' ideal points not to move too much from one term to the next.

8. Poole and Rosenthal conceive of their NOMINATE scores as reflecting underlying latent preference dimensions that typically do not change. The mapping of policies onto these dimensions does change, however, and the important changes that have occurred in the mapping of policy to the one- (and sometimes two-) dimensional policy space in the postwar era (Poole and Rosenthal 1997, 6; chapter 5) makes interpretation quite complex.

9. *Stanford* was overturned by *Roper v. Simmons* (2005), providing additional information for cross-temporal preference comparisons.

10. This parameter is standard in ideal point estimation theory and its precursor, item response theory (Baker 1992). Votes for which the alternatives are relatively close (meaning $(\lambda_v^C - \lambda_v^L)$ is relatively small) will have a low discrimination parameter as the non-spatial error term will be more likely to induce actors with preferences higher than the cutpoint to vote liberally and vice versa.

11. The years of service data are expressed in terms of deviations from mean years of service for computational convenience.

12. While Bailey and Chang (2001) used an EM algorithm, the sampling Bayes approach is more flexible and readily estimates standard errors (Clinton, Jackman, and Rivers 2004).

13. We do not use solicitor general positions on cases where the United States is a party. When the United States is a party to a case, precedent, the stakes of winning, the sometimes non-voluntary participation, or other non-ideological actors may be behind the position taken by the solicitor general.

14. The amicus filings were identified either in the *Supreme Court Compendium* or with Lexis-Nexus searches we performed. The statements are primarily from an extensive search of the *Congressional Record*.

15. A case was deemed "important" if it received news coverage in the *New York Times* or *Congressional Quarterly Almanac*. There was a twofold reason for limiting the cases in this manner. The effects we are interested in only truly matter if they affect important cases, broadly defined. In addition, limiting cases reduces the substantial MCMC estimation time. In order to ensure an adequate number of observations for every year, we include randomly selected cases that are not important for years that would otherwise have a small number of cases. We also do not use cases that cannot be coded on a liberal and conservative scale (Harvey and Woodruff 2011).

16. In the process of making clear his opposition to the decision, Senator Santorum stated, "Every society in the history of man has upheld the institution of marriage as a bond between a man and a woman. Why? Because society is based on one thing: that society is based on the future of the society. And that's what? Children. Monogamous relationships. In every society, the definition of marriage has not ever to my knowledge included homosexuality. That's not to pick on homosexuality. It's not, you know, man on child, man on dog, or whatever the case may be."

17. Of course, justices and members of Congress are not forced to vote, but it appears that abstention is costly. A justice who fails to vote without a good reason will probably lose the respect of his or her peers. A member of Congress who abstains may lose the respect of other members and may suffer campaign attacks based on low-voting rates.

18. Note that selection bias can occur even if there were no difference in preference distributions between commentators and all members of Congress. That is, a perfectly representative sample of legislators who made comments only when they were on the conservative side of cases would produce biased estimates.

19. Preference estimates and a methodological appendix are available at http://press.princeton.edu/titles/9598.html.

20. These scores were estimated with W-Nominate from Poole's Voteview website and using only congressional and presidential data. We fixed Senator Edward Kennedy (D, Massachusetts) as the "left" anchor and Representative Charles Stenholm (D, Texas) as the "up" anchor. Results differed with different dimensionality or anchoring assumptions, but the general pattern discussed here was stable.

21. One needs to be careful in ascribing a single median to the Court in a year. In years with an appointment, the median may shift considerably. In later chapters in this book when we need Court medians for analytical purposes, we calculate them on a case-by-case basis depending on who was on the Court.

CHAPTER 3   DISENTANGLING LAW AND POLICY PREFERENCES

1. For tractability reasons, our statistical model treats this second dimension as a valence dimension on which justices have heterogeneous weights; see discussion below.

2. Assuming all justices weight both dimensions equally, the cut-line is found by locating the line that bisects and is perpendicular to the line connecting the two outcomes (the petitioner and respondent outcomes).

3. For simplicity, we assume the "discrimination parameter" from Equation 2.1 is 1; it is easy enough to relax this assumption. For tractability we also treat the legal dimension as a valence dimension. See appendix in Bailey and Maltzman 2008.

4. Recall that one identifies this cut-line by drawing a line connecting P2 and R2, finding the midpoint of that line, and then drawing a perpendicular line through that point. This line divides the space into points that are closer to P2 and points that are closer to R2.

5. For more discussion of the Segal and Spaeth approach, see Songer and Lindquist 1996 and Brenner and Stier 1996, as well as the response in Segal and Spaeth 1996.

Chapter 4   Law Matters

1. We should note that the absence from our empirical model of some of the other legal values that could influence decision-making is not particularly troubling with regard to our broader project of trying to assess whether legal factors matter. These unmeasured legal factors are, to use the statistical terminology, "omitted variables," and omitted variables cause bias only if two conditions are met: the variable affects the dependent variable and it is correlated with other included variables. If the excluded legal concepts do not actually affect voting on the Supreme Court, then excluding them causes no bias. If, on the other hand, the excluded legal variables do affect Supreme Court voting, then law matters, contradicting the attitudinal model. We would not come to an incorrect conclusion about the influence of law although we could possibly mislabel the components of legal influences on the Court.

2. This is a standard part of ideal point estimation and item response theory. The higher the discrimination parameter, the better the vote is at distinguishing between liberals and conservatives.

3. We limit Supreme Court cases to those that involved criminal procedure, civil rights, the First Amendment, due process, or privacy. These cases were isolated using Spaeth's broad issue categories (2009). In particular, the Spaeth value variable had to be less than six. The cases selected include high-profile social issues such as abortion rights, the death penalty, and affirmative action and lead us to focus on the most salient areas of the Supreme Court agenda. We limit congressional and presidential roll calls to those focused on similar issues. The House and Senate roll-call votes are taken from Poole and Rosenthal's Voteview website (http://voteview.com/ [accessed December 30, 2010]). Details are available in the appendix. We have also estimated models including federalism cases and find generally similar results.

4. To identify the effect of stare decisis, we also employ observations of Supreme Court justices taking positions on previously decided cases. These are comments by justices that express support of or opposition to a prior ruling of the Court. Typically they were made by a justice about cases that were decided before the justice served on the bench. For example, Justices Breyer and Ginsburg noted in *Lawrence* (2003) that they would have voted with the minority in *Bowers* (1986). Another example is Stevens's assertion "I would have joined Rehnquist's dissent in *Weber* [*United Steel Workers v. Weber* (1979)] had I not been disqualified" (2006a, 1565). Thus, we created a *Bowers* observation for Breyer and Ginsburg and a *Weber* observation for Stevens.

5. We relied upon Spaeth's (2009) *authdec* variable. We also read each case identified in this manner to ensure that they involved the constitutionality of a law enacted by Congress and the president.

6. Cases are coded as implicating First Amendment speech rights if the Spaeth *authdec* variable of either the constitutional codes or the Spaeth issue code is in the 400s, excluding the codes for religious freedom (codes 455–62).

7. In the Bayesian context, a variable is significantly greater than 0 at the 1 percent level if at least 99 percent of the values in the posterior samples were above 0.

8. These results differ from those that appeared in Bailey and Maltzman 2008. The differences stem from a considerable expansion of the time frame in this analysis, adjustments to the coding protocol (see chapter 2), and correction of a coding error; see http://press.princeton.edu/titles/9598.html.

9. We also estimated the model based on a data set that included federalism cases. The results are very similar.

10. The number for each justice and each legal concept is calculated via simulations based on parameter estimates in Table 4.1. For each simulation, we calculated the average difference in the probability of a conservative vote when the legal concept (e.g., precedent) implies a conservative and a liberal vote. For each concept, we conducted simulations based on cutpoint values of $\kappa = -0.5$, $\kappa = 0.0$, and $\kappa = 0.5$. For example, for Justice O'Connor the difference that occurs when $\kappa = 0$ for the stare decisis can be seen in Figure 4.1 by subtracting the simulated probability O'Connor votes conservative on a liberal precedent (0.45) from the simulated probability O'Connor votes conservative on a conservative precedent (0.85), a difference of 40 percentage points.

11. See also Gerwirtz and Golder 2005. They characterized Thomas, followed by Kennedy and Scalia, as the justices least likely to practice judicial restraint. They also characterized Breyer as the justice most likely to practice judicial restraint. This claim does not hold up in our analysis.

12. We do not include Roberts and Alito in this figure or the next one because we have very few observations on which deference or speech law was implicated (at least in the manner we code these variables); their results are available in Table 4.1.

CHAPTER 5   CAUSES AND CONSEQUENCES OF DIVERSE LEGAL VALUES

1. Others have argued that Frankfurter was selective in how he exercised restraint; see the discussion in Cross 1997, 276.

2. Indeed, publications after Holmes's death revealed that Holmes was quite dismissive of much of the liberal social legislation he had famously voted to uphold, including the work-week law at issue in *Lochner* (Posner 2008, 25).

3. There are not enough free speech cases for Alito and Roberts to estimate their speech parameters with any precision.

4. There is a bump in the liberal precedent median in the early 1990s after Thomas replaced Marshall on the Court. This moved the median from O'Connor to White. While the two were very close ideologically (yielding little change in the policy median of the court), O'Connor placed greater weight on precedent. Moving from her to White moved the median on the liberal legal precedent cases to

the left. When White left, the median moved back to O'Connor and the considerable gap between the median on non-precedent cases and precedent cases opened up again.

CHAPTER 6   SEPARATION OF POWERS AND THE STRATEGIC CONSTRAINT

1. For other examples of the Court conceding to political branches, see Eskridge 1991; Spiller and Gely 1992; Marks 1989; and Epstein and Knight 1998.

2. We are assuming the Senate and House medians and the president define the pareto set. One could alter the model by recognizing the pivotal role of the senators whose support is needed to invoke cloture. To simplify the presentation, we highlight the role of the median senator. Likewise, we place all three branches on a single dimension. This assumption, too, could be relaxed.

3. Although the Court may have been within the 2007 pareto set, the Court's conservative ruling was not within the 2009 political pareto set. President Obama signed the Lilly Ledbetter Fair Pay Act of 2009 into law on his ninth day in office. If the Court had been far-sighted, it could have written a narrowly tailored opinion in Ledbetter's favor that would have been enough to forestall the more general policy that eventually became law.

4. Biographical accounts document personal friendships between Justice Harlan Fiske Stone and President Herbert Hoover (Mason 1956), Justice Felix Frankfurter and President Franklin Roosevelt (Hirsch 1981), and Justice Abe Fortas and President Lyndon Johnson (B. Murphy 1988). Likewise, members of the legislative and judicial branches frequently have social interaction.

5. Identifying the Court median on a case-by-case basis also allows us to account for differences associated with who is on the bench. In some terms, the Court median varies significantly. For example, the Court median in 1967 changed significantly after Justice Marshall replaced Justice Clark. Measuring Court medians for each case allows us to include Marshall when he was on the bench, Clark when he was on the bench, and neither when neither justice participated.

6. For seven justices (Reed, Jackson, Vinson, Minton, Goldberg, Alito, and Roberts) we have twelve or fewer instances where the SOP variable is not zero. Not surprisingly, our estimates' SOP variable effect for these justices is imprecise (for similar issues, see Lindquist and Cross 2009, 45).

7. These are cases for which the Spaeth *authdec1* variable is 4 and *authdec2* is not 1 or 2.

8. We implement this by assuming that the ρ parameters are zero for non-justices. As in chapter 4 we use members of Congress and presidents to pin down the ideological cutpoints of cases (the κs), which allows us to statistically identify non-ideological factors such as separation-of-power constraint.

9. A probabilistic voting theory model of Supreme Court decision-making would predict that every justice could move in response to a separation-of-power constraint. In such a model, movement by any justice could shift the expected median (Bailey and Chang 2003). For example, a non-median justice shifting to the right would mean that the probability of a liberal vote on a given case would decrease, shifting the expected Court median to the right.

10. For a discussion of the distinction between politically and legally salient, see Maltzman, Spriggs, and Wahlbeck 2000.

11. These results are different than those we saw in Figure 6.4. This is an artifact of one of two factors. First, we are less likely to secure significance because there are fewer observations of "constraint." Second, the movement we saw in Figure 6.4 of Whittaker and Stewart after the Kennedy election was driven by their actions on non-salient cases.

CHAPTER 7   SIGNALS FROM THE EXECUTIVE

1. Justices are not beyond criticizing others. After House Majority Leader Tom Delay (R, Texas) strongly criticized Justice Kennedy's use of foreign law and the Internet, Kennedy made a video for a reunion of Rehnquist clerks in which he was sitting at his computer and said he was doing research and then said goodbye in several languages (Toobin 2007, 231). And some justices are more willing to speak their mind than others. Scalia once characterized an O'Connor opinion as "perverse" and "bizarre" and wrote that it "invited chaos"—and he agreed with her on the result (Toobin 2007, 114).

2. This chapter builds on BKM but also has substantial differences including use of non-Court actors to identify ideological cutpoints, analysis of individual justices' responses to the solicitor general, and inclusion of more years and data. Some of the independent control variables utilized by BKM cannot be incorporated into the analysis here.

3. One important difference between the data employed in this chapter and previous chapters is that the positions of the solicitors general are now on the right-hand side of the equation and hence no longer used as bridging observations for presidential positions. Another difference is that judicial comments about previous cases are not included because it is unreasonable to code solicitors general positions for cases that occurred during a different period of time and under different political circumstances.

4. We do not look at the positions of the solicitor general when the United States is a party to a case as there is much less discretion for the solicitor general in taking the case. Starr (2002, 44) reports that "As the Solicitor General, I was duty bound to defend the constitutionality of a law passed by Congress if reasonable arguments could be mounted on its behalf. Inside the Solicitor General's office, we labeled the operative standard the 'straight-face' test. If the lawyer could argue a legal position with a straight face, then as the government's lawyer in the Supreme Court you had a moral and legal duty to do your best to defend the government's legal position."

5. We assume the solicitor general represents the policy views of the president in amicus briefs and thus is given the same ideological score as the president. As discussed in chapter 2, the president nominates the solicitor general and can fire him at will. There is considerable evidence that solicitors general have similar preferences as the presidents who choose them and that if there are conflicts, the president's views prevail. Others in the literature make the same assumption (Segal 1989; Stimson, Mackuen, and Erikson 1995). This assumption is at its

weakest when a solicitor general appointed by the previous president is serving a new president. For example, Robert Bork, Ford's solicitor general, continued to argue cases in the early part of the Carter administration. We therefore exclude cases argued by "transitional" solicitors general. This is, by and large, a fairly innocuous assumption except in the case of Erwin Griswold. Griswold was appointed by President Johnson in 1967 and served until 1973, the last four years serving under Nixon. He was frequently liberal and it is not clear how responsive he was to Nixon. John Dean (2001, 16) reports the following conversation on whether or not to consult Griswold on Supreme Court appointments: " 'My God, we can't talk to Griswold about these things,' [Attorney General] Mitchell said, wincing with chagrin when I [Dean] asked. Then he explained, 'While Griswold's a good Republican, he doesn't understand, [does] not always appreciate Richard Nixon's politics.' " Salokar (1992, 41) indicates that Nixon forced out Griswold because he was too liberal.

6. The ideological distance is calculated to include the legal variables we control for in chapter 3. For example, on a case with speech implying a liberal outcome, Scalia's distance from President Bush's solicitors general is different than on a case where speech is not implicated. Of course, our ideological distance measure would be tainted if the preferences of the solicitor general were allowed to affect the ideology measure we employ for justices. For example, if justices defer to solicitors general then there is a danger that the ideology measures of justices reflect, in part, their deference to the executive branch. Therefore, we estimate preferences and the absolute distance between the solicitor general and the justices based on a model from which we exclude cases where the solicitor general filed a brief.

7. There is some variation in the distance variable for Alito because of instances in which the precedent, deference, or free speech variable affects the distance.

8. Our Bayesian approach simulates the posterior distribution and allows us to calculate how much of the posterior distribution is less than zero (or, when the hypothesis being tested is that the coefficient is less than zero as for *SGDistance*, the proportion of the posterior that is greater than zero).

9. At the .05 level, the number of significant parameters is twelve, seven, and eight for, respectively, *SG*, *SGDistance*, and *SGOutlier* while the number significant for the three variables at the .01 level is seven, four, and five, respectively.

CHAPTER 8   CONCLUSION

1. Despite the lack of obvious structural incentives for lifetime-appointed justices to care about popular acceptance, existing scholarship establishes that high courts appear to care about and try to influence public opinion to increase the legitimacy of their decisions (see, e.g., Caldeira 1986; Staton 2006). Furthermore, scholars such as Hoekstra (2000) have demonstrated that the public (or at least portions of it) is attentive to Supreme Court decisions. Other research (e.g., Gibson, Caldeira, and Baird 1998) explores the nature of court legitimacy and public opinion regarding courts.

2. The random treatment was administered in the post-election survey immediately prior to the second thermometer question. In both the pre- and post-election surveys, respondents were given an opportunity to skip the question if they felt that they "Didn't know enough to rank." Respondents who did "not feel particularly warm or cold" were asked to rank Justice Scalia "50" on the feeling thermometer.

3. When the experiment was administered, the five-point ranking scale was randomly flipped (ranging from "I strongly disapprove" to "I strongly approve" and from "I strongly approve" to "I strongly disapprove"). This randomization was instituted to control for ordering effects. Rather than completing this question, respondents were given an opportunity to click "Not sure." We dropped these respondents from the analysis.

4. The trust question asked respondents, "In general, can the Supreme Court be trusted to make the correct decision?" Respondents answered on a five-point scale ranging from "Yes, it can be trusted" to "No, it can't be trusted." The anchors on the five-point scale were randomly reversed so as to control for any effect that question ordering induced. This question was given to them prior to being exposed to the experimental condition. The education variable groups respondents into six categories: no high school degree, high school graduate, some college, two-year college degree, four-year college degree, and post-graduate.

5. This finding seems to confirm the Gibson, Caldeira, and Baird (1998, 356) claim that "Perhaps diffuse support is a cause and not a consequence of specific support. That is, the level of commitment to an institution may color the views one holds of its performance."

Appendix   Statistical Details

1. This parameter is standard in ideal point estimation theory and its precursor, item response theory (Baker 1992). Votes for which the alternatives are relatively close (meaning $\lambda_v^C - \lambda_v^L$ is relatively small) will have a low discrimination parameter as the non-spatial error term will be more likely to induce actors with preferences higher than the cutpoint to vote liberally and vice versa.

2. The reason that the number of liberal precedent cases plus the number of conservative precedent cases does not sum to the number of total precedent cases is that there are a couple of cases for which the precedent variable took on different values depending on the time of the observation. For example, when *Rust v. Sullivan* (1991) was initially considered, the conservative side was seeking to overturn precedent, meaning the precedent variable was coded as −1. But when Justice Breyer took a position on the *Rust v. Sullivan* in 1995, the precedent was conservative (since the Court decided in the conservative direction in 1991); hence, the value of precedent for the Breyer observation is 1.

REFERENCES

Abraham, Henry J. 1999. *Justices, Presidents and Senators: A History of the U.S. Supreme Court Appointments from Washington to Clinton*. Lanham, MD: Rowman and Littlefield.

Ackerman, Bruce. 1991. *We the People: Foundations*. Cambridge, MA: Harvard University Press.

———. 2005. *The Failure of the Founding Fathers: Jefferson, Marshall, and the Rise of Presidential Democracy*. Cambridge, MA: Harvard University Press.

Adams, John, Samuel Adams, and James Bowdoin. 1780. Constitution of the Commonwealth of Massachusetts. http://www.mass.gov/legis/const.htm (accessed December 26, 2010).

Alexander, Larry, and Frederick Schauer. 1997. On Extrajudicial Constitutional Interpretation. *Harvard Law Review* 110, no. 7 (May): 1359–87.

Alito, Samuel. 2006. Statements at U.S. Senate Judiciary Committee Hearing on Judge Samuel Alito's Nomination to the Supreme Court. U.S. Senate Committee on the Judiciary, January 9–11.

Ansolabehere, Stephen, James Snyder Jr., and Charles Stewart III. 2001. Candidate Positioning in U.S. House Elections. *American Journal of Political Science* 45, no. 1 (January): 136–59.

Arnold, Douglas. 1990. *The Logic of Congressional Action*. New Haven: Yale University Press.

Bafumi, Joseph, Andrew Gelman, David Park, and Noah Kaplan. 2005. Practical Issues in Implementing and Understanding Bayesian Ideal Point Estimation. *Political Analysis* 13, no. 2: 171–87.

Bailey, Michael. 2001. Ideal Point Estimation with a Small Number of Votes: A Random Effects Approach. *Political Analysis* 9, no. 3: 192–210.

———. 2007. Comparable Preference Estimates across Time and Institutions for the Court, Congress and Presidency. *American Journal of Political Science* 51, no. 3 (July): 433–48.

Bailey, Michael, and Kelly Chang. 2001. Comparing Presidents, Senators, and Justices: Inter-Institutional Preference Estimation. *Journal of Law, Economics and Organization* 17, no. 2 (October): 477–506.

———. 2003. Extremists on the Court: The Inter-Institutional Politics of Supreme Court Appointments. Manuscript. Georgetown University.

Bailey, Michael, and Forrest Maltzman. 2008. Does Legal Doctrine Matter? Unpacking Law and Policy Preferences on the U.S. Supreme Court. *American Political Science Review* 102, no. 3 (August): 369–84.

Bailey, Michael, Brian Kamoie, and Forrest Maltzman. 2005. Signals from the Tenth Justice: The Political Role of the Solicitor General in Supreme Court Decision-Making. *American Journal of Political Science* 49, no. 1 (January): 72–85.

Baker, Frank. 1992. *Item Response Theory*. New York: Marcel Dekker.

Barnes, Jeb. 2004. *Overruled: Legislative Overrides, Pluralism and Contemporary Court-Congress Relations*. Palo Alto, CA: Stanford University Press.

—. 2007. Bringing the Courts Back In: Interbranch Perspectives on the Role of Courts in American Politics and Policy Making. *Annual Review of Political Science* 10 (June): 25–43.

Barnes, Robert. 2006. New Justices Take to the Podium, Putting Personalities on Display. *Washington Post*, November 20, A15.

Bartels, Brandon. 2009. The Constraining Capacity of Legal Doctrine on the U.S. Supreme Court. *American Political Science Review* 103, no. 3 (August): 474–95.

Baum, Lawrence. 1988. Measuring Policy Change in the U.S. Supreme Court. *American Political Science Review* 82, no. 3 (September): 905–12.

—. 1997. *The Puzzle of Judicial Behavior*. Ann Arbor: University of Michigan Press.

—. 1999. Recruitment and the Motivations of Supreme Court Justices. In Cornell W. Clayton and Howard Gillman, eds., *Supreme Court Decision-Making: New Institutionalist Approaches*. Chicago: University of Chicago Press.

—. 2006. *Judges and Their Audiences: A Perspective on Judicial Behavior*. Princeton: Princeton University Press.

Bawn, Kathleen, and Charles R. Shipan. 1997. Congressional Responses to Supreme Court Decisions: Imperfect Anticipation and Institutional Constraints. Manuscript. University of California, Los Angeles.

Benesh, Sara C., and Harold J. Spaeth. 2003. The Supreme Court Justice–Centered Judicial Databases: The Warren, Burger, and Rehnquist Courts. http://www.cas.sc.edu/poli/juri/sct.htm (accessed December 29, 2010).

Berkowitz, Peter, and Benjamin Wittes. 2001. The Professors and *Bush v. Gore*. *Wilson Quarterly* (Autumn): 76–89.

Bickel, Alexander. 1962. *The Least Dangerous Branch*. Indianapolis: Bobbs-Merrill.

—. 1986. *The Least Dangerous Branch*. 2nd ed. New Haven: Yale University Press.

Bingaman, Jeff. 2005. *Congressional Record*, 109th Cong., 1st Sess., September 21: S10268.

Biskupic, Joan. 2003. White House Says Target Is Quotas, Not Diversity. *USA Today*, January 16.

Black, Hugo. 1969. *A Constitutional Faith*. New York: Alfred Knopf.

Boot, Max. 1998. *Out of Order: Arrogance, Corruption, and Incompetence on the Bench*. New York: Basic Books.

Bork, Robert. 1990. *The Tempting of America*. New York: The Free Press.

Brandeis, Louis. 1932. *Burnet v. Coronado Oil and Gas Company*, 285 U.S. 293.

Brenner, Saul, and Harold J. Spaeth. 1995. *Stare Indecisis: The Alteration of Precedent on the Supreme Court, 1946–1992*. New York: Cambridge University Press.

Brenner, Saul, and Marc Stier. 1996. Retesting Segal and Spaeth's Stare Decisis Model. *American Journal of Political Science* 40, no. 4 (November): 1036–48.

Brenner, Saul, and Joseph M. Whitmeyer. 2009. *Strategy on the United States Supreme Court*. New York: Cambridge University Press.

Breyer, Stephen. 2005. *Active Liberty*. New York: Knopf.

———. 2010. *Making Democracy Work: A Judge's View*. New York: Knopf.

Bueno de Mesquita, Ethan, and Matthew Stephenson. 2002. Informative Precedent and Intrajudicial Communication. *American Political Science Review* 96, no. 4 (December): 755–66.

Burbank, Stephen, and Barry Friedman, eds. 2002. *Judicial Independence at the Crossroads: An Interdisciplinary Approach*. Thousand Oaks, CA: Sage Publications.

Bush, George W. 2003. Remarks on the Michigan Affirmative Action Case. http://www.presidency.ucsb.edu (accessed January 15, 2010).

Calabresi, Steven, and James Lindgren. 2006. Term Limits for the Supreme Court: Life Tenure Reconsidered. *Harvard Journal of Law and Public Policy* 29, no. 3 (Summer): 770–877.

Caldeira, Gregory A. 1986. Neither the Purse nor the Sword: Dynamics of Public Confidence in the Supreme Court. *American Political Science Review* 80, no. 4 (December): 1209–26.

———. 1987. Public Opinion and the U.S. Supreme Court: FDR's Court-Packing Plan. *American Political Science Review* 81, no. 4 (December): 1139–53.

Caldeira, Gregory A., and James L. Gibson. 1992. The Etiology of Public Support for the Supreme Court. *American Journal of Political Science* 36, no. 3 (August): 635–91.

Caldeira, Gregory A., and John R. Wright. 1988. Organized Interests and Agenda Setting in the U.S. Supreme Court. *American Political Science Review* 82, no. 4 (December): 1109–29.

Calvert, Randall. 1985. The Value of Biased Information: A Rational Choice Model of Political Advice. *Journal of Politics* 47, no. 2 (June): 531–55.

Cameron, Charles, Donald Songer, and Jeffrey A. Segal. 2000. Strategic Auditing in a Political Hierarchy: An Informational Model of the Supreme Court's Certiorari Decisions. *American Political Science Review* 94, no. 1 (March): 101–16.

Caplan, Lincoln. 1987. *The Tenth Justice: The Solicitor General and the Rule of Law*. New York: Knopf.

Clark, Tom S. 2009. The Separation of Powers, Court-Curbing and Judicial Legitimacy. *American Journal of Political Science* 53, no. 4 (October): 971–89.

Clinton, Josh, and Adam Meirowitz. 2001. Agenda Constrained Legislator Ideal Points and the Spatial Voting Model. *Political Analysis* 9, no. 3: 242–59.

Clinton, Josh, Simon Jackman, and Doug Rivers. 2004. The Statistical Analysis of Legislative Roll Call Data. *American Political Science Review* 98, no. 2 (May): 355–70.

Coburn, Tom. 2010. Dr. Coburn's opening remarks at the Judiciary Committee hearing of Elena Kagan. coburn.senate.gov/public/index.cfm/2010/6/dr-coburn-s-opening-remarks-at-the-judiciary-committee-hearing-of-elena-kagan (accessed September 21, 2010).

Cohen, Adam. 2006. Reining in Justice Scalia. *New York Times*, April 26. http://select.nytimes.com/2006/04/26/opinion/26talkingpoints.html (accessed December 21, 2010).

Connerly, Ward, and Edward Blum. 2002. Do the Right Thing. *Wall Street Journal,* December 4, sec. A, p. 18.

Cooper, James L. 1990. The Solicitor General and the Evolution of Activism. *Indiana Law Journal* 65 (Summer): 675–96.

Cox, Gary W., and Mathew D. McCubbins. 1993. *Legislative Leviathan: Party Government in the House*. Berkeley: University of California Press.

Crawford, Vincent, and Joel Sobel. 1982. Strategic Information Transmission. *Econometrica* 50, no. 6 (November): 1431–51.

Cross, Frank. 1997. Political Science and the New Legal Realism: A Case of Unfortunate Interdisciplinary Ignorance. *Northwestern University Law Review* 92, no. 1: 251–326.

Cross, Frank B., and Blake J. Nelson. 2001. Strategic Institutional Effects on Supreme Court Decisionmaking. *Northwestern University Law Review* 95, no. 4 (Summer): 1437–94.

Dahl, Robert. 1957. Decision-Making in a Democracy: The Supreme Court as National Policy Maker. *Journal of Public Law* 6 (Fall): 279–95.

Days, Drew. 1994. In Search of the Solicitor General's Clients: A Drama with Many Characters. *Kentucky Law Journal* 83, no. 2: 485–507.

Dean, John. 2001. *The Rehnquist Choice*. New York: The Free Press.

DeParle, Jason. 2004. *American Dream: Three Women, Ten Kids, and a Nation's Drive to End Welfare*. New York: Viking.

Devins, Neal, and Louis Fisher. 2004. *The Democratic Constitution*. New York: Oxford University Press.

Dickenson, Mollie. 2001. Lawyers Protest U.S. Supreme Court. http:// www .consortiumnews.com/2001/011501a.html (accessed September 21, 2010).

Dorf, Michael. 2009. Do the Supreme Court's Current Justices Hold Sincere Views about States' Rights: A Failure-to-Warn Case Reveals an Apparent Inconsistency. March 9, 2009. http://writ.news.findlaw.com/dorf/20090309.html (accessed August 1, 2010).

Douglas, William. 1949. Stare Decisis. *Columbia Law Review* 49, no. 6 (June): 735–58.

Downs, Anthony. 1957. *An Economic Theory of Democracy*. Reading, MA: Addison Wesley.

Dunne, Gerald. 1977. *Hugo Black and the Judicial Revolution*. New York: Simon and Schuster.

Dworkin, Ronald. 1978. *Taking Rights Seriously*. Cambridge, MA: Harvard University Press.

Edwards, Harry T. 1998. Collegiality and Decision Making on the D.C. Circuit. *Virginia Law Review* 84, no. 7 (October): 1335–70.

Ely, John Hart. 1980. *Democracy and Distrust: A Theory of Judicial Review*. Cambridge, MA: Harvard University Press.

———. 1991. Another Such Victory: Constitutional Theory and Practice in a World Where Courts Are No Different from Legislatures. *Virginia Law Review* 77, no. 4 (May): 833–79.

Epstein, Lee, and Jack Knight. 1995. Documenting Strategic Interaction on the U.S. Supreme Court. Paper presented at the Annual Meeting of the American Political Science Association, Chicago.

———. 1998. *The Choices Justices Make*. Washington, DC: CQ Press.

Epstein, Lee, and Jeffrey Segal. 2000. Measuring Issue Salience. *American Journal of Political Science* 44, no. 1 (January): 66–83.

———. 2006. Trumping the First Amendment. *Journal of Law and Policy* 21:81–121.

Epstein, Lee, Barry Friedman, and Nancy Staudt. 2008. On the Capacity of the Roberts Court to Generate Consequential Precedent. *North Carolina Law Review* 86, no. 5: 1299–1332.

Epstein, Lee, Jack Knight, and Andrew Martin. 2004. Constitutional Interpretation from a Strategic Perspective. In Mark C. Miller and Jeb Barnes, eds., *Making Policy, Making Law*. Washington, DC: Georgetown University Press.

Epstein, Lee, Valerie Hoekstra, Jeffrey Segal, and Harold Spaeth. 1998. Do Political Preferences Change? A Longitudinal Study of U.S. Supreme Court Justices. *Journal of Politics* 60, no. 3 (August): 801–18.

Epstein, Lee, Rene Lindstadt, Jeffrey A. Segal, and Chad Westerland. 2006. The Changing Dynamics of Senate Voting on Supreme Court Nominees. *Journal of Politics* 68, no. 2 (May): 296–307.

Epstein, Lee, Andrew Martin, Kevin M. Quinn, and Jeffrey Segal. 2009. Circuit Effects: How the Norm of Federal Judicial Experience Biases the Supreme Court. *University of Pennsylvania Law Review* 157, no. 3 (February): 833–80.

Epstein, Lee, Andrew Martin, Jeffrey A. Segal, and Chad Westerland. 2007. The Judicial Common Space. *Journal of Law, Economics and Organization* 23, no. 2 (June): 303–25.

Epstein, Lee, Jeffrey Segal, Harold Spaeth, and Thomas Walker. 2007. *The Supreme Court Compendium: Data, Decisions, and Developments*. Washington, DC: CQ Press.

Eskridge, William. 1991. Overriding Supreme Court Statutory Interpretation Decisions. *Yale Law School Journal* 101, no. 2 (October): 331–65.

Eskridge, William, John Ferejohn, and Neeta Gandhi. 2002. Strategic Voting in the Supreme Court: Civil Rights, the Court, and Congress in the 1970s and 1980s. Paper presented at the Midwest Political Science Association Meeting, Chicago.

Ferejohn, John. 1999. Independent Judges, Dependent Judiciary: Explaining Judicial Independence. *Southern California Law Review* 72, no. 2/3 (January and March): 353–84.

Ferejohn, John, and Larry Kramer. 2006. Judicial Independence in a Democracy: Institutionalizing Judicial Restraint. In John Drobak, ed., *Norms and the Law*. New York: Cambridge University Press.

Ferejohn, John, and Charles Shipan. 1990. Congressional Influence on Bureaucracy. *Journal of Law, Economics and Organization* 6, special issue (April): 1–21.

Ferejohn, John, and Barry Weingast. 1992. A Positive Theory of Statutory Interpretation. *International Review of Law and Economics* 12, no. 2 (June): 263–79.

Fisher, Louis. 1988. *Constitutional Dialogues: Interpretation as a Political Process*. Princeton: Princeton University Press.

Fraley, George III. 1996. Note, Is the Fox Watching the Henhouse? The Administration's Control of FEC Litigation through the Solicitor General. *Administrative Law Review* 9 (Winter): 1215–72.

Frank, Jerome. 2009 [1930]. *Law and the Modern Mind*. New Brunswick, NJ: Transaction Publishers, 2009.

Franken, Al. 2009. Opening Statement on Judge Sotomayor's Nomination. U.S. Senate Committee on the Judiciary, July 13. http://judiciary.senate.gov/hearings/testimony.cfm?id=3959&wit_id=8101 (accessed December 29, 2010).

Frankfurter, Felix. 1938. *Mr. Justice Holmes and the Supreme Court*. Cambridge, MA: Harvard University Press.

Friedman, Barry. 1990. A Different Dialogue: The Supreme Court, Congress and Federal Jurisdiction. *Northwestern University Law Review* 85, no. 1: 1–61.

———. 1998. The History of the Countermajoritarian Difficulty, Part One: The Road to Judicial Supremacy. *New York University Law Review* 73, no. 2 (May): 333–433.

———. 2006. Taking Law Seriously. *Perspectives on Politics* 4, no. 2 (June): 261–76.

———. 2009. *The Will of the People: How Public Opinion Has Influenced the Supreme Court and Shaped the Meaning of the Constitution*. New York: Farrar, Straus and Giroux.

Galanter, Marc. 1974. Why the "Haves" Come Out Ahead: Speculation on the Limits of Legal Change. *Law and Society Review* 9 (Fall): 95–160.

Gale Cengage Learning. 2005. *Making of Modern Law: U.S. Supreme Court Records and Briefs, 1832–1978*. Georgetown University Library Record number b458527.

Garbus, Martin. 2002. *Courting Disaster: The Supreme Court and the Unmaking of American Law*. New York: Times Books.

Gash, Alison, and Michael Murakami. 2009. Courts, Legislatures, and Ballot Initiatives: How Policy Venue Affects Public Acceptance. Paper presented at the Annual Meeting of the American Political Science Association, Toronto, Ontario.

Gelman, Andrew, John Carlin, Hal Stern, and Donald Rubin. 1995. *Bayesian Data Analysis*. Boca Raton: Chapman Hall.

Gely, Rafael, and Pablo Spiller. 1990. A Rational Choice Theory of Supreme Court Statutory Decisions with Applications to the State Farm and Grove City Cases. *Journal of Law, Economics and Organization* 6, no. 2 (Autumn): 263–300.

George, Tracy E., and Lee Epstein. 1992. On the Nature of Supreme Court Decision Making. *American Political Science Review* 86, no. 2 (June): 323–37.

Gerhardt, Michael. 2008. *The Power of Precedent*. New York: Oxford University Press.

Gewirtz, Paul, and Chad Golder. 2005. So Who Are the Activists? *New York Times*, July 6.

Geyh, Charles. 2006. *When Courts and Congress Collide: The Struggle for Control of America's Judicial System*. Ann Arbor: University of Michigan Press.

Gibson, James. 1977. Discriminant Functions, Role Orientations and Judicial Behavior: Theoretical and Methodological Linkages. *Journal of Politics* 39, no. 4 (November): 984–1007.

―――. 1978. Judges' Role Orientations, Attitudes, and Decisions: An Inter-active Model. *American Political Science Review* 72, no. 3 (September): 911–24.

―――. 1983. From Simplicity to Complexity: The Development of Theory in the Study of Judicial Behavior. *Political Behavior* 5, no. 1: 7–49.

―――. 1997. *United States Supreme Court Judicial Database, Phase II.* First ICPSR version. ICPSR Number 6987.

Gibson, James, and Gregory Caldeira. 2009. *Citizens, Courts, and Confirma-tions: Positivity Theory and the Judgments of the American People.* Princeton: Princeton University Press.

Gibson, James L., Gregory A. Caldeira, and Vanessa A. Baird. 1998. On the Le-gitimacy of National High Courts. *American Political Science Review* 92, no. 2 (June): 343–58.

Giles, Michael, Bethany Blackstone, and Rich Vining. 2008. The Supreme Court in American Democracy: Unraveling Linkages between Public Opinion and Decision-Making. *Journal of Politics* 70, no. 2 (April): 293–306.

Gillman, Howard. 2001. Review Essay: What's Law Got to Do with It? Judicial Behavioralists Test the "Legal Model" of Judicial Decision-Making. *Law and Social Inquiry* 26, no. 2 (Spring): 465–504.

Gillman, Howard, and Cornell Clayton. 1999. Beyond Judicial Attitudes: Institu-tional Approaches to Supreme Court Decision-Making. In Cornell W. Clayton and Howard Gillman, eds., *Supreme Court Decision-Making: New Institution-alist Approaches.* Chicago: University of Chicago Press.

Glick, Henry, and Kenneth Vines. 1969. Law-making in the State Judiciary: A Comparative Study of the Judicial Role in Four States. *Polity* 2, no. 2 (Winter): 142–59.

Gnagey, Laurel Thomas. 2003. Supreme Court Decisions Uphold Affirmative Ac-tion. *University Record Online.* http://www.ur.umich.edu/0203/June16_03/01 _decision.shtml (accessed September 21, 2010).

Goldberg, Carey. 1996. Wealthy Ally for Dissidents in the Drug War. *New York Times*, September 11.

Goldstein, Thomas C. 2007. Justice Thomas: Constitutional "Stare Indecisis." Symposium on Justice Thomas and the First Amendment. http://www.first amendmentcenter.org/analysis.aspxid=19133 (accessed November 26, 2007).

Greene, William. 2000. *Econometric Analysis.* 3rd ed. New York: Prentice Hall.

Greenhouse, Linda. 2003. Bush and Affirmative Action: News Analysis; Muted Call in Race Case. *New York Times*, January 17, sec. A, p. 1.

Groseclose, Timothy, Steven Levitt, and James Snyder. 1999. Comparing Interest Group Scores across Time and Chambers: Adjusted ADA Scores for the U.S. Congress. *American Political Science Review* 93, no. 1 (March): 33–50.

Hagle, Tim, and Harold Spaeth. 1992. The Emergence of a New Ideology: The Business Decisions of the Burger Court. *Journal of Politics* 54, no. 1 (February): 120–34.

―――. 1993. Ideological Patterns in the Justices' Voting in the Burger Court Business Cases. *Journal of Politics* 55, no. 2 (May): 492–505.

Hamilton, Alexander, James Madison, and John Jay. 2011. Reprint. *The Federal-ist Papers.* New York: Tribeca Books.

Hammond, Thomas H., Chris W. Bonneau, and Reginald S. Sheehan. 2005. *Strategic Behavior and Policy Choice on the U.S. Supreme Court*. Stanford, CA: Stanford University Press.

Hansford, Thomas G., and David F. Damore. 2000. Congressional Preferences, Perceptions of Threat, and Supreme Court Decision Making. *American Politics Research* 28, no. 4 (October): 490–510.

Hansford, Thomas G., and James F. Spriggs. 2006. *The Politics of Precedent on the U.S. Supreme Court*. Princeton: Princeton University Press.

Harlan, John Marshall. 1964. Dissenting Opinion in *Reynolds v. Sims*, 377 U.S. 533.

Harvey, Anna, and Barry Friedman. 2006. Pulling Punches: Congressional Constraints on the Supreme Court's Constitutional Rulings, 1987–2000. *Legislative Studies Quarterly* 31, no. 4 (November): 533–62.

———. 2009. Ducking Trouble: Congressionally-Induced Selection Bias in the Supreme Court's Agenda. *Journal of Politics* 71, no. 2 (April): 574–92.

Harvey, Anna, and Michael Woodruff. 2011. Confirmation Bias in the United States Supreme Court Judicial Database. Manuscript. New York University.

Hausegger, Lori, and Lawrence Baum. 1999. Inviting Congressional Action: A Study of Supreme Court Motivations in Statutory Interpretation. *American Journal of Political Science* 43, no. 1 (January): 162–85.

Heinemann, Ronald L. 1996. *Harry Byrd of Virginia*. Charlottesville: University of Virginia Press.

Hirsch, H. N. 1981. *The Enigma of Felix Frankfurter*. New York: Basic Books.

Hoekstra, Valerie J. 2000. The Supreme Court and Local Public Opinion. *American Political Science Review* 94, no. 1 (March): 89–100.

Howard, Robert, and Jeffrey A. Segal. 2004. A Preference for Deference: The Supreme Court and Judicial Review. *Political Research Quarterly* 57, no. 1 (March): 131–43.

Howe, M. D. 1953. *Holmes-Laski Letters: The Correspondence of Mr. Justice Holmes and Harold J. Laski: 1916–1935*. Cambridge, MA: Harvard University Press.

Jackman, Simon. 2000. Estimation and Inference via Bayesian Simulation: An Introduction to Markov Chain Monte Carlo. *American Journal of Political Science* 44, no. 2 (April): 375–404.

Johnson, Timothy R. 2003. The Supreme Court, the Solicitor General, and the Separation of Powers. *American Politics Research* 31, no. 4 (July): 426–51.

Johnson, Valen, and James Albert. 1999. *Ordinal Data Modeling*. New York: Springer.

Kagan, Elena. 2010. The Nomination of Elena Kagan to Be an Associate Justice of the Supreme Court of the United States. U.S. Senate Committee on the Judiciary, June 28–June 30.

Kahn, Ronald. 1999. Institutionalized Norms and Supreme Court Decision-Making: The Rehnquist Court on Privacy and Religion. In Cornell W. Clayton and Howard Gillman, eds., *Supreme Court Decision-Making: New Institutionalist Approaches*. Chicago: University of Chicago Press.

Kastellec, Jonathan P., and Jeffrey Lax. 2008. Case Selection and the Study of Judicial Politics. *Journal of Empirical Legal Studies* 5, no. 3: 407–446.

Katcher, Leo. 1967. *Earl Warren: A Political Biography*. New York: McGraw-Hill.

Katzmann, Robert. 1997. *Courts and Congress*. Washington, DC: Brookings/ Governance.

Kearney, Joseph, and Thomas Merrill. 2000. The Influence of Amicus Curiae Briefs on the Supreme Court. *University of Pennsylvania Law Review* 148, no. 3 (January): 743–854.

Keck, Thomas. 2007. Party, Policy or Duty: Why Does the Supreme Court Invalidate Federal Statutes? *American Political Science Review* 101, no. 2 (May): 321–38.

Knight, Jack, and Lee Epstein. 1996. The Norm of Stare Decisis. *American Journal of Political Science* 40, no. 4 (November): 1018–35.

Krauthammer, Charles. 2009. Sotomayor: Criticize, Then Confirm. *Washington Post*, May 29.

Krehbiel, Keith. 1998. *Pivotal Politics: A Theory of U.S. Lawmaking*. Chicago: University of Chicago Press.

———. 2007. Supreme Court Appointments as a Move-the-Median Game. *American Journal of Political Science* 51, no. 2 (April): 231–40.

Kronman, Anthony. 2006. Statement on Samuel Alito's Nomination. U.S. Senate Committee on the Judiciary, January 12. http://judiciary.senate.gov/hearings/ testimony.cfm?id=1725&wit_id=4907 (accessed December 25, 2010).

Kyl, Jon. 2009. Kyl Will Oppose Sotomayor Confirmation. Press release, Office of United States Senator Jon Kyl.

Landes, William, and Richard Posner. 1975. The Independent Judiciary in an Interest-Group Perspective. *Journal of Law and Economics* 18, no. 3 (December): 875–901.

Leahy, Patrick. 2005. *Congressional Record*, 109th Cong., 1st Sess., September 21: S10252.

———. 2009. Statement Regarding the Nomination of Judge Sonia Sotomayor to Be an Associate Justice on the U.S. Supreme Court. U.S. Senate Committee on the Judiciary, June 9.

Levi, Edward H. 1949. *An Introduction to Legal Reasoning*. Chicago: University of Chicago Press.

Levin, Mark R. 2005. *Men in Black: How the Supreme Court Is Destroying America*. Washington, DC: Regnery Publishing.

Levinson, Sanford. 1977. Review of *From the Diaries of Felix Frankfurter* by Joseph P. Lash. *American Journal of Legal History* 21, no. 1 (January): 80–83.

Lewis, Anthony. 2009. Justice Holmes and the Splendid Prisoner. *New York Review of Books*, July 2, 44–47.

Lewis, John. 2003. Bush's Strategy of Racial Innuendo: A Telling and Troubling Sign. *Atlanta Journal and Constitution*, January 20.

Li, Hao, and Suen Wing. 2004. Delegating Decisions to Experts. *Journal of Political Economy* 112, no. S1 (February): S311–35.

Lindquist, Stefanie, and Frank Cross. 2009. *Measuring Judicial Activism*. New York: Oxford University Press.

Lindquist, Stefanie, and Rorie Spill Solberg. 2007. Judicial Review by the Burger and Rehnquist Courts: Explaining Justices' Responses to Constitutional Challenges. *Political Research Quarterly* 60, no. 1 (March): 71–90.

Liptak, Adam. 2009. Roberts Sets Off Debate on Judicial Experience. *New York Times*, February 16.

———. 2010. Court under Roberts Is Most Conservative in Decades. *New York Times*, July 24.

Llewellyn, Karl. 1962. *Jurisprudence: Realism in Theory and Practice*. Chicago: University of Chicago Press.

Londregan, John. 1999. Estimating Legislators' Preferred Points. *Political Analysis* 8, no. 1: 35–56.

Loughlin, Sean. 2003. Santorum under Fire for Comments on Homosexuality. http://cnn.com/2003/ALLPOLITICS/04/22/santorum.gays/ (accessed September 20, 2010).

Maltzman, Forrest, and Paul J. Wahlbeck. 1996a. Strategic Policy Considerations and Voting Fluidity on the Burger Court. *American Political Science Review* 90, no. 3 (September): 581–92.

———. 1996b. May It Please the Chief: Opinion Assignments in the Rehnquist Court. *American Journal of Political Science* 40, no. 2 (May): 421–33.

Maltzman, Forrest, James F. Spriggs, and Paul J. Wahlbeck. 1999. Strategy and Judicial Choice: New Institutionalist Approaches to Supreme Court Decision Making. In Cornell W. Clayton and Howard Gillman, eds., *Supreme Court Decision-Making: New Institutional Approaches*. Chicago: University of Chicago Press.

———. 2000. *Crafting Law on the Supreme Court: The Collegial Game*. Cambridge: Cambridge University Press.

March, James G., and Johan P. Olsen. 1984. The New Institutionalism: Organizational Factors in Political Life. *American Political Science Review* 78, no. 3: 734–49.

Marks, Brian. 1989. A Model of Judicial Influence on Congressional Policymaking: *Grove City College v. Bell*. Ph.D. diss., Washington University.

Martin, Andrew. 2006. Statutory Battles and Constitutional Wars. In James R. Rogers, Roy B. Flemming, and Jon R. Bond, eds., *Institutional Games and the U.S. Supreme Court*. Charlottesville: University of Virginia Press.

Martin, Andrew, and Kevin Quinn. 2002. Dynamic Ideal Point Estimation via Markov Chain Monte Carlo for the U.S. Supreme Court, 1953–1999. *Political Analysis* 10, no. 2: 134–53.

———. 2009. Martin-Quinn Scores. http://mqscores.wustl.edu/measures.php (accessed January 4, 2011).

Martin, Andrew, Kevin Quinn, and Lee Epstein. 2005. The Median Justice on the U.S. Supreme Court. *North Carolina Law Review* 83, no. 5 (June): 1275–1322.

Mason, Alpheus Thomas. 1956. *Harlan Fiske Stone: Pillar of the Law*. New York: Viking Press.

McCarty, Nolan, and Keith Poole. 1995. Veto Power and Legislation: An Empirical Analysis of Executive and Legislative Bargaining from 1961 to 1986. *Journal of Law, Economics and Organization* 11, no. 2 (October): 282–312.

McCloskey, Robert. 1960. *The American Supreme Court*. Chicago: University of Chicago Press.

McGowan, Miranda O. 2008. Do as I Do, Not as I Say: An Empirical Investiga-
tion of Justice Scalia's Ordinary Meaning Method of Statutory Interpretation.
San Diego Legal Studies Paper No. 08-015.

McGrory, Mary. 2000. Supreme Travesty of Justice. *Washington Post*, December
14, A3.

McGuire, Kevin. 1998. Explaining Executive Success in the U.S. Supreme Court.
Political Research Quarterly 51, no. 2 (June): 505–26.

McGuire, Kevin, and James Stimson. 2004. The Least Dangerous Branch Revisited: New Evidence on Supreme Court Responsiveness to Public Preferences.
Journal of Politics 66, no. 4 (November): 1018–35.

McNollgast. 1995. Politics and the Courts: A Positive Theory of Judicial Doctrine
and the Rule of Law. *Southern California Law Review* 68, no. 6 (September):
1631–82.

Meernik, James, and Joseph Ignagni. 1997. Judicial Review and Coordinate Construction of the Constitution. *American Journal of Political Science* 41, no. 2
(April): 447–67.

Meinhold, Stephen S., and Steven A. Shull. 1998. Policy Congruence between the
President and the Solicitor General. *Political Research Quarterly* 51, no. 2:
527–37.

Mishler, William, and Reginald Sheehan. 1993. The Supreme Court as a Countermajoritarian Institution: The Impact of Public Opinion on Supreme Court Decisions. *American Political Science Review* 87, no. 1 (March): 87–101.

———. 1996. Public Opinion, the Attitudinal Model, and Supreme Court Decision Making: A Micro-Analytic Perspective. *Journal of Politics* 58, no. 1 (February): 169–200.

Mislevy, Robert, and R. Darrell Bock. 1990. *BILOG 3: Item Analysis and Test
Scoring with Binary Logistic Models*. Mooresville, IN: Scientific Software Inc.

Moraski, Bryon, and Charles Shipan. 1999. The Politics of Supreme Court Nominations: A Theory of Institutional Constraints and Choices. *American Journal
of Political Science* 43, no. 4 (October): 1069–95.

Murphy, Bruce Allen. 1988. *Fortas: The Rise & Ruin of a Supreme Court Justice*.
New York: Random House.

Murphy, Walter. 1962. *Congress and the Court: A Case Study in the American
Political Process*. Chicago: University of Chicago Press.

———. 1964. *Elements of Judicial Strategy*. Chicago: University of Chicago Press.

Murray, Frank. 2003. White House Set to Stay Out of Affirmative-Action Case.
Washington Times, January 9.

Nemachek, Christine. 2008. *Strategic Selection: Presidential Nomination of Supreme Court Justices from Herbert Hoover through George W. Bush*. Charlottesville: University of Virginia Press.

Nicholson, Chris, and Paul Collins. 2008. The Solicitor General's Amicus Curiae
Strategies in the Supreme Court. *American Politics Research* 36, no. 3 (May):
382–415.

Nixon, Richard. 1969. Conversation with Newsmen on the Nomination of the
Chief Justice of the United States. The American Presidency Project. May 22.
http://www.presidency.ucsb.edu/.

Noel, Hans. 2009. The Coalition Merchants: Testing the Power of Ideas with the Civil Rights Realignment. Manuscript. Georgetown University.

Norman-Major, Kristen A. 1994. *The Solicitor General: Executive Policy Agendas and the Court. Albany Law Review* 57 (Fall): 1081–1109.

Novak, Robert. 2003. Bush's First Justice. January 23. http://www.cnn.com/2003/ALLPOLITICS/01/23/column.novak.opinion.justice/ (accessed February 27, 2010).

O'Brien, David M. 2000. *Storm Center: The Supreme Court in American Politics.* 6th ed. New York: W. W. Norton.

———. 2003. *Constitutional Law and Politics.* 5th ed. New York: W. W. Norton.

O'Connor, Karen. 1983. The Amicus Curiae Role of the U.S. Solicitor General in Supreme Court Litigation. *Judicature* 66, no. 5 (December–January): 256–64.

Page, Scott E. 2007. *The Difference: How the Power of Diversity Creates Better Groups, Firms, Schools, and Societies.* Princeton: Princeton University Press.

Peabody, Bruce. 2005. Congressional Attitudes toward Constitutional Interpretation. In Neal Devins and Keith Whittington, eds., *Congress and the Constitution.* Durham: Duke University Press.

Peretti, Terri Jennings. 1999. *In Defense of a Political Court.* Princeton: Princeton University Press.

———. 2002. Does Judicial Independence Exist? In Stephen Burbank and Barry Friedman, eds., *Judicial Independence at the Crossroads: An Interdisciplinary Approach.* Thousand Oaks, CA: Sage Publications.

Perry, H. W. Jr. 1991. *Deciding to Decide: Agenda Setting in the United States Supreme Court.* Cambridge, MA: Harvard University Press.

Pickerill, J. Mitchell. 2004. *Constitutional Deliberation in Congress: The Impact of Judicial Review in a Separated System.* Durham: Duke University Press.

Pinello, Daniel R. 2003. *Gay Rights and American Law.* New York: Cambridge University Press.

Poole, Keith. 1998. Recovering a Basic Space from a Set of Issue Scales. *American Journal of Political Science* 42, no. 3 (July): 954–93.

———. 2004. Description of NOMINATE data. http://voteview.com/page2a.htm (accessed December 27, 2010).

———. 2005. *Spatial Models of Parliamentary Voting.* New York: Cambridge University Press.

Poole, Keith, and Howard Rosenthal. 1997. *Congress: A Political-Economic History of Roll Call Voting.* Oxford: Oxford University Press.

Posner, Richard. 2005. The Supreme Court 2004 Term, Foreword: A Political Court. *Harvard Law Review* 119, no. 1 (November): 31–102.

———. 2008. *How Judges Think.* Cambridge, MA: Harvard University Press.

Provine, Doris Marie. 1980. *Case Selection in the United States Supreme Court.* Chicago: University of Chicago Press.

Puro, Steven. 1981. The United States as Amicus Curiae. In S. Sidney Ulmer, ed., *Courts, Law and Judicial Processes,* 220–29. New York: The Free Press.

Rehnquist, William. 1987. *The Supreme Court.* New York: William Morrow.

Richards, Mark J., and Herbert Kritzer. 2002. Jurisprudential Regimes in Supreme Court Decision Making. *American Political Science Review* 96, no. 2 (June): 305–20.

Roberts, John G. 2003. Confirmation Hearings on Federal Appointments. U.S. Senate Committee on the Judiciary, serial no. J-108-1, part 3.

Robertson, Pat. 2004. *Courting Disaster: How the Supreme Court Is Usurping the Power of Congress and the People*. Wake Forest, NC: Integrity Publishers.

Rogers, James. 2001. Information and Judicial Review: A Signaling Game of Legislative-Judicial Interaction. *American Journal of Political Science* 45, no. 1 (January): 84–99.

Rohde, David W., and Harold J. Spaeth. 1976. *Supreme Court Decision Making*. San Francisco: W. H. Freeman.

Rosen, Jeffrey. 2000. The Supreme Court Commits Suicide. *The New Republic* 223 (December 25).

———. 2006. *The Most Democratic Branch: How the Courts Serve America*. New York: Oxford University Press.

Rosenberg, Gerald. 1991. *The Hollow Hope: Can Courts Bring about Social Change?* Chicago: University of Chicago Press.

———. 1992. Judicial Independence and the Reality of Political Power. *Review of Politics* 54, no. 2 (Summer): 369–98.

Sala, Brian R., and James F. Spriggs II. 2004. Designing Tests of the Supreme Court and the Separation of Powers. *Political Research Quarterly* 57, no. 2 (June): 197–208.

Salokar, Rebecca. 1992. *The Solicitor General: The Politics of Law*. Philadelphia: Temple University Press.

Sammon, Bill. 2003. Bush Set to Break Silence in Race Case. *Washington Times*, January 14.

Scalia, Antonin. 1998. *A Matter of Interpretation*. Princeton: Princeton University Press.

———. 2003. Dissent in *Lawrence v. Texas*. No. 02-102. Decided June 26.

———. 2004. Memorandum of Justice Scalia on *Cheney v. United States*. No. 03-475. Decided March 18.

Schaffer Library of Drug Policy. 1993. Senate Joint Resolution 8. http://www.druglibrary.org/Schaffer/hemp/sj8.htm (accessed September 20, 2010).

Scigliano, Robert. 1971. *The Supreme Court and the Presidency*. New York: The Free Press.

Segal, Jeffrey A. 1988. Amicus Curiae Briefs by the Solicitor General during the Warren and Burger Courts: A Research Note. *Western Political Quarterly* 41, no. 1 (March): 135–44.

———. 1989. Supreme Court Support for the Solicitor General: The Effect of Presidential Appointments. *Western Political Quarterly* 43, no. 1 (March): 137–52.

———. 1997. Separation of Powers Games in the Positive Theory of Congress and Courts. *American Political Science Review* 91, no. 1 (March): 28–44.

Segal, Jeffrey A., and Albert Cover. 1989. Ideological Values and the Votes of U.S. Supreme Court Justices. *American Political Science Review* 83, no. 2 (June): 557–65.

Segal, Jeffrey A., and Robert M. Howard. 2005. How the Supreme Court Justices Respond to Litigant Requests to Overturn Precedent in the U.S. Supreme Court, 1985–1994. In E. Slotnick, ed., *Judicial Politics: Readings from Judicature*, 431–41. 3rd ed. Washington, DC: CQ Press.

Segal, Jeffrey A., and Cheryl D. Reedy. 1988. The Supreme Court and Sex Discrimination: The Role of the Solicitor General. *Western Political Quarterly* 41, no. 3 (September): 553–68.

Segal, Jeffrey A., and Harold J. Spaeth. 1993. *The Supreme Court and the Attitudinal Model*. New York: Cambridge University Press.

———. 1994. The Attitudinal Model: The Authors Respond. *Law and Courts Newsletter* 4, no. 1: 10.

———. 1996. The Influence of Stare Decisis on the Votes of the United States Supreme Court Justices. *American Journal of Political Science* 40, no. 4 (November): 971–1003.

———. 2002. *The Supreme Court and the Attitudinal Model Revisited*. New York: Cambridge University Press.

Segal, Jeffrey, Chad Westerland, and Stefanie Lindquist. 2007. Congress, the Supreme Court and Judicial Review. Paper presented at Annual Meeting of Midwest Political Science Association, Chicago.

Shepsle, Kenneth A., and David Rohde. 2007. Advice and Consent in the 60-Vote Senate. *Journal of Politics* 69, no. 3 (August): 664–77.

Smith, Jean Edward. 1996. *John Marshall: Definer of a Nation*. New York: Henry Holt and Company.

Smith, Rogers M. 1988. Political Jurisprudence, the "New Institutionalism" and the Future of Public Law. *American Political Science Review* 82, no. 1 (March): 89–108.

Songer, Donald, and Stefanie Lindquist. 1996. Not the Whole Story: The Impact of Justices' Values on Supreme Court Decision-Making. *American Journal of Political Science* 40, no. 4 (November): 1049–63.

Sotomayor, Sonia. 2001. A Latina Judge's Voice. Address to the "Raising the Bar" Symposium at the University of California at Berkeley School of Law. http://www.berkeley.edu/news/media/releases/2009/05/26_sotomayor.shtml (accessed September 21, 2010).

———. 2009. Opening Statement before the Senate Judiciary Committee. U.S. Senate Committee on the Judiciary, July 13.

Sowell, Thomas. 2010. Another Judicial Power Grab. *Human Events*. May 19. http://www.humanevents.com/article.php?id=37087 (accessed September 21, 2010).

Spaeth, Harold. 1961. An Approach to the Study of Attitudinal Differences as an Aspect of Judicial Behavior. *Midwest Journal of Political Science* 5, no. 2 (May): 165–80.

———. 1964. The Judicial Restraint of Mr. Justice Frankfurter: Myth or Reality. *American Journal of Political Science* 8, no. 1 (February): 22–38.

———. 1965. Jurimetrics and Professor Mendelson: A Troubled Relationship. *Journal of Politics* 27, no. 4 (November): 875–80.

———. 1979. *Supreme Court Policy Making: Explanation and Prediction*. San Francisco: W. H. Freeman.

———. 2009. United States Supreme Court Judicial Database. http://scdb.wustl.edu/ (accessed December 25, 2010).

Spaeth, Harold J., and Michael F. Altfeld. 1986. Felix Frankfurter, Judicial Activism, and Voting Conflict on the Warren Court. In Sheldon Goldman and

Charles M. Lamb, eds., *Judicial Conflict and Consensus*. Lexington: University Press of Kentucky.

Spaeth, Harold J., and Jeffrey A. Segal. 1999. *Majority Rule or Minority Will: Adherence to Precedent on the U.S. Supreme Court*. New York: Cambridge University Press.

Spiller, Pablo, and Rafael Gely. 1992. Congressional Control or Judicial Independence: The Determinants of U.S. Supreme Court Labor-Relations Decisions, 1949–1988. *RAND Journal of Economics* 23, no. 4 (Winter): 463–92.

Spriggs, James F., and Thomas G. Hansford. 2001. Explaining the Overruling of U.S. Supreme Court Precedent. *Journal of Politics* 63, no. 4 (November): 1091–1111.

Spriggs, James F., and Paul J. Wahlbeck. 1997. Amicus Curiae and the Role of Information in the Supreme Court. *Political Research Quarterly* 50, no. 2 (June): 365–86.

Starr, Kenneth. 2002. *First among Equals: The Supreme Court in American Life*. New York: Warner Books.

Staton, Jeffrey. 2006. Constitutional Review and the Selective Promotion of Case Results. *American Journal of Political Science* 50, no. 1 (January): 98–112.

Stephenson, Matthew C. 2009. Legal Realism for Economists. *Journal of Economic Perspectives* 23, no. 2 (Spring): 191–211.

Stevens, John Paul. 2000. Opinion of the Court in *Apprendi v. New Jersey*. No. 99-478. Decided June 26.

———. 2006a. Learning on the Job. *Fordham Law Review* 74, no. 4 (March): 1561–67.

———. 2006b. Statement respecting the denial of the petitions for writ of certiorari. *Rangel-Reyes v. United States*. No. 05-10706. Decided June 12.

Stewart, Potter. 1966. Dissent. *Ginzburg v. United States*, 383 U.S. 463.

Stimson, James, Michael Mackuen, and Robert Erikson. 1995. Dynamic Representation. *American Political Science Review* 89, no. 3 (September): 543–65.

Stolberg, Sheryl Gay. 2009. Sotomayor, a Trailblazer and a Dreamer. *New York Times*, May 26.

Stout, David. 2005. Bush Nominee Continues Effort to Win over Senators. *New York Times*, July 22.

Sullivan, Kathleen M. 1998. The Jurisprudence of the Rehnquist Court. *Nova Law Review* 22, no. 3 (Spring): 743–61.

Sunstein, Cass R. 1999. *One Case at a Time: Judicial Minimalism on the Supreme Court*. Cambridge, MA: Harvard University Press.

———. 2005. The Rehnquist Revolution. *The New Republic*, January 10, 32–54.

Tamanaha, Brian Z. 2010. *Beyond the Formalist-Realist Divide: The Politics of Judging*. Princeton: Princeton University Press.

Tanenhaus, Joseph, Marvin Schick, Matthew Muraskin, and Daniel Rosen. 1963. The Supreme Court's Certiorari Jurisdiction: Cue Theory. In Glendon Schubert, ed., *Judicial Decision-Making*. New York: The Free Press.

Taylor, Stuart. 2005. What Kind of Justice? *National Journal* 37, no. 30 (July 23): 2352–57.

Thayer, James. 1893. The Origin and Scope of the American Doctrine of Constitutional Law. *Harvard Law Review* 7, no. 3: 129–56.

200 REFERENCES

Thomas, Clarence. 2006. Dissent from the denial of certiorari. *Rangel-Reyes v. United States.* No. 05-10706. Decided June 12.

Tiller, Emerson, and Frank Cross. 2006. What Is Legal Doctrine? *Northwestern University Law Review* 100, no. 1: 517–34.

Toma, Eugenia Froedge. 1991. Congressional Influence and the Supreme Court: The Budget as a Signaling Device. *Journal of Legal Studies* 20, no. 1 (January): 131–46.

Toobin, Jeffrey. 2007. *The Nine: Inside the Secret World of the Supreme Court.* New York: Anchor Books.

Tribe, Laurence. 1985. *God Save This Honorable Court: How the Choice of Supreme Court Justices Shapes Our History.* New York: Random House.

Tsebelis, George. 2002. *Veto Players: How Political Institutions Work.* Princeton: Princeton University Press.

Turner, Kathryn. 1961. The Midnight Judges. *University of Pennsylvania Law Review* 109, no. 4 (February): 494–523.

Tushnet, Mark. 1999. *Taking the Constitution Away from the Courts.* Princeton: Princeton University Press.

———. 2005. *A Court Divided: The Rehnquist Court and the Future of Constitutional Law.* New York: W. W. Norton.

Ulmer, S. Sidney. 1973. Social Background as an Indicator to the Votes of Supreme Court Justices in Criminal Cases: 1947–1956 Terms. *American Journal of Political Science* 17, no. 3 (August): 622–30.

———. 1984. The Supreme Court's Certiorari Decisions: Conflict as a Predictive Variable. *American Political Science Review* 78, no. 4 (December): 901–11.

Ulmer, S. Sidney, and David Willison. 1985. The Solicitor General of the United States as Amicus Curiae in the U.S. Supreme Court: 1969–1983 Terms. Paper presented at the annual meeting of the American Political Science Association, New Orleans, Louisiana.

UM Lawyer. 2003. Subject to Interpretation. University of Mississippi, Spring/Summer edition. http://www.law.olemiss.edu/UM LAW SPR03/UMlaw/interpretation.htm (accessed November 20, 2007).

Urofsky, Melvin. 1991. *Felix Frankfurter: Judicial Restraint and Individual Liberties.* Boston: Twayne Publishers.

U.S. Congress. 1971. *Memorial Addresses and Other Tributes in the Congress of the United States on the Life and Contributions of Hugo LaFayette Black.* 92nd Cong., 1st Sess.

Wald, Patricia M. 1999. A Response to Tiller and Cross. *Columbia Law Review* 99, no. 1 (January): 235–61.

Ward, Artemus. 2003. *Deciding to Leave: The Politics of Retirement from the United States Supreme Court.* Albany: State University of New York Press.

Wechsler, Herbert. 1959. Toward Neutral Principles of Constitutional Law. *Harvard Law Review* 73, no. 1 (November): 1–35.

West, Diana. 2003. Bush Must Take a Stand on Affirmative Action. January 6. http://townhall.com/columnists/DianaWest/2003/01/06/bush_must_take_a_stand_on_affirmative_action (accessed September 21, 2010).

Whittingon, Keith. 1999. *Constitutional Construction: Divided Powers and Constitutional Meaning.* Cambridge, MA: Harvard University Press.

———. 2005. Congress before the Lochner Court. *Boston University Law Review* 85, no. 3 (Summer): 821–57.

———. 2009. *Political Foundations of Judicial Supremacy: The Presidency, the Supreme Court, and Constitutional Leadership in U.S. History.* Princeton: Princeton University Press.

Yalof, David A. 1999. *Pursuit of Justices: Presidential Politics and the Selection of Supreme Court Nominees.* Chicago: University of Chicago Press.

Zavodnyik, Peter. 2007. *The Age of Strict Construction: A History of the Growth of Federal Power, 1789–1861.* Washington, DC: Catholic University of America Press.

Zeppos, Nicholas S. 1993. Deference to Political Decisionmakers and the Preferred Scope of Judicial Review. *Northwestern University Law Review* 88, no. 1: 296–335.

INDEX

Abington v. Schempp, 165

abortion, 22, 34, 41, 56, 57; and bridge observations, 30; and inter-institutional examples, 30; and *Roe v. Wade,* 17; state regulation of, 11, 30

Abraham, Henry J. 1999, 17

Ackerman, Bruce. 1991, 153

Ackerman, Bruce. 2005, 96

ADA, 22, 176n5

Adams, John, 4, 95

Adams, John, Samuel Adams, and James Bowdoin. 1780, 4, 111

Adarand v. Pena, 164

ADA scores, 21, 37, 101–2

Adkins v. Children's Hospital (1923), 80

affirmative action, 35, 121

African Americans, 26, 169

Aiken, George, 111, 112

Akron v. Akron Center for Reproductive Health, 165

Alexander, Larry, and Frederick Schauer. 1997, 154

Alexander v. Holmes County, 165

Alito, Samuel, 175n1, 180n6, 182n7; and conservative v. liberal vote, 76; and deference, 75; and free speech, 75, 179n3, 179n12; ideal points for, 39; and precedent, 75, 77, 82, 84, 85; and separation of powers, 105; and solicitor general, 132, 133, 134, 135

Alito, Samuel. 2006, 10

Allegheny v. ACLU (1989), 167

Almendarez-Torres, Hugo, 64

Almendarez-Torres v. United States (1998), 64–65

American Civil Liberties Union (ACLU), 80

American Civil Rights Institute, 122

Americans for Democratic Action, 21

Ansolabehere, Stephen, James Snyder Jr., and Charles Stewart III. 2001, 37

anti-sodomy law, 47

anti-subversion acts, 80

appointment: lifetime, 6, 182n1; process of, 3

Apprendi v. New Jersey (2000), 64

Arnold, Douglas. 1990, 69

Ashbrook, John, 165

Atkins v. Virginia (2002), 27, 168

attitudinal model, 15, 49, 119, 143, 175n1; characteristics of, 4–6; and sentencing guideline cases, 65; and solicitor general, 124–25; and *Texas v. Johnson,* 140

Austin v. Michigan Chamber of Commerce (1990), 168

Bafumi, Joseph, Andrew Gelman, David Park, and Noah Kaplan. 2005, 156, 158

Bailey, Michael. 2001, 20, 31

Bailey, Michael. 2007, 18, 40, 80, 101, 102, 103, 141, 159, 175n1

Bailey, Michael, and Forrest Maltzman. 2008, 177n3, 179n8

Bailey, Michael, and Kelly Chang. 2001, 28, 32, 102, 176n12

Bailey, Michael, and Kelly Chang. 2003, 180n9

Bailey, Michael, Brian Kamoie, and Forrest Maltzman. 2005, 125, 181n2

Bailey v. Drexel Furniture (1922), 80

Baker, Frank. 1992, 27, 158, 176n10, 183n1

Baker v. Carr (1962), 161, 163, 167

Bank of the United States, 11–12

Barnes, Jeb. 2004, 5, 14

Barnes, Jeb. 2007, 83

Barnes, Robert. 2006, 67

Baucus, Max, 26, 118

Baum, Lawrence. 1988, 24

Baum, Lawrence. 1997, 7, 89, 175n3

Baum, Lawrence. 2006, 14, 124

Bawn, Kathleen, and Charles R. Shipan. 1997, 14

Bayesian Markov Chain Monte Carlo methods, 19, 33, 43, 70, 104, 131

Bayesian sampling, 32

Bayh, Evan, 26

Baze v. Rees (2008), 66

Benesh, Sara C., and Harold J. Spaeth. 2003, 71

Bentsen, Lloyd, 116

Berkowitz, Peter, and Benjamin Wittes. 2001, 1
Bickel, Alexander. 1962, 153
Biden, Joseph, 114
Bilbo, Theodore, 25, 26
Bill of Rights, 12, 66
Bingaman, Jeff. 2005, 10
birth control, 12
Biskupic, Joan. 2003, 121, 122
Black, Hugo, 81; and deference, 74, 75–76, 78, 82; and free speech, 74, 77, 79, 82; ideal points for, 39; and liberalism vs. conservatism, 89; and precedent, 74, 77, 82, 84; and *Schwartz v. Texas*, 167; and separation of powers, 105, 106, 107, 111, 112, 113, 119; and solicitor general, 132, 134, 135, 137, 138; as strict constructionist, 13; and strict interpretation of First Amendment, 68; and Truman, 124
Black, Hugo. 1969, 13, 68
Blackmun, Harry: and *Brown v. United States*, 167; and conservative vs. liberal vote, 76; and deference, 75, 76, 78, 82; and free speech, 75, 79, 82; ideal points for, 39; and precedent, 74, 75, 77, 82; and *Roe v. Wade*, 24; and separation of powers, 105, 106, 107, 113, 114, 115, 116, 119; and solicitor general, 132, 134, 135, 137, 138; and *Texas v. Johnson*, 140, 141; and *Webster v. Reproductive Health*, 24
Boot, Max. 1998, 1
Borah, William, 69
Bork, Robert, 1, 84, 181–82n5
Bork, Robert. 1990, 11, 12, 89
Bork Hearings I, 164
Bowers v. Hardwick (1986), 47, 178n4
Brandeis, Louis, 67, 68
Brandeis, Louis. 1932, 8
Brennan, William, 19, 81; and deference, 74, 75, 78, 82; and free speech, 74, 79, 82; ideal points for, 39, 40; and *Lee v. U.S.*, 167; and precedent, 74, 77, 82; and *Roe v. Wade*, 24; and separation of powers, 105, 106, 107, 111, 113, 114, 115, 119; and solicitor general, 132, 134, 135, 136, 137, 138; and strict interpretation of First Amendment, 68; and *Texas v. Johnson*, 140, 141; and *Webster v. Reproductive Health*, 24

Brenner, Saul, and Harold J. Spaeth. 1995, 6, 66
Brenner, Saul, and Joseph M. Whitmeyer. 2009, 175n4
Brenner, Saul, and Marc Stier. 1996, 178n5
Breyer, Stephen, 11; and *Almendarez-Torres v. United States*, 64; and *Bowers v. Hardwick*, 178n4; and conservative vs. liberal vote, 76; and deference, 75, 78, 82; and free speech, 75, 76, 79, 82; and *Gonzales v. Raich*, 51, 52; *and Granholm v. Heald*, 89; ideal points for, 39; and judicial restraint, 10, 179n11; and *Lawrence v. Texas*, 47; and legal values, 145; and precedent, 75, 77, 82; and *Rust v. Sullivan*, 183n2; and separation of powers, 105, 106, 107, 116, 118, 119; and solicitor general, 132, 135, 137, 138; and *Virginia v. Black*, 142
Breyer, Stephen. 2005, 3, 10
Breyer, Stephen. 2010, 95, 145
bridge observations, 170–73; across institutions, 19; and Congress, 36, 58, 60, 70; and legal doctrine, 65; and legal values, 159–60; method of, 27–31, 33, 34, 40–41, 43; and presidents, 70; and separation of powers, 102, 104, 109–10; and time, 19, 29
Brooke, Edward, 26
Brown v. Board of Education (1954), 31, 34, 35, 36, 37, 161, 163, 176n6
Brown v. United States (1959), 167
Buckley v. Valeo (1976), 162, 168
Bueno de Mesquita, Ethan, and Matthew Stephenson. 2002, 8, 66
Burbank, Stephen, and Barry Friedman, eds. 2002, 124
Burger, Warren, 12, 74; and conservative vs. liberal vote, 76; and deference, 75, 76, 78, 82; and free speech, 75, 79, 82; ideal points for, 39; and precedent, 75, 77, 82; and *Roe v. Wade*, 24; and separation of powers, 105, 106, 107, 114, 115, 119; and solicitor general, 132, 134, 135, 137, 138
Burger Court, 17, 18, 42, 90
Burton, Harold: and deference, 74, 75, 76, 78, 82; and free speech, 74, 79, 82; ideal points for, 39; and precedent, 74; and separation of powers, 105, 106, 107; and solicitor general, 132

Bush, George H. W., 25, 34–35, 159, 162
Bush, George W., 133, 162; and affirmative action, 121–23; and *Brown v. Board of Education*, 34; and *Bush v. Gore*, 1; and conservatism, 42, 48; and *Grutter v. Bollinger*, 35; and *Ledbetter v. Goodyear Tire & Rubber Company*, 99; and liberalism, 90; and separation of powers, 115, 117, 118; solicitors general of, 182n6; and strict constructionism, 12
Bush v. Gore (2000), 1–2, 6
busing, 26, 31
Byrd, Harry, 25–26, 113, 116

Cable Television Consumer Protection and Competition Act (1992), 159–60
Caldeira, Gregory A. 1986, 182n1
Caldeira, Gregory A., and John R. Wright. 1988, 96, 123, 124, 175n4
California, 50–51
Calvert, Randall. 1985, 127
Cameron, Charles, Donald Songer, and Jeffrey A. Segal. 2000, 128
campaign finance, 160, 162
Caplan, Lincoln. 1987, 124
Carter, Jimmy, 90, 113, 161, 181–82n5
Center for Equal Opportunity, 121
Chase, Salmon, 96
checks and balances, 13
Cheney, Richard, 114, 115, 124
child labor laws, 80
Church, Frank, 114, 115
Citizens United v. F.E.C (2010), 84
civil rights, 11, 30–31, 34, 41, 104, 130, 160, 178n3
Civil Rights Act (1957), 29
Civil Rights Act (1960), 29, 170
Civil Rights Act (1964), 29, 31, 41, 99, 169
Civil Rights Act (1991), 25, 30–31, 41
Civil Rights Restoration Act, 25
Clark, Tom C., 102, 180n5; and deference, 74, 76, 78, 82; and free speech, 74, 79, 82; ideal points for, 39; and precedent, 74, 75, 77, 82; and separation of powers, 105, 106, 107, 111; and solicitor general, 132, 133, 134, 135
Clark, Tom S. 2009, 97, 98, 101, 117
Clegg, Roger, 121, 122
Clinton, Josh, and Adam Meirowitz. 2001, 29, 70

Clinton, Josh, Simon Jackman, and Doug Rivers. 2004, 20, 31, 70, 158, 176n12
Clinton, William Jefferson, 35, 42, 90, 114–15, 162
Coburn, Tom, 165
Coburn, Tom. 2010, 12–13
Cohen, Adam. 2006, 124
Coleman, Mary Sue, 122
Cole v. Young, 163
Collins, Susan, 118
commerce clause, 66, 88, 89
common sense, 11
Common Space scores, 40, 41
communism, 80
Congress, 3, 21, 30, 32–33, 34; and bridge observations, 27–28, 58, 60, 70, 104; comments by members of, 159, 163–64, 165–66; constituencies of, 69; as constraining, ix; deference to, 10, 11, 15, 67, 164, 166; desire to avoid conflict with, 14; distribution of ideal points for, 174; and ideology, 68, 69, 88; influence of, x, 6, 153; inter-temporal preference estimation for, 24–25; and judicial restraint, 10; and justice according to morality, 12; and legal doctrine, 69; legitimacy of, 4; and positions on Supreme Court cases, 19; and precedent, 90; preference estimates for, 38; public approval of, 85; public positions of, 27–28; and restraint, 10; and Roberts, 10; roll call votes of, 37, 38, 68, 104, 159–60, 166, 168, 170, 178n3; and Roosevelt's Court packing plan, 96–97; and separation of powers, 13, 14, 103, 107, 108, 109–19, 120; statements on floor of, 37; strategic influence of, 155; threat of unfavorable reaction by, 98–101; votes of, 28, 36; voting vs. non-voting positions of, 37–38
Connerly, Ward, and Edward Blum. 2002, 122
conservatism, 20, 21, 23, 28, 40, 49, 50, 56, 59, 61; and affirmative action, 121–22; and *Almendarez-Torres v. United States*, 64; and Burger Court, 18, 42; and deference, 72; and First Amendment free speech principle, 72; and free speech, 85; and *Gonzales v. Raich*, 51, 52; and influence of elected branches, 153; and Martin and Quinn estimates, 24; and Martin and Quinn ideology scores, 17; and

conservatism (*cont.*)
    Nixon, 18; and originalism, 84; and precedent, 71; and Scalia, 74; and separation of powers, 89, 90, 91, 98, 99, 103, 104, 106, 107, 108, 110, 111, 112, 113, 114, 115, 116, 117, 118, 119; and solicitor general, 126, 127, 128, 129–30, 131, 133, 137
Constitution, 4, 66; amendments to, 11, 14, 108; and Bank of the United States, 11–12; commerce clause of, 88, 89; as contract, 12; coordinate construction of, 153; and judicial restraint, 9, 10, 11; and originalism, 84; originalist reading of, 11; and public opinion, 146–52; and strict constructionists, 12; and strict interpretation, 67; textualist reading of, 11
constitutional cases: and influence of elected branches, 153; and separation of powers, 97, 102, 103, 108, 120
constitutionality, 72, 166
constitutional order, 3, 5
Cooper, James L. 1990, 35
Cooperative Congressional Election Study (CCES), 146–52
Cox, Archibald, 35
Cox, Gary W., and Mathew D. McCubbins. 1993, 69
Crawford, Vincent, and Joel Sobel. 1982, 126, 127
crime, 34, 41
criminal procedure, 104, 129–30, 160, 178n3
criminal sentencing requirements, 64
Cross, Frank. 1997, 5, 7, 77, 88
Cross, Frank B., and Blake J. Nelson. 2001, 14
cross-burnings, 141–42

Dahl, Robert. 1957, 2
Daschle, Thomas, 116
Days, Drew. 1994, 35
Dean, John. 2001, 31, 34, 83, 181–82n5
death penalty, 17, 27, 29, 31, 66–67, 80
Debs, Eugene, 67–68
deference, x, 70, 73, 131, 164, 166, 171, 172, 173; changing importance of, 83; by individual justices, 74, 75–76, 78, 81, 82, 85; and judicial restraint, 9; and legal experience, 87; and liberalism vs. conservatism, 72; likelihood of, 15; and policy

change, 67; to solicitors general, 124; and textualists, 11; and Thomas, 67. *See also* restraint; separation of powers
Delay, Tom, 181n1
democracy, 2, 9, 66, 154
Democratic party, 25, 40, 41, 99, 109, 113; and judicial appointments, 101, 102; southern, 27, 36, 40, 41
Denver Area Educational Telecommunications Consortium v. Federal Communications Commission (1996), 159–60
DeParle, Jason. 2004, 26
Devins, Neal, and Louis Fisher. 2004, 153
Dickenson, Mollie. 2001, 1
Dickerson v. United States (2000), 2
Dirksen, Everett, 111, 112
District of Columbia v. Heller, 27
Dodd, Christopher, 111, 114, 115
Dole, Robert, 113, 114
Dorf, Michael. 2009, 51
Douglas, Paul, 36
Douglas, William O., 12, 81; and deference, 75–76, 78, 82; and free speech, 74, 79, 82; ideal points for, 39; and precedent, 74, 77, 82, 84; and *Roe v. Wade,* 24; and separation of powers, 105, 106, 107, 111, 113; and solicitor general, 132, 134, 135, 137, 138
Downs, Anthony. 1957, 20
drug testing, 169
Ducat, Craig R. 2004, 169
due process, 104, 130, 160, 178n3
due process clause, 47
Dunne, Gerald. 1977, 9, 69, 77, 88, 124
Dworkin, Ronald. 1978, 8, 66

Eastland, James, 25, 26, 40, 41, 111, 112, 114, 163
economy, 11, 34, 51, 89
educational testing, 27, 109
Edwards, Harry T. 1998, 2
Eisenhower, Dwight, 35, 112, 118
elected branches: influence of, 97–120. *See also* Congress; president
elected officials, ix, 7, 42; and bridge observations, 58, 63, 65; influence of, 4; and judicial restraint, 9, 10, 16; and legal values, 65, 88. *See also* bridge observations; deference; separation of powers
elections, 4; and separation of powers, 109–17

Ellender, Allen, 25, 41
Ely, John Hart. 1980, 10, 13, 80
Ely, John Hart. 1991, 4
Engel v. Vitale, 164
Epstein, Lee, and Jack Knight. 1995, 4
Epstein, Lee, and Jack Knight. 1998, 13, 95, 96, 98, 143, 175n4, 180n1
Epstein, Lee, and Jeffrey Segal. 2000, 117, 160
Epstein, Lee, and Jeffrey Segal. 2006, 85
Epstein, Lee, Andrew Martin, Jeffrey A. Segal, and Chad Westerland. 2007, 175n2
Epstein, Lee, Andrew Martin, Kevin M. Quinn, and Jeffrey Segal. 2009, 86
Epstein, Lee, Barry Friedman, and Nancy Staudt. 2008, 24
Epstein, Lee, Jack Knight, and Andrew Martin. 2004, 14, 108
Epstein, Lee, Jeffrey Segal, Harold Spaeth, and Thomas Walker. 2007, 2, 159
Epstein, Lee, Valerie Hoekstra, Jeffrey Segal, and Harold Spaeth. 1998, 32, 33
Escobedo v. Illinois (1964), 3
Eskridge, William. 1991, 13, 159, 180n1
Eskridge, William, John Ferejohn, and Neeta Gandhi. 2002, 13
Espionage Act, 67, 68
executive branch, 3; deference to, 11; influence of, 6; and judicial restraint, 9, 10; legitimacy of, 4. *See also* president
Exon, J. J., 25, 41
Ex parte Milligan (1866), 96

FEC v. Colorado Republican Fed. Campaign Comm. (2001), 168
FEC v. Wisconsin Right to Life (2007), 168
federalism, 51, 52, 85, 130
Federalist 78, 2
Federalists, 95
Federal Trade Commissioners, 96
Ferejohn, John. 1999, 13, 14
Ferejohn, John, and Barry Weingast. 1992, 7, 14, 98
Ferejohn, John, and Charles Shipan. 1990, 13, 98, 99
Ferejohn, John, and Larry Kramer. 2006, 9
First Amendment, 130, 160, 178n3, 179n6; and flag burning, 140; and liberal or conservative vote, 72; and precedent, 66; strict interpretation of, x, 13,

15, 65, 67–68; and *Texas v. Johnson,* 140; and *Virginia v. Black,* 142. *See also* freedom of speech; strict construction
First National Bank, 11
Fisher, Louis. 1988, 153
flag burning, 68, 72, 103, 140
Flag Protection Act, 103
Food Employees v. Logan Valley Plaza (1968), 167
Ford, Gerald, 181–82n5
Fortas, Abe, 17, 180n4; and conservative vs. liberal vote, 76; and deference, 75, 78, 82; and free speech, 75, 76, 79, 82; ideal points for, 39; and legal values, 73; and precedent, 75, 77, 82; and separation of powers, 105, 106, 107, 113, 119; and solicitor general, 132
Founders, 6
Fourteenth Amendment, 47
Fowler, Wyche, 160
Fraley, George III. 1996, 35
Frank, Jerome. 2009 [1930], 5
Franken, Al. 2009, 10
Frankfurter, Felix, 179n1, 180n4; and conservatism vs. liberalism, 88; and deference, 74, 75, 76, 78, 82; and free speech, 74, 79, 82; and Goldberg, 42; and Hughes, 69; ideal points for, 39; and judicial restraint, 9–10, 85; and liberal vs. conservative values, 80–81; and precedent, 74, 77, 82, 84; and separation of powers, 105, 106, 107, 111; and solicitor general, 132
Frankfurter, Felix. 1938, 81
freedom of speech, 34, 41, 70, 72, 73, 74, 76–77, 81, 131, 172, 173, 179n6; and Alito and Roberts, 179nn3, 12; and Court ideology vs. Congress and presidents, 90–91; emphasis on, 85; and Espionage Act, 68; ideal points for, 39; and legal experience, 87; and liberals vs. conservatives, 85; protection of, 85; and separation of powers, 102, 103; steady postwar importance of, 83; and strict construction, 13; and *Texas v. Johnson,* 140–41. *See also* First Amendment; strict construction
Fried, Charles, 35
Friedman, Barry. 1990, 14
Friedman, Barry. 1998, 14
Friedman, Barry. 2006, 1, 4, 70

Friedman, Barry. 2009, 3, 13, 68, 69, 80, 81, 84, 85, 89, 91, 99
Fulbright, William, 111, 112
Fullilove v. Klutznick, 161
Furman v. Georgia (1972), 3, 17, 31, 163

Galanter, Marc. 1974, 124
Gale Cengage Learning. 2005, 71
Garbus, Martin. 2002, 89
Gash, Alison, and Michael Murakami. 2009, 145–46
Gelman, Andrew, John Carlin, Hal Stern, and Donald Rubin. 1995, 157, 158
Gely, Rafael, and Pablo Spiller. 1990, 13, 98
George, Tracy E., and Lee Epstein. 1992, 8, 66
Gerhardt, Michael. 2008, 84, 141
Gewirtz, Paul, and Chad Golder. 2005, 179n11
Geyh, Charles. 2006, 124
Gibson, James. 1977, 7
Gibson, James. 1978, 7
Gibson, James. 1983, 7
Gibson, James. 1997, 159
Gibson, James L., Gregory A. Caldeira, and Vanessa A. Baird. 1998, 182n1, 183n5
Gillman, Howard. 2001, 6, 50
Gillman, Howard, and Cornell Clayton. 1999, 7, 8, 66
Ginsburg, Ruth Bader, 81; and *Almendarez-Torres v. United States,* 64; and conservative vs. liberal vote, 76; and deference, 75, 78, 82; and free speech, 75, 79, 82, 85; and *Gonzales v. Raich,* 51, 52; and *Granholm v. Heald,* 89; ideal points for, 39; and *Lawrence v. Texas,* 47; and precedent, 75, 77, 82; and separation of powers, 105, 106, 107, 116, 118, 119; and solicitor general, 132, 135, 137, 138; and *Virginia v. Black,* 142
Ginsburg Bowers v. Hardwick, 178n4
Glick, Henry, and Kenneth Vines. 1969, 7
Gnagey, Laurel Thomas. 2003, 122
Goldberg, Arthur, 42, 81, 180n6; and conservative vs. liberal vote, 76; and deference, 74, 78, 82; and free speech, 74, 79, 82; ideal points for, 39; and *Kent v. Dulles,* 167; and precedent, 74, 77, 82; and separation of powers, 105; and solicitor general, 132–33

Goldberg, Carey. 1996, 51
Goldstein, Thomas C. 2007, 75
Gonzales, Alberto, 35, 122
Gonzales v. Raich (2005), 50–52
Goodyear, 99
Granholm v. Heald (2005), 88–89
Grassley, Charles, 116
Gratz, Jennifer, 121
Gratz v. Bollinger, 122–23
Greene, William. 2000, 38
Greenhouse, Linda. 2003, 123
Gregg, Judd, 116
Gregg v. Georgia (1976), 31
Griswold, Erwin, 36, 181–82n5
Griswold v. Connecticut (1965), 12, 164
Groseclose, Timothy, Steven Levitt, and James Snyder. 1999, 21
Grove City College v. Bell, 165
Grutter, Barbara, 121
Grutter v. Bollinger, 35, 122–23
gun control, 27

Hagle, Tim, and Harold Spaeth. 1992, 4
Hagle, Tim, and Harold Spaeth. 1993, 4
Hamilton, Alexander, 11
Hamilton, Alexander, James Madison, and John Jay. 2011, 6
Hammond, Thomas H., Chris W. Bonneau, and Reginald S. Sheehan. 2005, 143
Hansford, Thomas G., and David F. Damore. 2000, 97, 101
Hansford, Thomas G., and James F. Spriggs. 2006, 8, 9, 66–67
Harlan, John Marshall, II, 10; and deference, 67, 74, 78, 82; and free speech, 74, 79, 82; ideal points for, 38, 39, 40; and precedent, 74, 77, 82; and separation of powers, 105, 106, 107, 111, 113; and solicitor general, 132, 133, 134, 135
Harlan, John Marshall. 1964, 67
Harper v. Virginia Board of Elections (1966), 12
Harvard Law Review, 160
Harvey, Anna, and Barry Friedman. 2006, 97, 101, 102, 103, 108
Harvey, Anna, and Barry Friedman. 2009, 97, 101, 102
Harvey, Anna, and Michael Woodruff. 2011, 97, 101, 176n15
Hatch, Orrin, 114, 116

Hausegger, Lori, and Lawrence Baum. 1999, 67
Heinemann, Ronald L. 1996, 26
Helms, Jesse, 25, 114, 115, 159
Hirsch, H. N. 1981, 180n4
Hoekstra, Valerie J. 2000, 182n1
Hollings, Fritz, 25, 26, 33, 40, 41, 113, 176n6
Holmes, Oliver Wendell, Jr., 9, 67–68, 81, 179n2
homosexuals, 47
Hoover, Herbert, 180n4
House of Representatives, 32, 98, 99, 103, 114, 115
Howard, Robert, and Jeffrey A. Segal. 2004, 76
Howe, M. D. 1953, 9
Hudgens v. NLRB (1976), 167
Hughes, Charles Evans, 69
Humphrey, Hubert, 111, 112
Humphrey's Executor v. United States (1935), 96
Hurley v. Irish American Gay, Lesbian and Bisexual Group of Boston (1995), 162
Hutchison, Kathryn Ann Bailey, 118

ideal point, 48–49
identification, 15; and bridge observations, 58, 60, 62; and legal values and policy preferences, 53–55; and non-Court actors, 58–62, 63
ideology, ix, 15, 20, 53, 68, 175n1; and Congress, 68, 69, 88; and *Gonzales v. Raich,* 52; and legal factors, 48; measurement of, 15; and policy, 62–63; and presidents, 68, 69; and solicitor general, 125, 126, 129, 136, 137, 139; and *Texas v. Johnson,* 140; and *Virginia v. Black,* 141–42
income tax, 80
institutional boundaries, 43
institutional constraint, 16
institutional position, 7
institutions, comparison across, 18–19, 20–22, 23, 27, 30, 102

Jackman, Simon. 2000, 19, 157
Jackson, Robert, 81, 180n6; and deference, 74; and free speech, 74, 79, 82; ideal points for, 39; and legal values, 73; and

precedent, 74; and separation of powers, 105; and solicitor general, 132
Jaffee v. Redmond (1996), 125
Javits, Jacob, 163
Jefferson, Thomas, 11–12, 95
Jefferson administration, 96
Johnson, Gregory Lee, 68, 140
Johnson, Lyndon, 17, 180n4, 181–82n5
Johnson, Timothy R. 2003, 123
Johnson, Valen, and James Albert. 1999, 157, 158
Jones, W., 25
judicial review, 95
Judiciary Act (1789), 96
Judiciary Act (1801), 95
Judiciary Act (1802), 95
jury deliberations, 88

Kagan, Elena, 6–7, 13, 69
Kagan, Elena. 2010, 7, 10, 69
Kahn, Ronald. 1999, 7, 8, 9, 66, 89
Karcher v. Daggett (1983), 167
Kastellec, Jonathan P., and Jeffrey Lax. 2008, 57
Katcher, Leo. 1967, 81
Kearney, Joseph, and Thomas Merrill. 2000, 123, 125, 175n4
Kefauver, Estes, 163
Kelo v. New London, 166
Kennedy, Anthony: and *Almendarez-Torres v. United States,* 64; and *Bush v. Gore,* 1; and *Casey,* 75; and conservative vs. liberal vote, 76; and deference, 75–76, 78, 82; and Delay, 181n1; and free speech, 75, 79, 82; and *Gonzales v. Raich,* 51, 52; and *Granholm v. Heald,* 89; ideal points for, 39; and judicial restraint, 179n11; and *Lawrence v. Texas,* 47; and *Lynch v. Donnelly,* 167; and precedent, 75, 77, 82; and *Roe v. Wade,* 75; and *Roper v. Simmons,* 36; and separation of powers, 105, 106, 107, 115, 116, 118; and solicitor general, 132, 134, 135, 136, 137, 138; and *Stanford v. Kentucky,* 36; and *Texas v. Johnson,* 140, 141, 142; and *Virginia v. Black,* 142; and *Webster v. Reproductive Health,* 24
Kennedy, Edward, 25, 116, 163, 177n20
Kennedy, John, 35, 112, 118, 161, 181n11
Kent v. Dulles (1958), 167
Kerrey, Joseph Robert, 118

Kirkpatrick v. Preisler (1969), 167
Knight, Jack, and Lee Epstein. 1996, 8, 95
Krauthammer, Charles. 2009, 144
Krehbiel, Keith. 1998, 99
Krehbiel, Keith. 2007, 102
Kronman, Anthony. 2006, 9
Kyl, Jon. 2009, 144

labor rulings, 101
Landes, William, and Richard Posner.
    1975, 8
Lawrence, John, 47
Lawrence v. Texas (2003), 47, 67, 178n4
Laxalt, Paul, 164
Leahy, Patrick, 115, 116
Leahy, Patrick. 2005, 10
Leahy, Patrick. 2009, 144–45
Ledbetter, Lilly, 99
*Ledbetter v. Goodyear Tire & Rubber
    Company* (2007), 99
Lee, Rex, 35
Lee v. Florida (1968), 167
Lee v. U.S. (1952), 167
Lee v. Weisman (505 U.S. 577), 169
Lee v. Weisman (1992), 35, 164
legal doctrine, 143; as affecting most jus-
    tices, 73; and bridge observations, 65;
    and difference from elected officials, 58;
    and elected officials, 65; as guiding deci-
    sions, ix, 2, 7, 64–79; and historical re-
    gimes, 81–86; and ideological behavior,
    15; modeling and estimating the role of,
    68–70; and policy positions, 91, 154. *See
    also* legal values; precedent; stare decisis;
    strict construction
Legal Information Institute, 160
legalism, 143, 144, 147
legal realism, 5, 6
legal values, x, 2, 6–13; and bridge obser-
    vations from Congress, 58, 60; causes
    and consequences of diverse, 80–92;
    conflicting, 11, 78; data on, 70–72; as
    evolving, 85–86; and experience, 86–87,
    91–92; and *Gonzales v. Raich,* 51; het-
    erogeneity in, 78; and historical regimes,
    81–86; and ideology, 48; importance of,
    143–52; as influential for most justices,
    78; and non-Court actors, 130; and pol-
    icy, 15, 47–64, 83; and politics, 85; and
    public opinion, 146–52; Segal and Spa-
    eth's test for, 55–58; and sentencing

guideline cases, 65; and separation of
    powers, 102–3, 119; and *Texas v. John-
    son,* 140; and unanimity, 3; using non-
    court actors to identify the effect of,
    58–62. *See also* legal doctrine
lethal injections, 66
Levi, Edward H. 1949, 8, 66
Levin, Mark R. 2005, 89
Levinson, Sanford. 1977, 81
Levy, Leonard, 69
Lewis, Anthony. 2009, 68
Lewis, John. 2003, 121
Li, Hao, and Suen Wing. 2004, 126
liberalism, 18, 20, 21, 23, 28, 40, 42, 49,
    50, 56, 59, 61; and *Almendarez-Torres v.
    United States,* 64; and deference, 72; and
    First Amendment free speech principle,
    72; and free speech, 85; and *Gonzales v.
    Raich,* 51, 52; and influence of elected
    branches, 153; and Martin and Quinn
    ideology scores, 17; and New Deal, 91;
    and precedent, 71, 84; and separation of
    powers, 90, 91, 98, 99, 101, 103, 104,
    106, 108, 109, 110, 111, 112, 113, 114,
    115, 116, 117, 118, 119; and solicitor
    general, 126, 127, 128, 130, 131, 132–
    33, 137; and Souter, 84; and *Virginia v.
    Black,* 141, 142
Lieberman, Joseph, 164
Lilly Ledbetter Fair Pay Act of 2009,
    180n3
Lindquist, Stefanie, and Frank Cross. 2009,
    17, 76, 90, 175n2, 180n6
Lindquist, Stefanie, and Rorie Spill Solberg.
    2007, 78
Liptak, Adam. 2009, 86, 154
Liptak, Adam. 2010, 17
Llewellyn, Karl, 97
Llewellyn, Karl. 1962, 5
Lochner v. New York (1905), 3, 80, 179n2
Londregan, John. 1999, 29
loose construction, 11
Lopez v. U.S. (1962), 167
Lott, Trent, 116
Loughlin, Sean. 2003, 37
*Louisville Joint Stock Land Bank v. Rad-
    ford* (1935), 96
Lynch v. Donnelly (1984), 161, 167

Madison, James, 95
Mallory v. U.S., 163

Maltzman, Forrest, James F. Spriggs, and Paul J. Wahlbeck. 1999, 5
Maltzman, Forrest, James F. Spriggs, and Paul J. Wahlbeck. 2000, 143, 175n4, 181n10
Marbury, William, 95–96
Marbury v. Madison (1803), 95–96, 120
marijuana, 50–52
Marks, Brian. 1989, 14, 180n1
Marshall, John, 95–96
Marshall, Thurgood, 4, 102, 180n5; and conservative vs. liberal vote, 76; and deference, 78, 82; and *Food Employees v. Logan Valley Plaza,* 167; and free speech, 75, 79, 82; ideal points for, 39; and precedent, 75, 77, 82, 179n4; and *Roe v. Wade,* 24; and separation of powers, 105, 106, 107, 113, 114, 115, 119; and solicitor general, 132, 134, 135, 136, 137, 138; and *Texas v. Johnson,* 140, 141; and *Webster v. Reproductive Health,* 24
Martin, Andrew. 2006, 101
Martin, Andrew, and Kevin Quinn, 17–18, 19, 22, 24, 26, 33, 40, 43, 175n4, 176n5, 176n7
Martin, Andrew, and Kevin Quinn. 2002, 17, 32, 34, 80, 141, 175n2
Martin, Andrew, and Kevin Quinn. 2009, 40
Martin, Andrew, Kevin Quinn, and Lee Epstein. 2005, 20
Mason, Alpheus Thomas. 1956, 180n4
Massachusetts Constitution of 1780, 4
Mazzoli, Romano, 165
McCain, John, 147, 148
McCain-Feingold campaign finance bill, 166
McCardle, William, 96
McCarthy, Joseph, 163
McCarty, Nolan, and Keith Poole. 1995, 36
McConnell, Mitch, 166
McConnell v. FEC (2003), 72
McGovern, George, 163
McGowan, Miranda O. 2008, 65
McGuire, Kevin. 1998, 123, 124
McGuire, Kevin, and James Stimson. 2004, 143
McNollgast. 1995, 14
Meernik, James, and Joseph Ignagni. 1997, 101

Meinhold, Stephen S., and Steven A. Shull. 1998, 35
Merrill, Thomas W., 123, 124
Mikulski, Barbara, 165
Milliken v. Bradley (418 U.S. 717), 169
minimum wage, 3, 80, 97
Minnesota v. Carter (525 U.S. 83), 169
Minnesota v. Olson (495 U.S. 91), 169
minorities, 11, 31
Minton, Sherman, 180n6; and deference, 74, 75, 78, 82; and free speech, 74, 79, 82; ideal points for, 39; and precedent, 74; and separation of powers, 105; and solicitor general, 132
Miranda v. Arizona (1966), 2, 3
Mishler, William, and Reginald Sheehan. 1993, 143, 175n4
Mishler, William, and Reginald Sheehan. 1996, 143
Mislevy, Robert, and R. Darrell Bock. 1990, 158
Mondale, Walter, 113
morality, 12
Moraski, Bryon, and Charles Shipan. 1999, 21, 102
Morehead v. New York (1936), 80
Morella, Connie, 19
Moseley-Braun, Carol, 164
Murphy, Bruce Allen. 1988, 180n4
Murphy, Walter. 1962, 34
Murphy, Walter. 1964, 7, 13, 14, 98, 108, 143
Murray, Frank. 2003, 121, 122
Mushroom Promotion, Research and Consumer Information Act (1990), 100
Muskie, Edmund, 114

National Industrial Recovery Act, 80, 96
National Labor Relations Act, 97
National Labor Relations Board v. Jones & Laughlin (1937), 97
National-Republicans, 95
National Treasury Employees v. Von Raab (489 U.S. 656), 169
Nelson, Ben, 116
Nemachek, Christine. 2008, 102
New Deal, 3, 34, 69, 80, 81, 84, 89, 91, 96, 97
New York Times, 117, 162, 176n15
Nicholson, Chris, and Paul Collins. 2008, 129

Nixon, Richard, 12, 17, 18, 36, 83, 112, 161, 181–82n5
Nixon, Richard. 1969, 12
Noel, Hans. 2009, 88
Norman-Major, Kristen A. 1994, 35
Novak, Robert. 2003, 35, 122

Obama, Barack, 48, 147, 148, 180n3
O'Brien, David M. 2000, 95
O'Brien, David M. 2003, 31
O'Connor, Karen. 1983, 123
O'Connor, Sandra Day, 181n1; and *Almendarez-Torres v. United States,* 64; and *Bush v. Gore,* 1; and *Casey,* 75; and conservative vs. liberal vote, 76; and deference, 75–76, 78, 82; and free speech, 75, 79, 82; and *Gonzales v. Raich,* 51, 52; and *Granholm v. Heald,* 89; ideal points for, 38, 39, 40; and *Lawrence v. Texas,* 47; and precedent, 73–74, 75, 77, 82, 179–80n4, 179n10; and separation of powers, 105, 106, 107, 115, 116, 118, 119; and solicitor general, 132, 134, 135, 136, 137, 138; and *Texas v. Johnson,* 140, 141; and *Virginia v. Black,* 142; and *Webster v. Reproductive Health,* 24
Olsen, Ted, 122
originalism, 11, 66, 84, 85

Packwood, Robert, 113, 114
Page, Scott E. 2007, 154
Peabody, Bruce. 2005, 69
Penry v. Lynaugh (1989), 27
Percy, Charles, 163
Peretti, Terri Jennings. 1999, 4, 9, 14, 98
Perry, H. W., Jr. 1991, 124
Phillips v. Washington Legal Foundation, 166
Pickerill, J. Mitchell. 2004, 69
Pickering, John, 95
Pinello, Daniel R. 2003, 47
Planned Parenthood v. Ashcroft (1983), 56
Planned Parenthood v. Casey (1992), 29, 75, 168
policy, ix, x, 3, 4, 6, 18; and attitudinal model, 5; and bridge observations from Congress, 58, 60; changing, 26; and *Gonzales v. Raich,* 51; and ideology, 62–63; implications for Supreme Court cases, 70; as influencing legal values, 83;

and legal model claim, 7; and legal values, 15, 48–53; motivation by, 15–16; precedent to indirectly pursue, 8–9; and sentencing guideline cases, 65; and separation of powers, 13
political science, 86, 154–55
Pollack v. Farmers Loan and Trust (1895), 80
poll taxes, 12
Poole, Keith, 177n20
Poole, Keith. 1998, 25, 36
Poole, Keith. 2004, 25
Poole, Keith, and Howard Rosenthal, 22, 26, 41, 43, 175nn2, 4, 176n5, 178n3
Poole, Keith, and Howard Rosenthal. 1997, 19, 20, 24–25, 33, 37, 69, 88, 176n8
Posner, Richard. 2005, 5
Posner, Richard. 2008, 7, 17, 143, 179n2
Pound, Roscoe, 97
Powell, Lewis: and conservative vs. liberal vote, 76; and deference, 75, 76, 78, 82; and free speech, 75, 79, 82; ideal points for, 39; and *Kirkpatrick v. Preisler,* 167; and precedent, 75, 77, 82; and *Roe v. Wade,* 24; and separation of powers, 105, 106, 107, 113–14, 115, 119; and solicitor general, 132, 134, 135, 137, 138
precedent, x, 6, 70, 71–72, 85, 131, 162, 164, 179–80n4, 179n10; and *Almendarez-Torres v. United States,* 64–65; and Blackmun, 74; and bridge observations, 65, 171, 172, 173; after Burger as Chief Justice, 74–75; changing importance of, 83, 84; and comments by justices, 178n4; and Court ideology vs. Congress and presidents, 90; and identification problem, 60, 61, 62; influence of, 154; instrumental value of, 66; and Kennedy, 75; and legal experience, 87; and liberalism vs. conservatism, 91; and liberal or conservative vote, 71; and New Dealers, 84; and O'Connor, 73–74; and originalism, 84; and political context, 84; and Scalia, 65, 74, 75; Segal and Spaeth test for effect of, 55–58; and Stevens, 65, 66; and Thomas, 65, 74–75; and Tom C. Clark, 75; and White, 75
president, 23, 42, 99; and bridge observations, 19, 34–35, 70, 104; comments of,

161–62; data on, 33, 34–36; deference to, 15; desire to avoid conflict with, 14; and ideology, 68, 69; influence of, ix, x, 6, 153; and justice according to morality, 12; positions on Senate and House votes, 36; and precedent, 90; preference estimates for, 38; and separation of powers, 13, 14, 103, 107, 109, 117, 119, 120; and solicitor general, 35–36, 121–39, 181–82n5; strategic influence of, 155; threat of unfavorable reaction by, 98–101
privacy, 12, 34, 47, 104, 130, 160, 169, 178n3
Provine, Doris Marie. 1980, 123
public opinion, 15, 32, 100, 143, 145–52, 183nn2, 3, 4
Puro, Steven. 1981, 123

Quillen, James, 165

race, 34
racial covenants, 12
Ramstad, James, 166
Rangel, Charles, 165
Rangel-Reyes v. United States (2006), 65
rational choice, 7, 100
Reagan, Ronald, 35, 90, 114, 161
Reed, Stanley, 81, 180n6; and deference, 74, 75, 78, 82, 85; and free speech, 74, 79, 82; ideal points for, 39; and precedent, 74; and separation of powers, 105; and solicitor general, 132
Regents of the University of California v. Bakke (1978), 3, 160
regime theory, 83
Rehnquist, William, 2, 4, 83; and *Almendarez-Torres v. United States,* 64; and *Bush v. Gore,* 1; and conservative vs. liberal vote, 76; and deference, 75, 78, 82; and free speech, 75, 76, 79, 82; and *Gonzales v. Raich,* 51–52; and *Granholm v. Heald,* 89; ideal points for, 38, 39; and *Lawrence v. Texas,* 47; and legal vs. policy perspective, 154; and precedent, 75, 77, 82; and *Roe v. Wade,* 24, 168; and separation of powers, 105, 106, 107, 114, 115, 116, 118; and solicitor general, 132, 134, 135, 136, 137, 138; and *Stanford v. Kentucky,* 168; and *Texas v. Johnson,* 140, 141; and *United Steel Workers v. Weber,* 178n4; and *Virginia v. Black,* 142; and *Webster v. Reproductive Health,* 24
Rehnquist, William. 1987, 96, 97
Reid, Harry, 26
religion, 34
religious freedom, 169
Republican party, 102, 113, 114, 115
restraint, 9–11, 15, 16, 107, 166, 175n3, 179n11; and bridge observations, 65; changing emphasis on, 85; and conditions, 10; and legitimacy, 9; and separation of powers, 102. *See also* deference
Richards, Mark J., and Herbert Kritzer. 2002, 66
Riegle, Donald, 165
right to life amendment, 30
Roberts, John G., Jr., 175n1, 180n6; and conservative vs. liberal vote, 76; and deference, 75; and experience, 86–87; and free speech, 75, 179nn3, 12; ideal points for, 39; and judicial deference, 67; and legal values, 143–44; and legal vs. policy perspective, 154; and precedent, 75, 77, 82, 84–85; and separation of powers, 105; and solicitor general, 132, 133, 134, 135; as strict constructionist, 12
Roberts, John G. 2003, 10, 143–44
Roberts, Owen, 3
Robertson, Pat. 2004, 89
Roe v. Wade (1973), 17, 22–24, 37, 161, 163, 165, 168; and Kennedy, 75; and *Planned Parenthood v. Ashcroft,* 56; and states, 30; and Thomas, 29, 36; and *Webster v. Reproductive Health,* 71
Rogers, James. 2001, 101, 154
Rohde, David W., and Harold J. Spaeth. 1976, 4
Romer v. Evans (1996), 47
Roosevelt, Franklin, 3, 80, 89, 96–97, 180n4
Roper v. Simmons (2005), 36, 176n9
Rosen, Jeffrey. 2000, 1
Rosen, Jeffrey. 2006, 4, 9
Rosenberg, Gerald. 1991, 14, 98
Rosenberg, Gerald. 1992, 108
Roth, William, 114, 115
Rove, Karl, 121
Russell, Richard, Jr., 25
Rust v. Sullivan (1991), 183n2

Sacco, Nicola, 80
Sala, Brian R., and James F. Spriggs II. 2004, 97, 101
Salokar, Rebecca. 1992, 36, 123, 124, 181–82n5
Sammon, Bill. 2003, 121, 122
Santorum, Richard, 37, 116, 177n16
Scalia, Antonin, 20, 81, 102, 181n1; and *Almendarez-Torres v. United States,* 64; and amicus briefs, 125; and *Austin v. Michigan Chamber of Commerce,* 168; and Bush, 182n6; and *Bush v. Gore,* 1; and conservatism, 74; and conservative vs. liberal vote, 76; and deference, 75–76, 78, 82; and free speech, 75, 79, 82, 85; friendships of, 124; and *Gonzales v. Raich,* 51–52; and *Granholm v. Heald,* 89; ideal points for, 39; and judicial restraint, 179n11; and jury deliberations, 88; and *Lawrence v. Texas,* 47; and originalism, 88; and precedent, 74, 75, 77, 82, 84; and public opinion about legal values, 147–50; and sentencing guideline cases, 65; and separation of powers, 105, 106, 107, 115, 116, 118; and social relationships, 100; and solicitor general, 132, 135, 136, 137, 138; and strict constructionism, 68; and *Texas v. Johnson,* 140, 141; and textualism, 12; and *Virginia v. Black,* 142; and *Webster v. Reproductive Health,* 24
Scalia, Antonin. 1998, 11, 65
Scalia, Antonin. 2003, 75
Scalia, Antonin. 2004, 100
Schechter Poultry v. United States (1935), 80, 96
Schiavo, Terri, 100
Schlesinger, Arthur, 76
school prayer, 26
Schwartz v. Texas (1952), 167
Scigliano, Robert. 1971, 124
search and seizure, 88
Segal, Jeffrey A., and Harold Spaeth, 55–58
Segal, Jeffrey, Chad Westerland, and Stefanie Lindquist. 2007, 101
Segal, Jeffrey A., 175n3
Segal, Jeffrey A. 1988, 123, 124
Segal, Jeffrey A. 1989, 35, 181n5
Segal, Jeffrey A. 1997, 21, 97, 100, 101, 102, 103
Segal, Jeffrey A., and Albert Cover. 1989, 4, 21

Segal, Jeffrey A., and Cheryl D. Reedy. 1988, 123
Segal, Jeffrey A., and Harold J. Spaeth. 1993, 1–2, 4, 6, 175nn1, 4
Segal, Jeffrey A., and Harold J. Spaeth. 1994, 3
Segal, Jeffrey A., and Harold J. Spaeth. 1996, 55, 66, 178n5
Segal, Jeffrey A., and Harold J. Spaeth. 2002, 5, 6, 7, 14–15, 125
Segal, Jeffrey A., and Robert M. Howard. 2005, 71
segregation, 26, 27, 169
Senate, 23, 30, 32, 36, 38, 98, 99; evolution of preferences of, 42; public statements and amicus filings of, 38; and separation of powers, 103, 110, 115
sentencing guidelines, 65
separation of church and state, 88
separation of powers, 13–14, 15, 16, 95–120, 175n4; and attitudinal model, 143; and comparison across institutions, 18–19; and cross-institutionally comparable preference measures, 101; and election periods, 109–17; models of, 97–101; skeptics of, 99–100; and statutory vs. constitutional cases, 103; and strategic behavior, 13, 14, 100, 101, 102; and strategic constraints, 103. *See also* deference
Shaw v. Hunt, 162
Shelley v. Kramer (1948), 12
Shepsle, Kenneth A., and David Rohde. 2007, 102
signaling model, 15, 16, 136, 137
signaling theory, 126, 139
Simpson, Alan K., 164
Sixth Amendment, 64, 88
Skinner v. Railway Labor Exec. Assoc., 162
Slochower v. Board of Education, 163
Smith, J. 1996, 95
Smith, Margaret, 113
Smith, Rogers M. 1988, 7
Smith Act of 1940, 80
solicitor general, 15, 121–39, 143, 181nn3, 4, 182n6; amicus briefs of, 123, 124, 125, 126–27, 130, 131, 132–33, 159, 181n5; case selection by, 129; general success of, 123–26; as ideological signal, 126–29; influence of, 138–39; information from, x, 125–29, 130; and judicial

deference, 124; and president, 35–36, 181–82n5; signaling influence of, 155; and signaling model, 125–26

Songer, Donald, and Stefanie Lindquist. 1996, 178n5

Soros, George, 51

Sotomayor, Sonia, 144–45

Sotomayor, Sonia. 2001, 144

Sotomayor, Sonia. 2009, 10

Souter, David, 81; and *Almendarez-Torres v. United States,* 64; and *Casey,* 75; and conservative vs. liberal vote, 76; and deference, 75, 78, 82; and free speech, 75, 79, 82, 85; and *Gonzales v. Raich,* 51, 52; and *Granholm v. Heald,* 89; ideal points for, 38, 39, 40; and *Lawrence v. Texas,* 47; and liberalism, 84; and precedent, 75, 77, 82, 84; and separation of powers, 105, 106, 107, 115, 116, 118, 119; and solicitor general, 132, 134, 135, 136–37, 138; and *Virginia v. Black,* 142

Southern Manifesto, 26, 36

Sowell, Thomas. 2010, 1

Spaeth, Harold, 180n7

Spaeth, Harold. 1961, 4

Spaeth, Harold. 1964, 4

Spaeth, Harold. 1965, 5

Spaeth, Harold. 1979, 4, 6

Spaeth, Harold. 2006, 72

Spaeth, Harold. 2009, 36, 71, 160, 162, 164, 178n3, 178n5

Spaeth, Harold J., and Jeffrey A. Segal. 1999, 6, 55, 56, 66

Spaeth, Harold J., and Jeffrey A. Segal. 2001, 8

Spaeth, Harold J., and Michael F. Altfeld. 1986, 80

Sparkman, John, 111, 112

Specter, Arlen, 115, 116

Spiller, Pablo, and Rafael Gely. 1992, 13, 101, 180n1

Spriggs, James F., and Paul J. Wahlbeck. 1997, 124

Spriggs, James F., and Thomas G. Hansford. 2001, 97, 101

Stanford v. Kentucky (1989), 29–30, 36, 168, 176n9

stare decisis, 32, 57, 60, 61, 66–67, 71, 178n4; and *Almendarez-Torres v. United States,* 65; influence of, 15; and liberalism vs. conservatism, 91; and political

context, 84; principle of, 8–9; and separation of powers, 102

Starr, Kenneth. 2002, 5, 154, 181n4

states, 9, 30, 85, 89

statistical details, 156–74

statistical model, 31–33

Staton, Jeffrey. 2006, 182n1

statutory cases, 98; and influence of elected branches, 153; and separation of powers, 97, 101, 103–8, 120

Stearns, Cliff, 166

Stenholm, Charles, 25, 177n20

Stennis, John, 114, 115

Stephenson, Matthew C. 2009, 5, 6, 62

Stevens, John Paul, 20; and *Almendarez-Torres v. United States,* 64–65; and *Baker v. Carr,* 167; and *Baze v. Rees,* 66; and conservative vs. liberal vote, 76; and deference, 75, 78, 81, 82; and free speech, 75, 79, 82; and *Gonzales v. Raich,* 51, 52; and *Granholm v. Heald,* 89; ideal points for, 38, 39, 40; and *Lawrence v. Texas,* 47; and precedent, 75, 77, 82; and *Rangel-Reyes v. United States,* 65; and sentencing guideline cases, 65; and separation of powers, 105, 106, 107, 114, 115, 116, 118, 119; and solicitor general, 132, 134, 135, 137, 138; and *Texas v. Johnson,* 140, 141; and *United Steel Workers v. Weber,* 178n4; and *Virginia v. Black,* 142; and *Webster v. Reproductive Health,* 24

Stevens, John Paul. 2000, 64–65

Stevens, John Paul. 2006a, 178n4

Stevens, John Paul. 2006b, 65

Stewart, Potter, 181n11; and deference, 75, 78, 82; and free speech, 75, 77, 79, 82; ideal points for, 39; and precedent, 74, 77, 82; and *Roe v. Wade,* 24; and separation of powers, 105, 106, 107, 111, 112, 113, 114, 115, 119; and solicitor general, 132, 134, 135, 137, 138

Stewart, Potter. 1966, 77, 81

Stimson, James, Michael Mackuen, and Robert Erikson. 1995, 35, 181n5

Stolberg, Sheryl Gay. 2009, 144

Stone, Harlan Fiske, 9, 10–11, 180n4

Stone v. Graham, 162

Stout, David. 2005, 12

strict construction: and Black, 13, 68; and Brennan, 68; and bridge observations, 65;

strict construction (*cont.*)
  and Constitution, 12, 67; and First
  Amendment, x, 13, 15, 65, 67–68; and
  George W. Bush, 12; and Roberts, 12;
  and Scalia, 12, 68
Sunstein, Cass R. 2005, 75
Swann v. Charlotte-Mecklenburg (402
  U.S. 1), 169
*Swann v. Charlotte-Mecklenburg County
  Board of Education,* 161

Tamanaha, Brian Z. 2010, 1, 4, 5, 6, 62, 97
Tanenhaus, Joseph, Marvin Schick, Mat-
  thew Muraskin, and Daniel Rosen.
  1963, 123
Taylor, Stuart. 2005, 12
temporary assistance for needy families,
  170
term limits, 3–4
Texas, 47
Texas Court of Criminal Appeals, 140
Texas v. Johnson (1989), 3, 68, 71, 140–41,
  142, 164
Texas v. Lawrence (2003), 37
textualism, 11, 12, 65
Thayer, James. 1893, 9
Thomas, Clarence, 29, 81; and *Almendarez-
  Torres v. United States,* 64, 65; and *Apprendi v. New Jersey,* 64; and *Buckley v.
  Valeo,* 168; and *Bush v. Gore,* 1; and
  conservative vs. liberal vote, 76; and deference, 75–76, 78, 82; and free speech,
  75, 79, 82, 85; and *Gonzales v. Raich,*
  51–52; and *Granholm v. Heald,* 89; ideal
  points for, 38, 39; and judicial restraint,
  179n11; and *Lawrence,* 67; and *Lawrence v. Texas,* 47; and precedent, 74–75,
  77, 82, 84, 179n4; and *Roe v. Wade,* 36;
  and separation of powers, 105, 106, 107,
  115, 116, 118; and solicitor general,
  132, 135, 136, 137, 138; and *Virginia v.
  Black,* 142
Thomas, Clarence. 2006, 65
Thompson v. Oklahoma (1988), 29–30
Thurmond, James Strom, 113, 164
Tiller, Emerson, and Frank Cross. 2006, 7,
  66
time, 18, 19, 22–27, 29–30, 33, 40–41, 43
Toma, Eugenia Froedge. 1991, 98
Toobin, Jeffrey. 2007, 66, 75, 89, 181n1
Tower, John, 111

Traditional Values Coalition, 51
Tribe, Laurence. 1985, 3
Truman, Harry, 124
Tsebelis, George. 2002, 99
Turner, Kathryn. 1961, 95
Tushnet, Mark. 1999, 4
Tushnet, Mark. 2005, 68
Twenty-first Amendment, 88–89

Ulmer, S. Sidney. 1973, 7
Ulmer, S. Sidney. 1984, 123
Ulmer, S. Sidney, and David Willison. 1985,
  124
United States v. Carolene Products (1938),
  10–11
United States v. Eichman (1990), 68
United States v. U.S. Food (2001), 100
United Steel Workers v. Weber (1979),
  178n4
University of Michigan, 121–23
Urofsky, Melvin. 1991, 10, 80
U.S. Congress. 1971, 13
U.S. v. Booker (2005), 88
U.S. v. Eichman (1990), 103
U.S. v. Lopez, 162
U.S. v. Robel, 165
U.S. v. Wilson (1975), 167
utility maximization, 7

Vanzetti, Bartolomeo, 80
Vinson, Fred, 180n6; and deference, 74;
  and free speech, 74; ideal points for, 39;
  and legal values, 73; and precedent, 74;
  and separation of powers, 105; and solicitor general, 132
Vinson Court, 34
Virginia v. Black (2003), 141–42
voting rights, 26
Voting Rights Act of 1965, 170

Wald, Patricia M. 1999, 2, 7–8
Ward, Artemus. 2003, 17
Warren, Earl, 17, 102; and deference, 74,
  78, 82; and free speech, 74, 79, 82; ideal
  points for, 39; and precedent, 74, 77, 82;
  and separation of powers, 105, 106, 107,
  111, 113; and solicitor general, 132,
  134, 135, 137, 138
Warren Court, 17, 84, 90
Webster v. Reproductive Health (1989),
  22–24, 30, 71

Wechsler, Herbert. 1959, 9
welfare legislation, 170
West, Diana. 2003, 121
West Coast Hotel Company v. Parrish
    (1937), 3, 97
White, Byron: and conservative vs. liberal
    vote, 76; and deference, 74, 75, 76, 78,
    82; and free speech, 74, 76, 79, 82; ideal
    points for, 39; and precedent, 74, 75, 77,
    82, 179–80n4; and *Roe v. Wade,* 24; and
    separation of powers, 105, 106, 107,
    113, 114, 115, 116, 119; and solicitor
    general, 132, 134, 135, 136–37, 138;
    and *Texas v. Johnson,* 140, 141; and
    Webster v. Reproductive Health, 24
White v. Weiser (1973), 167
Whittaker, Charles, 76, 181n11; and
    deference, 74, 75, 78, 82; and free
    speech, 74, 79, 82; ideal points for, 39;

and precedent, 74, 77, 82; and separa-
    tion of powers, 105, 106, 107, 111, 112;
    and solicitor general, 132
Whittington, Keith. 1999, 153
Wilson, Pete, 51
Wirth, Tim, 160
women, in military, 169
work week, 80
Wyden, Ron, 116

Yalof, David A. 1999, 81
Youngstown Sheet & Tube Co. v. Sawyer,
    124

Zavodnyik, Peter. 2007, 11
Zelman v. Simmons-Harris, 162
Zemel v. Rusk (1965), 167
Zeppos, Nicholas S. 1993, 67
Zorinsky, Edward, 25